DON'T CALL ME MUM!

A MOTHER'S STORY OF BEING PUSHED TO THE BRINK

MARIA FRANKLAND

AUTONOMY PRESS

CONTENTS

First published by Autonomy Press 2021

Second edition

Cover art by Darran Holmes

This book is dedicated to other parents still searching for help and support and the professionals who will hopefully give it to them.

FOREWORD

PRAISE FOR DON'T CALL ME MUM!

I am an art psychotherapist working with adults and children, and a mother of three beautiful boys. This book is intriguing and insightful - written in such a way where you can read it any time of the day, and pick up from where you left off, then be instantly interested and consumed with what you are reading.

I found it to be extremely heart-felt, thoughtfully written and relatable in lots of ways, particularly with some of the young people that are in therapy with me. Each chapter was emotive and I enjoyed reading it, safe to say it only took me a few sittings to finish it - I couldn't put it down! I was left wanting to read more and know of the later years - what happened next - which to me is the sign of a great read!

Maria is a talented author and I would highly recommend this story; personally and professionally.

Rachel Bentley, Art Psychotherapist

JOIN MY 'KEEP IN TOUCH' LIST

If you'd like to be kept in the loop about new books and special offers, join my 'keep in touch list' by visiting www.autonomypress.co.uk. You will receive a free novella as a thank you for joining.

INTRODUCTION

I blame the parents! This is something I have often heard.

"It's not always their fault!" I want to yell in response. "Some parents have tried absolutely *everything.*"

I am the mother of a son who had juvenile convictions for thefts, class B drug possession, criminal damage and public disorder. In addition to this, he was permanently excluded from mainstream school and ostracised from almost everyone we knew.

What people who blame the parents don't know is that at the age of one-and-a-half, when my son would not sleep, destroyed everything he laid his hands on, and threw Oscar-winning tantrums, I began trailing him around every available 'expert' in the field of childhood behavioural problems.

Health visitors blamed my separation from his father in infancy; our GP suspected maternal depression, whilst the 0-19 Team conceded his conduct to be a result of my youth and inexperience.

Further down the line, child psychologists asserted his diet as a contributory factor, meanwhile child psychiatrists held *my* background responsible. Teachers delved into his home life,

Social Services suspected abuse and the Youth Offending Team attributed peer pressure. The police blamed him, and the courts punished me.

This is our story. I hope other parents take some comfort from it (you are not alone!) I also hope that health professionals, whatever their expertise, can learn from it.

COUNTING THE COST

I LIKE WRITING LISTS. They keep me straight. Sometimes, I write a list of lists I need to write! Today, I'm listing all the things my fifteen-year-old son has broken this year:

1. kettle
2. bathroom door
3. microwave
4. fridge freezer
5. PlayStation control pad
6. Playstation
7. glasses and cups - too many to count
8. outside security light
9. drainpipe at front of house
10. drainpipe at back of house
11. cupboard door
12. hinges on bathroom window
13. two holes punched in wall
14. my heart

I could list all the things he has stolen and sold too. But I'll come to that later.

MY PROBLEM

OCTOBER 2009 (AGED 15 YEARS, 10 MONTHS)

"Social Services are unlikely to do anything," the woman stated gently as I howled in anguish down the telephone.

"He can't come back here!" I paced the room as I stated my case. "We're going to lose our home because of him!" *I can't take it anymore!*

I replaced the receiver, sinking with it into the floor. Now my voice had stilled; the house was eerily quiet. All fight was slipping from me. The plan had been to tell them straight that breaking point had been reached.

I could not tolerate sitting in the same room as him. I could not bear to look at him. *Either he went, or I did.* I no longer felt guilty for feeling this way.

The teacher at his pupil referral unit had listened patiently as I ranted, and she made all the right sympathetic noises. Yet I detected an undercurrent of disbelief in her replies. She obviously thought I was exaggerating.

I caught sight of myself in the bedroom mirror. I was spending a lot of time in my room. Trying to escape my son's name calling, taunts and threats, not to mention the constant bullying for money I did not have and could not give. However, he was not choosy who he would then steal from to ensure his insatiable demands were met; family, friends, shops, neighbours or strangers.

The taste of tears trickled into my mouth as I observed my pallid reflection.

Was that really me?

I barely recognised myself anymore. Clad in baggy tracksuit bottoms and a shapeless jumper, I had become lost between the deepening lines on my face. Lines that should belong to a woman ten years my senior, instead of a thirty-five-year-old.

Night-after-night I was becoming more depleted; repeatedly awoken by Tom's nocturnal homecomings or his hooded associates. Instead of sleep, fear would stand guard. Unlike my son's degenerate 'friends' whose faceless existence brought him security; my constant companion had two faces of fear. One face reflected uncertainty; where he was, who he was with, whether he was OK. The other reflected hatred for the miserable life he was forcing me to lead.

Anyway, this latest attempt at seeking help was as futile as all the previous ones I had made. He was nobody else's problem. Mine and mine alone.

He did not reappear that day. The phone call I had made would probably have been made known to him. Maybe he felt ashamed at the disgusting names he had called me that morning, or the threat to smash up my car.

As was usually the case, it took an eternity to drop off to sleep that night. As his mother, I was forced to endure endless images, all consisting of my darkest fears intruding into my extremely shattered mind.

Most fifteen-year-olds would be warm in their beds on a chilly October night. The heating had clicked off long ago. It was after 2 am ... I startled at every noise. Just as I eventually dozed, I was alerted to something being thrown to his window from our driveway. Leaping up to investigate, I saw them: the associates, concealed in hoods. I strained to hear their conversation.

"He's ignoring us."

"Maybe he's not there."

"I'm not having this."

"But he owes me."

"We could just press the doorbell."

"He told me he'd have some."

"Nah, he'll keep."

Crouching under the window, I hoped they had not seen me peering. Why wouldn't they give up and leave our fractured family in peace? I had not yet turned off the lamp outside the front door. Until he was in, I always left it switched on. It cast unwelcome shards of light, stabbing me through the venetian blind.

Becoming Tom's mother had always robbed me of the right to sleep. Fifteen years on, I was still alone, in the dark, in the middle of the night. A solitary figure, enveloped in darkness, longing to be allowed to rest like everyone else.

THE FIRST SLEEPLESS NIGHT

JANUARY 1994 (AGED 0.5 DAYS)

AT LEAST THEY *can go back to sleep,* I thought, bitterly, as I observed the rest of the ward in the darkness around my own illuminated bed. It was 1.45 am. Tom writhed on my bed, all flailing arms and legs. But at least he had stopped crying for now. I had been worried about him disturbing everyone else too.

By 2.30 am, I was desperate. I had fed and changed him three times, cuddled him and tried laying him down, both in his cot and in bed with me. Tugging my dressing gown around me, I lowered my bare feet onto the cold floor. I gathered him up and lay his tiny, warm form upright against my shoulder. A little walk around was bound to settle him and stop him crying.

The ward was in darkness except for a dim lamp at the nurses' station and the fairy lights on the Christmas tree. I held him towards them, hoping for distraction. He quietened and fastened his stare upon the twinkling colours. The ward was in silence apart from the low hum of conversation that occasionally passed between the nursing staff. A whiff of coffee and toast made my stomach inadvertently rumble. It must have been thirty-six hours since I had eaten, before my contractions had started. I had been so excited about meeting my baby for the first time, now I felt guilty for wishing he would be quiet.

"Shall we take him for a while?" Offered one of the nurses, standing up behind the high desk. "You need to rest. He should settle soon. Being born usually wears them out!"

"Well, it's certainly worn me out!" I walked to the side of the desk. "Are you sure?"

"Of course." She held her arms out for him. "Pass him here."

I scuttled back to bed. Flicking off the overhead lamp, I burrowed gratefully beneath the blanket and closed my eyes. Sleep washed over me as easily as tumbling water over stones. But what only seemed like moments later, I was awoken to a snuffling sound in the cot beside me. Like a hedgehog rooting for food.

Rubbing my eyes, I grappled on the bedside cabinet for my watch. 4.20 am. The nurse must have returned him as I slept. Lifting him from the cot, I tried to feed him again, hoping he would fall asleep as he took his milk. He didn't. After a while, I decided to take him back to the nurses' station.

I climbed back into bed and tried to fall back asleep. But his high-pitched wail was echoing through the ward. I sighed as I heard footsteps 'click-clacking' towards my bed.

"I thought I'd better bring him back before he wakes everybody! He wants his Mum."

Taking him from her, I scanned the darkened room. The moonlight was filtering in between the blinds. It cast wobbly shadows over the sleeping forms; five other mothers and five babies in cots beside them. I fed Tom again. The silence of the night was only broken by the occasional snore or a momentary small cry. This would be answered with milk, swiftly resulting in a contented baby.

But not mine. If any of the other new mothers had glanced over at my bed, they would have peered through the thin curtain, pulled around in a fruitless attempt to mask the wails of an un-pacified child. They would have seen me, a jostling silhouette, trying to cajole my baby into sleep. Envy was not in their eyes. It was in mine.

I had been desperate for motherhood. I had spent my teenage years in local authority care and missed my siblings hugely. Taking responsibility for myself meant I had grown up to be resilient and self-sufficient.

But I had wanted to recreate my own family. One that could not be snatched from me. Since my nineteenth birthday, Peter and I had endured month after month of disappointment when I hadn't fallen pregnant.

I looked down at my wide-awake newborn. Yes, he was gorgeous and everything I had yearned for. I had not been prepared for our first night together to be so hard. Perhaps everything would get easier as I adjusted to my new role.

THE SECOND AND THIRD SLEEPLESS NIGHTS

THE DOCTOR WAS CONDUCTING her ward round on our fourth day on the ward when we were due to be discharged. "It is most unusual," she said. "New babies are normally *exhausted* after birth. They barely wake in the first few days, apart from to be fed or changed. I'm sure he'll settle down for you soon." She briskly moved to the next bed.

Tom had fallen asleep at about 5.30 am that morning. Minutes later, or so it felt, the breakfast trolley had begun to rattle around. Feeling nauseous with exhaustion, I had just about managed a bit of toast and marmalade. Its tang lingered in my mouth as I rested back onto the pillows.

I peeked into Tom's cot. Still he slept. He was now into his fourth hour of sleep which felt like a gift from God. The only time he had really slept since his birth three days prior, was when our friends and Peter's family had come to visit him.

As I lay down amidst the warm ward, I was so worn out that I could hardly hear the chattering of the other mums to each other. The doorbell to the ward buzzed constantly. I could hear it, but it all felt miles away.

Peter's voice made me jump.

"Come on sleepy, the doctor has come to see you both." He peered into the cot. "Hello little man."

"What, again?" I hauled myself up from the pillows. "She's already checked him."

"You're coming home son!" He scooped Tom up. "He needs a final once over, that's all."

"Do you have to wake him?" I said weakly. "You don't know what a battle it is to get him to sleep!"

He had brought Tom's car seat, all-in-one coat and bobble hat. Once we had been checked and discharged, a nurse accompanied us to the hospital foyer to help us into the taxi. My eyes ached, hit by the sudden glaze, as I exchanged the artificial light for winter sunshine. It was a beautiful day, perfect to take our baby home.

The peace and warmth would enable Tom to settle better. I eagerly anticipated being back in my own home with Peter to lend a hand with the night feeds. But I was to be disappointed.

Peter slept nonchalantly through Tom's nocturnal noise, ensuring even less sleep was afforded to me than had been in hospital, where at least the nurses had helped a little. I fed him until I was sore and rocked him until I wept. Exasperated and powerless, I was desperate to close my eyes and sleep.

At some point I must have fallen asleep because I awoke to find the room in stillness. Jumping up, I lunged towards Tom's sleeping basket. It was empty. I ran into the kitchen and spotted a note by the kettle.

"Have taken Tom to meet my mum. Get some rest."

Of course, he meant well. But fury speared me. We should have *both* taken Tom to meet his grandma. Looking around our home, it seemed rest would be the last thing I could get. The place was a tip. Every available surface was covered in baby paraphernalia. Laundry and the dishes needed sorting. Peter must have done absolutely *nothing* before heading out with Tom. I sobbed as I clattered around. The cleaner and tidier things became, the more my mood darkened. I could not shake it.

It continued all day. Peter ran me a bath later that evening. I wallowed in it, weeping as I listened to the bubbles in the foam popping. My tears were as warm as the bath water.

"I'm going to buy milk powder so I can feed him tonight. You're going to get a proper night's sleep." His voice suddenly cut into my thoughts from the bathroom door.

It made me feel like a failure to be depriving Tom of breast milk. This self-reproach threatened to overpower me. However, he seemed to like the formula and guzzled greedily from the bottle, gazing wide-eyed at Peter as he suckled. I tunnelled beneath the bedclothes, appreciative that he was having a turn at being kept awake.

By ten past four, the formula had run out. There were no more bottles sterilised. Peter nudged me as Tom squawked from his basket.

"You'll have to sort him Sarah. I've had enough." He turned and faced the other way. "I need some sleep."

Bleary eyed, I retrieved him. There was no more sleep for me that night.

As the weeks limped over each other, Peter and I became different people. We no longer laughed. In fact, we barely civilly conversed. We snapped. Fought. Compared. And blamed.

Peter slept. I didn't. He worked. I coped. The gulf between us widened and by the time Tom was five months old, reality had to be faced.

"I need a break from you." I bawled at him, overwhelmed by fatigue and responsibility. "I can't stand you near me at the moment."

"I'll stay at my mum's for a couple of weeks." After thundering from the room, he slammed around for a while as he packed his possessions.

His leaving came too easily. I sensed a whiff of relief. Respite from his newly acquired middle-aged lifestyle.

THE 182ND SLEEPLESS NIGHT

AUGUST 1994 (AGED 8 MONTHS)

ME, I just had to get on with it. After Peter's departure, Tom 'slept' in bed with me. Six, seven or eight times a night, he would wake, for twenty to thirty-minute periods. Then, he would doze for about twenty minutes before stirring again. I don't know why he kept waking. His nappy did not need changing and milk would be rejected. It was necessary to accept this situation and resign myself to this way of life. In hindsight, I do not know how I kept functioning. I missed Peter though I didn't want him to come back. I was barely surviving myself. Sometimes I could barely believe I had become a single mum at the age of twenty-one. All the dreams I'd had for having my own happy family had been destroyed. I lived on Income Support and was barely managing. Plus, I'd never known loneliness like it.

The weather had improved so our windows were often ajar. Tom's incessant crying must have disturbed the neighbours. If this was the case, no one ever protested. They may have felt sorry for me. Or wondered what I was doing wrong.

Had they looked out; they would have witnessed us in the street on many a night. As early dawn broke, Tom would bawl from his buggy as I paced up and down the pavement, trying to lull him to sleep using the wheeled motion.

I hope nobody saw me on one occasion. My mood was as black as the night. Neighbours may have questioned why I was alone and where Tom was.

Has she left her baby on his own? I'd had to. I had come close to hurting him. My rage had been so powerful, I had tasted it. It had tingled in my nose with the ferocity of a nosebleed. A white madness had engulfed me before I had fled from the upstairs room, aware that if I did not get away from him, I might have hurled him against the wall.

"Will you shut up?" I had shoved him a little too roughly into his cot. In complete anguish, I then circled the street, regret consuming me. *I had nearly hurt my baby!* I had allowed anger to devour exhaustion and adrenaline had cascaded through my veins.

After I'd calmed enough to return, he'd cried himself out. So had I. Drawing him towards me, I kissed the top of his head.

"I'm sorry sweetie. Please forgive me. I could never hurt you. Ever. Rocking him in the darkness, I wept into his hair, breathing his powdery scent. There was no way that could ever happen again. I *had* to come to terms with my new existence.

The next day I made a remorseful fuss of him; playing and singing with him more than usual. Despite the angst, I adored Tom. My world revolved around him. Every spare penny was spent on new toys and lovely outfits for my blue-eyed, white-haired *everything.*

SURELY MOTHERHOOD SHOULDN'T BE THIS HARD??

AN ACTIVE CHILD

OCTOBER 1994 (AGED 10 MONTHS)

LIKE AN OLYMPIC SWIMMER, Tom mastered the crawl with speed and finesse. He could not, even momentarily, be left unattended. Everything had to be moved. *Everything.* Ornaments, photographs, magazines, the cat's dish, and anything that could be spilt. I could never have foreseen the requirement to have to do a *risk assessment* every time I averted my eyes. Anything within his grasp was at his mercy. It was as though he organised his next onslaught in his mind whilst I changed his nappy.

Each day was like a scene from 'The Great Escape.' As I held him *prisoner* in my arms, I became accustomed to his ferocious wriggling and determined attempts to break free; his usual response to being detained. As soon as he was free, he would escape across the room at a breathtaking pace towards anything inadvertently left out. On hands and knees, he would hurtle towards any item that he could wrench apart, pour or throw. Even the cat, once curious at him, now kept a safe distance.

The health visitor was amazed at his ten-month mobility.

"He's advanced for his age. "She watched in astonishment as he waddled towards her. "I can't believe he's walking *already.*"

Welcome to my world! I wanted to reply. Instead, I breathed deeply and fixed my expression; a strange combination of acceptance and exhaustion. "Oh yes! I've got my hands full now." I shuffled around the room, collecting discarded items as I spoke.

"How's he sleeping?" She yanked her handbag away from Tom. "Dare I ask?"

"Still badly, but I'm used to it." I slung toys into his toy box and wondered if she detected the resignation in my voice.

"Has he slept through the night yet?" She tugged a form and a pen from her bag. I chuckled before disappearing into the kitchen to pour coffee.

"I think the longest he's slept is for an hour!" I called back.

"It must be difficult."

Of course not! He's a breeze! What makes you think that having a child who sleeps for an hour a night is difficult? The sarcasm bubbled inside me, but I remained my jovial self, leaving the veil that cloaked the reality of my feelings firmly in place.

"I'm used to it." I no longer questioned my life. It was my normality. I returned with our drinks; she placed hers on the low table beside her.

"Will it be OK there?"

"No! Quick! Grab it!" She rescued it before Tom took full swing.

This was one of his favourite games. He loved to swipe at cups and glasses and would approach them at remarkable speed. Before I had any chance of preventing him, he would usually have reached his target. Anything left within his grasp would be smashed. Digging up plants and ripping into books were also amongst his favourite pursuits.

"Do you have any support?" She asked.

I shook my head.

"A mum? Any family?"

"Not really. I used to be in care."

She wrote something down. "I'll put you forward for some nursery provision. You could do with a break."

"I'd love to go to college or to work," I said. "I left school with one G.C.S.E. I was getting bullied there so I didn't go." I felt my shoulders sag at the memory. "But I'm in charge of my life now. And I want to make things better for us. Me and Tom, I mean."

"Leave it with me. I'll see what I can do."

Being confined to the bath was something Tom detested. He would try to clamber out or thrash about in the water with an intensity that resembled a beached fish. Inevitably, I and the bathroom floor would be saturated. Baths became a brief affair.

For all 'simple' tasks such as nappy changing, dressing and the putting on of shoes. restraint was necessary. Tom was strong and would squirm to be free. To watch me trying to strap him into his pushchair could be likened to a policeman trying to handcuff a newly captured criminal. It was a challenging situation, but one I had to resign myself to. *Surely this was how it must be for all mums of toddlers.*

Around this time, I exchanged my back-to-back council house which was riddled with damp and needed decoration I could not possibly manage or afford, into a ground floor flat. The flat gave us a much nicer environment and I quickly settled there. It was directly on a bus route and close to a park, so I vowed to make the effort to get us out more.

However, if I tried to visit friends with Tom, excuses were politely made. Like '*we're on our way out*' or '*I'm not well*' or '*we're expecting visitors in ten minutes.*' That kind of thing.

One friend was not so gracious. She had two boisterous

daughters and Tom would be wild with anticipation whenever he encountered them. They fed off each other's enthusiasm and would have fared better if given space to rampage in, rather than the confines of a lounge.

One day, my friend invited me in.

"Mark's decided Tom must stay strapped in his buggy whilst you're here. "She avoided eye contact with me as she informed me of her partner's wishes. "Every time he comes, he breaks things or pours something. Or both. Perhaps it's better if *we* visit *you* in future."

Making my excuses, I left soon after, blinking back tears as I trudged round to another friend's house to repeat the conversation. She was sympathetic. But her partner wasn't.

"I don't blame him for saying that," he muttered as Tom threw his bottle of juice at one of their framed pictures, smashing it. As I left, I decided not to visit in future if her partner's car was outside.

It was becoming like that everywhere. I was increasingly isolated. People insisted on visiting me, rather than risking the damage that my son might inflict. At least in my own home, it was *my* stuff getting smashed. Not that I had much left!

Nor could I afford to replace it. Living on benefits with no family support was a nightmare. *Yet how could I go back to work? Who on earth would look after Tom, especially with the behaviour he displayed?* I couldn't afford a childminder and the health visitor hadn't been in touch about a nursery place. Peter helped minimally at that time and only took him out for an hour or two at a time. Admittedly, we'd had Tom too young. We'd had a romantic idea of what parenthood would be like and had learned a hard lesson.

Some weeks I had to make difficult choices. Which was more important for an extra couple of pounds on the meter – gas or electricity? Nappies or an extra seven pounds worth of food. I am ashamed to say that some weeks, I was so desperate that I would put a bag of nappies on the back of the pushchair and cover them with my coat. If anyone had challenged me, I would have blamed *baby brain*, or something.

I am forever indebted to Vicky, my friend who would invite us around for dinner at least once a week and let me take a load of laundry as I did not have a washing machine. Her partner would even run Tom and I home in the evening. She was the only friend at the time who made us welcome.

It became fruitless attempting the launderette, meeting a friend for a drink in a café, or even queuing in the post office. Every activity would be blighted by Tom's screams for attention. Arching his back in temper, he would repeatedly hurl his head against the back of his buggy. God only knows how he did not injure himself. People would gawp at us and mutter about his behaviour or try to offer advice. I felt more and more like a social outcast.

Especially one Sunday when we attended church. We didn't go often as it was too much of an ordeal. However, there were some Sundays when I felt compelled to go. I loved the peace and stillness. The scent of incense would wash over me as soon as I entered. It was a relief just to sit and be. If only Tom would have permitted this.

We stayed at the back, so as not to interrupt the service. I was armed with juice, biscuits and a couple of quiet toys. Five minutes into the service, the commotion he made forced me to take him outside. My teeth clattered in the icy air as I attempted to calm him down. Our coats, of course, were inside.

Whilst a hymn was being sung, we ventured back in. As soon as it was over, Tom fired up again. He squawked an excruciatingly loud 'NO!!' and writhed in anger, as I tried to keep a hold on his squirming little body. My face burned and I knew I had to get us out of there. Every eye was on me, in silent condemnation, or so it felt.

Just as I was gathering our things together, an elderly

woman stormed over, coming so close to us that her perfume penetrated the incense.

"What do you think you're doing? I've come here to listen to the service, not the likes of that!" Her finger jabbed sharply towards me. She glared at Tom as though he was diseased. It was a reaction I was getting used to. The pain in the top of my chest felt as though I had swallowed a sob and it had gone down the wrong way.

"What is it Jesus said?" remarked another woman, jumping to my defence. "*Suffer the little children who come unto me.* Ignore her," she said. "You're as welcome as she is."

But the damage was done. It was years before I ventured back into a church.

BABY'S FIRST CHRISTMAS

DECEMBER 1994 (AGED 11 MONTHS AND 3 WEEKS)

"Look at our gorgeous tree!" Balancing Tom's weight on my hip, we walked over to where it proudly presided. For several seconds, he stared at the lights, the colours reflecting onto the perfection of his face. I was suddenly transported back a year, to the nurses' station where he had, as a newborn, gazed at the tree there. He swung his arm at one of the baubles.

"No Tom!" I caught hold of his arm. "Don't spoil the tree!" He wriggled in order to get me to lower him to the floor.

"I'll get you a drink," I announced, finally putting him down. He had to get used to the tree, and would probably tug at its ornaments but seriously, what damage could he do?

If you slowly count to twenty now, you will get an idea of the length of my absence from the room. As I made the short journey back from the kitchen to the living room, there was a crash, not a loud one but a 'tinselly' one.

"Tom!" I raced back into the room. "No!"

He stepped back from the tree, still aglow on the floor and appeared to be admiring his handiwork.

"That's naughty!" He giggled as I tapped his hand. Leading him to his bedroom, I plonked him in his cot, ignoring his wails as I put the tree back together. I was reminded of the year before when heavily pregnant, Peter and I had put the tree up together, full of excitement about our baby. We had got engaged earlier that year and though we were young, we thought we would always be together. If anyone had told us that becoming parents would push us apart and that we would fall out of love with each other, we would never have believed them.

On releasing Tom, I shouted "*no!*" whenever he approached the tree and tapped his hand when he was about to make a grab for it. But as I prepared his tea, he got another chance. Once again, the tree sprawled forlornly upon the carpet. Protecting it became tiresome and I was relieved when 'bedtime' was approaching.

This night, like every night, after his tea, I bathed him, and tried to settle him in his room with a bottle. As I sang nursery rhymes, he would whinge, all too aware of the inevitable. Then I would have to 'peel' him from me. His fingers would grip my jumper, like an abandoned chimpanzee, trying to prevent me from laying him down.

Back in the living room, I cranked up the TV to drown his screaming. Next, he repeatedly threw his head against the bars of his cot. This was impossible to ignore so I had to give in and retrieve him. This process lasted throughout the evening, into the early hours. It wasn't a one off – it was like this every night.

His bedroom was gradually being ruined. Tom enjoyed ripping the wallpaper within reach around his cot. Both of his musical cot mobiles had been pulled down along with other toys I had secured to the cot bars.

~

Christmas Eve was not as I would have envisaged. Tom's first Christmas. It should have been Peter and I putting presents for him under the tree which stood bedraggled and unlit, worn out from being mercilessly thrown. Not as worn out as me though. I was twenty-one years old yet felt about seventy-one. Other girls would be out partying tonight. Unlike me: huddled on the sofa, surrounded by darkness, with a glass of wine for company. I often wondered what I'd done wrong. I thought of Peter, probably out enjoying himself and began to cry.

The only light wavered in the corner of the room, from the TV. Closing my eyes and scrunching them tightly did not eliminate the screaming and endless banging coming from the little bedroom. But I had to ignore it. Enough was enough. And I was lonely. I suspected that no man was likely to come near me with such a handful of a baby. There had been one that had stuck around for a few weeks in September, just before I moved, taking me out a little and ringing me up regularly.

Vicky had again, been a Godsend and looked after Tom to free me up sometimes. Shaun was away at college through the week but receiving letters and phone calls from him reminded me that I was more than Tom's mum and he really brought a light into my life.

Then Shaun had paid for us to have a few days in a caravan at the coast. There had been an occasion where he'd offered to have Tom so I could do a bit of shopping. When I returned, it transpired that Tom had not stopped screaming since my departure. My short-lived boyfriend ended things after that, saying that he was not old or responsible enough to take on someone else's baby. I couldn't blame him.

~

It was a relief to welcome the arrival of the New Year; and with it, Tom's first birthday. This would be the year when I would get myself back to work. Find a nursery or a childminder. By July all my secretarial courses would be passed. I lived for

Wednesdays, the day when I went to college and Tom went into crèche. The young crèche assistants coped well with him, though they would always be full of tales of his antics when I picked him up. Once July had passed, I resolved I would find a part time job as a secretary. Earn some proper money and get my brain into something other than coping with motherhood.

Just after Tom's first birthday, he managed to 'break out' of his cot. I could not believe it when he came tearing into the living room one night, waving his bottle.

"Bot-bot!" he demanded. I re-filled it with orange juice and hauled him back to bed, where I was astonished to find that he had snapped two of the bars on his cot. After that, there was no hope of confining him in his room at bedtime. They were completely unfixable. I had no choice other than to convert the cot into its second phase – a toddler bed.

"Bot-bot!" he would bawl as he raced out of his room up to eight times every night. I would present him with orange juice and return him to his room. His thirst concerned me. It was unquenchable and his nappies were saturated!

I slept on a knife's edge, poised the whole time for disturbance. People commented on my sunken face and dark eyes, caused by a year of no sleep. I wondered if it was ever going to end. I had desperately wanted a baby of my own. The joy of unconditional love between us, yet I could not believe the reality of it.

One February morning, I awoke with a start and glanced at the clock. 7:45 am. Tom had not woken since midnight! I shot across the hallway of our flat into his room and shook him. He remained in stillness.

For a moment I thought he was dead.

"Tom!" Panic speared me as I shook him again. He sprang

up like a jack-in-a box. “Bot-bot!” He thrust the bottle at me. I hugged him in relief.

Happily, two or three times each week, he began to sleep through the main part of the night and was starting to allow me five to six hours of uninterrupted sleep. Rather than wake in a blind panic, I was grateful. However, I knew I would never take sleep for granted again.

DOES ORANGE JUICE CAUSE HYPERACTIVITY?

MORE BOYS than girls are hyperactive. Figures show a ratio of 3:1 (high percentage of blonde blue-eyed boys). There are, of course, degrees of the problem, and not every child will have all the symptoms described below.

SYMPTOMS OF HYPERACTIVITY

IN INFANCY

- Crying, screaming, restless, needs little sleep.
- Colic. Difficult to feed, whether breast or bottle.
- Cannot be pacified or cuddled… spurns affection.
- Excessive dribbling … may be VERY THIRSTY.
- Head banging, cot rocking, fits and tantrums.

OLDER CHILDREN (in addition to symptoms in infancy)

- Clumsy, impulsive, accident prone.
- Erratic disruptive behaviour.
- Compulsive 'touching.'
- Constant motion.
- Disturbs other children.
- May be aggressive.

- Lacks concentration and may be withdrawn.
- Normal or high IQ but fails at school.
- Poor appetite.
- Poor hand and eye co-ordination.
- Uncooperative, defiant and disobedient.
- Self abusive (pulling hair/picking skin etc.).
- Continued problems with sleep.

(Source: Hyperactive Children's Support Group)

HE SHOULD BE MUZZLED!

MAY 1995 (1 YEAR, 5 MONTHS)

AS THE DAYS LENGTHENED, I was more positive. I coerced myself out of the flat with Tom, even if it was just to the park so he could let off steam. Here I would sometimes bump into a friend and we could chat as Tom ran amok. I realised that I had started to feel depressed, I still felt isolated all the time and far older than my twenty-two years. I longed to be able to buy new clothes or get my nails done. I yearned to be able to go out for a drink or for a dance. I was never going to meet someone new stuck inside my flat with Tom every night.

One friend, Cathy, was someone I met up with regularly. Her son, Jack, was only six weeks older than Tom. He was also an absolute handful but not in the same league as Tom. I noticed one difference the first time I invited them around for tea and gave the boys spaghetti and sausages. Jack sat still at the table and fed himself with a spoon, albeit messily. But he concentrated on what he was doing.

Tom, however, had to be fastened into his highchair. As always, his meal was served in a bowl with a 'suction plate,' and stuck to his highchair tray. Within three seconds of receiving his meal, however, it lay splashed around the feet of the highchair on the plastic sheeting I used to protect the carpet. I scooped the sausages and spaghetti up and tried again. Once again, he threw it down.

I spooned it back into the bowl and tried to feed it to him. Screaming, he arched his back in temper and spat out the food that did make it into his mouth.

"Is he always like this?" Cathy looked astonished as she wiped Jack's mouth.

"I'm afraid so." I let a jagged breath out. "I don't even try to eat my meal with him anymore!"

"Perhaps he's not hungry," she frowned.

"He must be!" I held the spoon again against his clamped mouth. "He's not eaten for hours. I'd hoped he might improve with Jack setting such a good example."

"Maybe that's why he's doing it?" She lifted Jack out of the chair and clasped him towards her. "Maybe he's showing off!"

"No, he's like this every single mealtime!" I put the bowl aside, finally admitting defeat.

"Poor you. Maybe you should take the food away when he launches his bowl. He'll soon learn that he goes hungry when he does that."

"I've tried that already. He doesn't seem to learn anything, no matter what I do."

"Then keep trying. After a couple of days, he'll get the message."

"I know you're only trying to help Cathy but honestly, I know what I'm doing." *Did I really?*

Because our sons were similar in age, we often got together. We would feed the ducks or go to a soft indoor play area. Early one morning, Cathy phoned me with a suggestion.

"How about we catch the bus to the coast?"

I glanced out of the window. "Well it's certainly sunny enough for it."

"I'll meet you at the bus stop in an hour."

My mood was cheerier than the day outside as I bundled together everything we would need. It would be wonderful to get some sea air! As I bustled around the flat, Tom sprawled before the TV, nibbling at his toast. *He was still!* Perhaps the fact that I had changed what he was drinking was starting to take effect?

"No!" As I re-entered the room, I caught him stuffing toast into the video recorder.

Every ounce of strength was required to strap him into his buggy. But eventually, we were organised. Cathy and Jack were waiting at the bus stop.

Throughout the first bus ride, Tom squirmed on my knee, yearning for escape. Cathy twisted herself so that her upper half and Jack were almost facing into the aisle between the seats in what, I suppose, was an attempt to distance herself from us as all the other passengers were staring at Tom and me. I prayed he would sleep on the longer trip we were to embark on. It was to take ninety minutes so surely; he would get bored.

Cathy and I sat on the second bus with our sons on our laps. Ten minutes into the journey, Tom was on a mission to be free. This was obviously not possible. His body grew tense with rage, and I had to shield my face as he repeatedly flung his head backwards. Then he leaned forwards and yanked the hair of a passenger in front.

"I'm sorry!" I gasped. "Are you alright?"

She raked some of the hair that he had torn from her scalp and held it in front of me.

"That," she hissed, "is disgusting! You need to get him sorted out!" She wrenched her bag from the overhead rack before shifting to an upstairs seat.

Tom's behaviour was having a terrible effect on Jack, who was beginning to wriggle and grimace in a similar way. At one point they were causing such a commotion that the bus driver screeched the bus to a halt.

"You're going to have to control those kids!" Turning around, he surveyed us in revulsion. "I can't concentrate on the road! What's bloody wrong with em both? Have you given em drugs or something?"

"Hear, hear!" echoed a couple behind us. I glanced at Cathy. Clearly unfamiliar to being shamed in this way, she concealed her crimson face behind Jack's head.

"I'll move to the seat in front with him I think," she muttered, sliding towards it without looking at me. For the rest of the journey, we didn't speak. I doubt I'd have been able to hear her above the din Tom kept making anyway.

Had I been on a local bus, I would have got off and waited for the next one. The day seemed to be ruined before it had begun. I had never been so grateful when we finally reached Scarborough.

"He should be muzzled." A man snapped as we descended.

"You can say that again." An elderly woman surveyed me coldly, shaking her head. "I hope we're on a different bus to you when we go home!"

"Do you really have to be so nasty?" Tears swam into my eyes. "Haven't you had kids of your own?"

"Not like him."

"Have you ever heard of parenting classes?" A younger woman shouted after me.

I had barely opened my mouth in response when Cathy grabbed my arm.

"Just ignore them. I've had enough embarrassment for one day!"

The prospect of the return journey blighted our day out. Cathy was cool towards me and barely spoke to Tom. She even took herself off with Jack's buggy for an hour, her reasoning being that Jack was unable to take his afternoon nap around Tom.

Thankfully, our return home was less problematic. Jack

slept for most of it. Again, Cathy sat in a different seat. Any other passengers would have assumed we were strangers rather than two friends having the day out with our children.

I was surprised that Tom did not nod off, given his day of relentless activity in the sea air. However, he was more manageable than earlier that day, tantrumming only a handful of times, as opposed to constantly. The bus was only half-full, allowing people to move away from us if they wished.

FIRST BID FOR FREEDOM

TOM SEEMED weary as we arrived home that evening. It was nearly nine pm so he was not in his usual frenzied mood. Although the journey had been dreadful, the fresh air had obviously done the trick. It had done me good to get out for the day too. Sometimes I felt as though I might climb the walls with frustration. There were not too many places I could take Tom because of his behaviour, nor did I have the money to do much anyway.

I read him a story as he guzzled milk from his bottle, then I kissed him before drawing his curtains. The fading sunlight seeped around their edges like an eclipsed moon.

Being a muggy evening, I opened his window slightly then clicked his door shut behind me. Momentarily, he grizzled but he did not pursue me out of the room for a change. Within ten minutes, all was peaceful. Tucking my feet under me, I curled up gratefully in front of the TV, wondering whether to celebrate my success at getting him to sleep with a glass of wine that I knew I had left, or a bar of chocolate. I glanced happily at an untouched magazine that I had not had a moment yet to enjoy. *Until tonight.*

About five minutes later, at the edge of my vision, I noticed a woman hauling a child across the grassed area that our flat overlooked. My heart began hammering against my rib cage as I realised it was Tom. Time seemed to slow as I scrambled out of my chair and began fumbling beyond the red mist that had descended, for my door keys. *How on earth had this woman managed to abduct my son?*

I pelted to the door and darted across the grass towards her.

"Stop! Stop!" My shrieks sounded as though they belonged to someone else.

"Is he yours?"

Tom was tugging to escape.

"Yes. What the-" I snatched him from her, scarcely able to breathe.

"You stupid woman! Can't you look after your own child? I've just stopped him being killed."

Reality quickly dawned on me. "I thought he was asleep!" My face was smouldering as I clutched him against me. "Honestly, I only tucked him into bed ten minutes ago." I sounded pathetic. "He must have climbed through his window."

"Well thanks a lot anyway!" She began striding away, shaking her head. "I've missed my bus because of you."

"I'm so sorry!" Tears flamed my eyes. Tears of humiliation.

"You can fish your own kid off the road next time." She shouted back over her shoulder. "You're a disgrace!"

Open mouthed, I stared after her. It was horrendous being yelled at, being blamed. Yet I realised how I must have appeared. *How could I have argued with her?*

Tom, pyjama-clad, was a picture of innocence. It was a feat to keep a grip of him as I carted him back to the flat; he was battling to get free again.

He *had* climbed out of his bedroom window. It was an absolute mercy that we lived in the ground floor flat of the high-rise block. He must have climbed from his bed to his windowsill and descended the five feet onto the grass outside. *How on earth could an eighteen-month-old child safely drop five feet? Thank God that woman had seen him! The alternatives did not bear contemplating!* Nestled within my relief was guilt that I had not pre-empted this possibility. After that, I never left his window ajar again.

GOOD MORNING

SEPTEMBER 1995 (1 YEAR, 9 MONTHS)

I HAD BY THIS TIME, had a month at my new job. I was working as a secretary at the Leeds Dental Institute each weekday afternoon. I loved it. Finally, I had a reasonable wage coming in and a renewed sense of purpose to my life. And I began the next levels of my secretarial qualifications on two weekday mornings. Tom was attending a local day nursery as the health visitor had written a letter to help me get a place. They gave preference to working single mums anyway.

For five afternoons and two mornings each week, I became 'me' again. I could do my hair, put on a bit of make-up and wear a skirt and blouse. I loved using my new secretarial skills – typing and shorthand. It was a good job that I only worked in the afternoon as mornings were incredibly tough. I was always late for the two mornings I had at college. Within minutes of waking, Tom would pelt into my room and demand the replenishment of his 'bot-bot.' I had started to give him blackcurrant instead of orange. Then he established a new routine.

The first time it occurred, I had laid half asleep, listening to a scuffling in the kitchen. I was not awake enough to act upon it. But after an almighty crash, I flew in to investigate. Flinging open the door, the sight before me made me gasp.

Covered in cat food and smeared in margarine, Tom sprawled, cross-legged, in a heap of tipped-out Persil. (I had finally been able to afford a washing machine!) The kitchen looked as though it had been burgled. In a sense, I suppose, it had. All six yogurts had been devoured and the cheese block gnawed at. Most of the fridge's contents lay strewn across the floor. A cup of tea was not an option as the carton of milk had been emptied everywhere.

This became a regular occurrence, so within days, I fitted fridge and cupboard locks, also ensuring everything in the kitchen was out of Tom's reach.

The morning after the locks had been installed; another jolt awaited me upon awakening.

I emerged from my room, stunned to realise that he was still in his bedroom.

"Tom, breakfast time." I opened his door. Then I discovered what he had done. "You naughty boy!"

The contents of his nappy had been smeared all over his bed, walls, the floor and himself. The overpowering stink made me gag. Closing the door for a moment gave me the space to take a few gulps of air and compose myself.

Then, when I reopened the door, with my jumper over my face, I was primed for the stench that whacked me like a sledgehammer.

Pinning him down, I scraped the worst from him with baby wipes as I waited for the bath to fill. Unfortunately, this little 'game' also grew habitual. It was as though he was trying to punish me.

"Perhaps he's trying to tell you he's ready to be potty trained," suggested the health visitor, wrapping her fingers around her mug of tea. By now, she had learned to keep hold of it. Although when I recounted his other escapades, particularly his tendency to escape, she was alarmed.

"You must make sure you keep all the doors and windows locked." Her gaze flashed around the room as she spoke.

"I do." I scooped Tom up and dumped him on my knee. I sensed he was about to investigate the contents of the health visitor's handbag by how he was appraising it. "But then he head-bangs when he can't have his own way."

"Now that is worrying." Placing her cup down, she slid a notebook from her bag. "How often is he doing that?"

"Every day." I lowered Tom back to the floor. He did not want to sit on my knee. "Sometimes he bangs his head on his wall, sometimes it's against the floor or if we are out, he throws his head back against the buggy. It's particularly bad at bedtime."

We both watched Tom as he hurtled to his toy box and began flinging his toys onto the floor with great gusto.

"How do you feel about me putting in a referral to the 0-19 Team?"

I chewed my bottom lip and nervously raised my eyes to hers. "What does that mean?"

"They're specialists with problem behaviour. Hopefully they'll be able to give you some advice and strategies." She was scribbling onto her notepad as she spoke.

"I'm not sure." I paused. "I'm doing all I can with him." I glanced around at my cluttered and unkempt living room, which smelt of old milk and baby wipes. "I tell him off. I watch him like a hawk." My voice faded. "I'm scared they'll blame me."

"Of course they won't." Reaching over, she rested her hand on my arm. "You're doing a wonderful job. But you do need support. I've said this all along."

"I know." I felt drained. I reluctantly agreed she could refer him. There was certainly nothing else on offer.

SECOND BID FOR FREEDOM

TOM WAS PLAYING in his room with his cars one Saturday. It was the middle of the day and he had seemed subdued after lunch, so I hoped he might take a nap which would enable me to get a few jobs done as I had been working all week. As I folded laundry, I glanced absently out of the window, dropping it all when I spotted a man dragging Tom from the road.

This time, I knew abduction was not a possibility, he must have undone the catch on his window himself. I tore across the grass, berating myself and trying to ready myself for another onslaught from a stranger.

"I'm sorry!" I tried to say before the man could unleash his condemnation. It was already evident in his expression.

"He's done this before! I'm going to nail his window down!" I struggled to get my words out between my gasps for air.

"You want reporting, you do. Look at the size of him! Thank God I saw him when I did."

"I know how it must look. I'm really sorry!"

"You will be when he gets run over. You ought to be ashamed."

I could not hold back the tears as I trudged away, wrestling to hang onto my son. There would have been no point trying to convince the man. He held a common opinion. I was useless, useless, useless, useless!

The tears rolled down my cheeks and the more I tried to quell them, the faster they came. I longed for someone to be at home for me to offload with. I was sick of having no one to talk to. Even at work, I was in my own office so only spoke to the consultant I was secretary to or to people on the phone. I still missed Peter but had heard rumours that he had a new girlfriend.

THE 0-19 TEAM

"What causes him to bang his head?" The man peered over his glasses as Tom tipped out the entire toy box with a crash. His pen was poised above his clipboard.

"Usually when he's upset about something."

Tom sifted through the toys, presumably searching for one which appealed to him.

"What sort of things is he upset by?" The man crossed his legs; his trousers boasted a pristine crease down the centre, his socks sported a diamond pattern and he wore the shiniest shoes I had ever seen.

I shuffled awkwardly. "Mealtimes, bedtimes, bath times; being made to sit in his buggy." Tom was becoming restless as he lolled among the discarded toys. I resisted the urge to attend to him. "Anything."

"Do you tell him off?" As he posed the question, he ducked in time to allow a carefully aimed toy to skim the top of his head. His expectant expression conveyed that he expected me to do something about this.

"Of course I tell him off – it's all I ever seem to do." I leaned over to where Tom sat, beaming mischievously at a pair of scissors he had discovered in the toy box. I took them and thrust them at the man, resisting the urge to say something.

"Do you smack him?" He placed the scissors in a drawer.

"I sometimes shout or smack his hand." I expected him to approve but he stared at me.

"We don't condone smacking." I tried to see what he was scribbling on his clipboard but he raised it towards his chest.

"I meant *tap* his hand." Perhaps in adding that he would alter *shocking mother* to *not-so-bad mother!*

"He is lively." Tom was amusing himself by grabbing and hurling items from the man's desk. "No, please don't do that," the man implored as he bent to retrieve a hole punch from his grasp. Normally I would have intervened, but I wanted him to experience Tom in all his glory.

"I'm worried there's something wrong with him." I said.

The man, seemingly giving up, allowed Tom to have the hole punch.

"He's constantly on the go, as you can see. He sleeps terribly and destroys whatever he can get his hands on."

"I see. And he's not even two yet?" The man looked irked as a million tiny white circles littered his immaculate green carpet.

"No." I outstretched my hand to Tom for the hole punch.

"Have you thought about a parenting course?" The man fished around in his briefcase.

I chewed my lip to quell the expletive that threatened to be spoken. What an utter waste of time. The man was useless. I rose from my seat to retrieve Tom, adamant that I would sort him out myself.

I would be stricter; enforce a tighter routine. Everything would be kept out of his way and more locks would be fitted. Whatever it took to manage him better would be implemented. But there were always going to be occasions when my vigilance might lapse.

When we got home, I poured Tom a drink and switched on the TV. Normally I would have put on a video tape to amuse him. Unfortunately, days before, the machine had grown exhausted of being stuffed with food and toys. It was ready to join the growing list of Tom's breakages.

"Just sit there sweetheart. Mummy's nipping to the loo. Won't be a moment."

Within seconds, there was a deafening bang. Sprinting back into the room, I saw that Tom had lodged himself behind the cabinet and pushed the TV to the floor. It smoked and sparked like a volcano.

I flew towards Tom, grabbed him and raced with him over to the door. The TV made a peculiar popping noise before it died its death.

"Great. Thanks very much." I inhaled the scent of the smoking TV. There went the one thing that kept me going in the evening. I would have to try and buy a new one on credit as my monthly wage wouldn't cover the one-off purchase of a TV. Listening to the radio was not an option either as Tom had previously snapped the aerial. He always targeted items that would be expensive to replace. It was soul destroying.

EXTRA PARENT ONE

NOVEMBER 1995 (AGED 1 YEAR, 10 MONTHS)

"HELLO STRANGER!" I flung the door open to find Martin standing there. He had lived in my former street and I had occasionally looked after his daughters when he and his wife were stuck. I had Tom literally under one arm, battling to get free. After a moment, I released him and he bolted off towards the lounge.

"I'm sorry," heat rose to my face as I glanced down at my floor length skirt with my nightie still over the top of it. I dragged my fingers through my wild hair. "I haven't had chance to get dressed properly yet!"

"Don't worry." He twisted car keys within his fingers. "I should've rung first."

"Come in." I opened the door a little wider. "I'll put the kettle on." He was a nice man and I was sure he wouldn't judge me for the mess. Besides, ten minutes of adult conversation would be a welcome distraction.

He followed me to the lounge. Tom was racing in a zigzag fashion from one wall of the room to the other and back again. Looking at my lounge, I saw what Martin must be seeing. Curtains were half hung and cups were overturned. Strewn toys and clothes carpeted the floor. God knows what was smeared on a window, I hadn't had chance to wipe it, and a picture had been smashed. It was as though a tornado had ripped through the room, damaging everything in its path. But my little tornado was still escalating.

"Enough!" I screeched at him.

"You make some tea." Martin stepped towards him. "I'll keep an eye on this one."

I watched them through the serving hatch between the lounge and the kitchen. Martin caught Tom in mid-flight and bent down. "Hello there, you've grown since I last saw you." Then his phone fell from his top pocket. I was surprised to see someone with a mobile phone in 1995. Tom immediately seized it.

"No. No Tom!" Backing away with Martin's phone, Tom had an evil sneer on his lips. "Give it to me," he coaxed, moving towards him. Raising his arm, he launched it at the wall. Bolting towards it, Martin managed to retrieve it before Tom did.

"It's alright – it's unscathed!" Martin's expression was loaded with sympathy as I returned to the living room bearing two mugs of tea. Tom was now vaulting from the windowsill onto the sofa. "You've got your hands full!"

"I know." I passed Martin a mug before sinking onto a chair.

"Perhaps I could call round one evening when he's in bed?" he suggested, as we sipped our tea. "We can have a *proper* catch up." *Then* he added, "I'll bring wine."

"What about Louise?" I was still puzzled as to what Martin was doing *here,* without her.

"We've split up. We're getting a divorce."

"I'm sorry." Inadvertently, a bubble of excitement rose in my stomach. Martin was a good-looking man. I tried to quell it.

"Don't be. I'm not. I found out where you'd moved to from Peter."

"*Peter?*"

"Yes. He's got a new girlfriend, hasn't he?"

So the rumours had been true then. "A glass of wine one night would be lovely," I agreed. "Only be warned, it's not always simple to get Tom to bed."

~

On Friday evening, Martin returned. I had asked him not to come until nine so I might have some chance of getting Tom to sleep. I had purposely woken him early and asked nursery to only let him have a short nap if he'd needed one. Not that he normally did!

"Ssssh." I said as I answered the door. "He's asleep." I'd made sure I looked a bit better than last time Martin had seen me. I was wearing my new top with my short denim skirt. I'd even managed to find time whilst Tom was watching Teenage Mutant Ninja Turtles to blow dry my hair.

We tiptoed through the hallway and I clicked the living room door behind us.

"I'll get some glasses," I announced, spotting the wine he was clutching. The living room was in much better shape than it had been last time he was here too. As he poised to perch on the sofa, there were several blobs of dried nail varnish. Martin gingerly lowered himself next to it.

"Oh, I stupidly left a bottle of nail varnish out," I explained, placing the glasses on the coffee table. "It was so upsetting; the sofa was new. I've not even finished paying for it yet!"

Martin pointed next, to the cracked window. "Don't tell me he's done that as well!"

"I'm afraid so!" I followed his gaze. "He lobbed his bottle at it."

He shook his head. "How old is he now?"

"He'll be two in six weeks!" I passed him a corkscrew and he began uncorking the wine.

Tom must have sensed he was being discussed, for at that moment, he burst in through the door.

"Bot-bot!" The bottle he launched nearly struck me. Retrieving it, I headed to the kitchen.

For ten minutes, he screamed fiercely whilst I tried to settle him back into bed. No amount of coercion or offers to read a story were going to work. Tom knew Martin was in the lounge and was probably scared of missing something. I had been looking forward to Martin coming around – I'd never really viewed him as 'boyfriend' material before, but he was single, I was single, and we'd always got along with each other. *What harm was there in spending a bit of time together.* Finally, I gave up. I was looking forward to my glass of wine and chatting to Martin. I balanced Tom on one hip and walked back to the lounge.

"It's no good. He's wide awake!" I gestured towards the glass Martin clutched. "Just make sure you keep that in your hand!"

Martin left after one glass. It was difficult to talk over Tom and it was apparent he was not going to settle back down and go back to bed.

"Can you get a babysitter sometime?" He asked as I saw him out.

"I can try." Then, gathering all the courage I could muster, I said, "are you asking me out?"

"Yes. I suppose I am." He smiled at me. "Sarah, would you like to get a babysitter and come out with me as soon as possible?"

As I shut the door behind him, excitement tugged at me. I was pleased he seemed to like me, but he looked more than just a bit repelled by Tom. I hoped that he would not be scared off like the last one.

THIRD BID FOR FREEDOM

I WAS TAKING no chances with Tom's safety after his previous 'break-outs' and had therefore nailed down his bedroom window. Of course, he discovered an alternative escape route: the balcony, which our external living room door opened onto. Never would I have imagined he could possibly climb over the railings, let alone negotiate the six-foot drop at the other side.

Visiting friends looked sceptical when I showed them the height from which Tom had jumped or lowered himself. Martin had, by now, become a regular visitor but I noticed he tended to arrive late, after Tom had gone to bed. By now, we'd had three evenings out together. Once to the pub, once for a meal and once out clubbing. Peter had taken Tom on these occasions.

I suspected his new girlfriend was taking part in these overnight stays, but I had to push that to the back of my mind. It was wonderful to get dressed up and put make up on again, to go out and be twenty-two with the attention of a good-looking man. Martin rang me all the time when we weren't together, even at work.

I was having to be careful that the consultant, my boss, didn't catch me on the phone when I was supposed to be working. Still, I had butterflies every time I thought about him – something I couldn't even recall feeling with Peter.

One evening, I was washing the dishes whilst Tom was surrounded by the contents of his upturned toy box. Whether he played with them or launched them over the balcony was debatable, but he was momentarily quiet. Inhaling the floral scent of washing up liquid, I gazed absently through the window. My attention was suddenly diverted to yelling voices and car horns. I tried to see what was going on, suspecting that there must have been an accident.

An all-too-familiar blonde head became visible amongst several stationary vehicles. Even though I knew it was him, I still glanced into the living room in case I was mistaken, and he was innocently playing with his toys. I could barely catch my breath as I hurtled from our flat, towards the commotion.

It was as though time slowed as I ran to him, terrified he'd been hurt. Within moments, I was in the centre of the road, scooping him into my arms. Angry rants from the cars' occupants echoed all around me. I longed to defend myself, though I knew it would be futile. Tom was safe – that was the main thing. I gripped him tightly as words of fury continued to be flung. He writhed in my arms like an abducted child, in fact, I was surprised no one challenged me about whether I was even his mother.

I placed one foot in front of the other, not daring to look back. Each jeer forced a fresh tear behind my eyes, and I hoped to make it back into the flat before I let them slide down my face.

"You naughty, naughty boy!" Tom continued to wriggle.

In retrospect, I can understand the opinions of the onlookers; what an incompetent, irresponsible parent I must have seemed.

Fresh air within our home became a luxury I was forced to forsake. Any opportunity such as a door left ajar or a slightly open window obviously would prove too much for Tom to resist.

Aaargh!

EXTRA PARENT TWO

JANUARY 1996 (2 YEARS)

I HAD a tea-party for Tom on his second birthday. One of his friends brought along an electronic Buzz Lightyear he had received at Christmas. When he wasn't allowed to keep it, Tom jealously wrenched an arm from its socket.

He bit two children, trapped the finger of another and pulled a fistful of a little girl's hair when he wanted a cake she had picked up. Another of my living room windows met its demise when Tom hurled his new truck at it, then he narrowly avoided burning himself when he made a sudden grab at his lit birthday cake. There was food splattered everywhere and I was relieved beyond words when the 'party' ended.

The other mothers, all friends to me, must have sensed my stress and maintained a polite silence. One friend though, Tina, made a comment as she left that afternoon;

"Sarah, I'm not sure how you cope!" Wide-eyed, she appeared to survey all the debris. "Is Tom's behaviour always this bad?"

"Hopefully he'll grow out of it," I held the door open for her.

"I don't think I could manage." She clutched the hand of

her well-behaved daughter. "You're brave for attempting a party!"

Later, Tom's dad arrived with his new girlfriend. It was a moment I had been dreading but was inevitable. She looked younger than me. Having said that, I was so stressed; *anyone* would have looked younger than *me*!

"Sarah, this is Elizabeth." Peter looked nervous.

"Nice to meet you." I tried to smile as I offered my hand. "Can I get you a drink?"

"No," Elizabeth seemed unsure of me. "Thanks, but we can't stay long."

"You'd be lucky to drink it anyway," laughed Peter. "Drinks don't last long around Tom!"

"So, are you going to spend some time with him?" I asked Peter. "I'd prefer it if you could take him out." I held the door ajar so he could view Tom's handiwork. "I had a party and have a lot of cleaning to do."

"Oh my God," gasped Peter. "Did you leave them all unattended?"

"Don't be stupid!" I began gathering food remains. "Anyway, it wasn't all of them. It was mainly Tom!"

"Do you need a hand?" offered Elizabeth. I warmed to her then, feeling perhaps we might have been friends if we had met in different circumstances.

"No, I'll be OK, but thanks." I scraped something dubious looking from the carpet.

"Would you like us to take Tom overnight," she continued, bending down beside him as he tore open the last of his presents. "I bet you could do with a break. We're staying at my parents tonight. I'm sure they'd love to meet him."

"Are you sure that's a good idea?" Peter looked reluctant. "You can see what he's capable of!"

"We can keep him in line between us, *surely*?" She began squashing wrapping paper into a carrier bag.

I suddenly felt possessive. "It's fine. Don't worry." Rising from the floor, I wiped my hands on a paper napkin. "Just take him for a couple of hours so I can have a break."

We deliberated for a while. Eventually I relented and packed an overnight bag for him. I was devoid of all energy as I watched Peter wrestle him into his coat, then fasten him into his pushchair.

There was now an option between ringing Martin and perhaps having a night out. Or I could have a peaceful evening in and a restful night's sleep. I surveyed in sadness as Peter, Elizabeth and Tom strolled across the grass, away from my flat. To an unknown observer, they appeared like the little family unit that I, myself, had forever yearned for. I had to prevent myself bolting after them and demanding that Elizabeth hand my baby back. For a moment it was like she was stealing him from me. Tears flooded my eyes as she took over pushing the buggy. *She had my baby!* I was bereft as I realised people would assume *she* was Tom's Mum.

I decided to ring Martin. Young and carefree was in order. But he didn't answer.

WHAT BEHAVIOUR COULD GET YOU BARRED FROM A PUB?

1. Fighting?
2. Being in possession of illegal substances?
3. Being drunk and disorderly?
4. Vandalism?
5. Theft?
6. Underage drinking?
7. Climbing up onto a pool table, pulling down your trousers and urinating all over the pool table?

If anyone has a tale of someone getting barred from a pub younger than two-and-a-half, please let me know.

MARBLE UP MY BUM!

JULY 1996 (2 YEARS, 7 MONTHS)

"MARBLE UP MY BUM!" Tom sang from where he squatted on the carpet. "Marble up my bum!"

I peered at him. Surely not. A sensation of dread stole around me as I envisaged a trip to the accident and emergency department. Fortunately, I was spared the humiliation. After an hour of coaxing and bribery on my part, he pushed it back out into his potty.

His messing himself was relentless. I grew tempted to revert to nappies. But he was potty trained and would go several days without 'an accident.' Whilst at nursery, he never *once* soiled or wet himself.

Because of his frequent accidents, it was necessary to bath him twice daily, which was a nightmare. Although the clamouring to get out of the bath had subsided, he still poured water *everywhere.* Most problematic was that he had started to conduct his toileting whilst in the bath. I would sense from his face that he was 'straining.' I would whisk him out of the water and dump him on the toilet. Once, however, I momentarily left him, whilst I got shampoo from the cupboard. I re-entered the bathroom and was baffled to see him stood inside the toilet bowl. Meanwhile, particles of poo were floating around the bath.

"Do you think there might be something wrong with him?" Martin once asked. I became extremely protective at this. Tom was just naughty – *how dare Martin suggest there might be something wrong with him!* Martin had two daughters from his marriage and his ex-wife had already said they weren't allowing them around Tom as he bullied them. In suggesting something might be wrong though, Martin was only echoing my own worries.

Whenever, I tried to keep a tight rein of Tom in a shop or at a bus stop he would bite me like an angry dog. But more worrying was his biting of other children. His nursery reported daily occurrences of it. Then a horrible incident happened at my flat when Cathy had brought Jack to play. She hadn't been around so much since the Scarborough day out, so it was always nice to see her. She seemed to prefer conducting our conversations as friends by telephone.

As we chatted, the boys fought over a toy. Jack was bent forwards, so Tom dropped his head onto Jack's back. I watched, rooted to the spot in horror as Tom dug his teeth into exposed skin above Jack's waistband. The skin whitened, stretched taut as the bite deepened. Cathy leapt to her feet and literally had to hook her fingers in between Tom's teeth and her son's skin to release his grip.

Jack howled in agony. Cathy barely looked at me as she left our flat with her sobbing son. Apparently, the injury took weeks to heal.

THE URINALS

SCENE - *The Royal public house tap room, football match on, me returning from ladies' loos.*

Man: Is that your son with the blond hair?

Me: (frantically looking around) Eh? Yes. My boyfriend is looking after him. Just whilst I was in the loo.

Man: Well he's not doing a very good job. Your son is currently in the gents. I think he'll need a bath when you get him home.

Martin: (jumping to feet) Oh no, I was engrossed in the match, I'm sorry!

. . .

Man: (displaying expression of disgust) He's been climbing in the urinals and throwing air fresheners around.

Me: (upon observation of a drenched and pungent Tom) Look at the state of you! Martin! Why weren't you watching him?

Martin: I can take my girls anywhere - they'd never behave like that. I'm telling you now; you need help. *He's not right.*

MORE ABOUT MORNINGS

AUGUST 1996 (AGED 2 YEARS, 8 MONTHS)

RESPITE WAS AFFORDED by virtue of three Godsends:

1. My job
2. Tom's fortnightly overnight stay with his dad
3. Our fortnightly babysitter

Of course, we took full advantage of these Tom-free evenings and would try to have a night out. After all, I was twenty three and Martin was twenty six. We practically lived together by now but argued when Tom was around. I wanted his help but then didn't want it at the same time. He judged us and I hated him for it. And he always compared Tom to his own daughters.

However, we had a great time when it was the two of us. Inevitably we would progress to a nightclub and return home a little worse for wear at a ridiculous hour of the night. Looking back, this was madness when I had Tom to face the next day!

The flat would be wrecked when we returned to the babysitter, however, the full horror of his destruction would not become apparent until we had sobered up the following morning.

Tom would sometimes get up unheard. We must have been comatose not to be alerted as he rampaged through the flat. Balancing on his slide, he would then be able to reach the elevated kitchen door lock in order to empty the fridge and cupboards.

~

As dawn broke one summer's day, I, in my semi-intoxicated state, felt increasingly sick. At first, I blamed wine from the previous evening. Then it became apparent that Tom had smeared my hair with butter as I slept. This was heating up and emitting an awful stink!

Closer inspection of the kitchen revealed that he had gnawed at the cheese, devoured all the yogurts and the contents of the cat bowl. Any form of liquid that could be poured, had been. It was 5.30 am.

Martin and I ended up rowing. He told me what I had long since suspected. That Tom repulsed him, and I would be hard pressed to find any man who would take us on. By six o'clock, he had stormed out, leaving me to clean up the mess with tears streaming down my face.

THE HYPERACTIVE CHILDREN'S SUPPORT GROUP

HAVING FELT LESS than enamoured with the 0-19 Team, I set about doing my own research and stumbled across the HCSG in a pamphlet. The following letter shone a light into my darkness.

*Dear Sally Bunday, (*This is the founder of the group)

I feel compelled to write to you, as with your help I have now got an adorable 4-year-old boy, whom I now love very much. This was not the case six months ago. He has gone from being an aggressive, spiteful child with more tantrums in a day than I care to remember, to a loving, affectionate, bright and intelligent little boy - all because of his diet.

Following the advice given in the booklet, we have eliminated the 'culprits' from his diet - mainly 'colours', chocolate, orange and many preservatives. We have occasional 'blips' as we call them, but these are usually caused by M. having foodstuffs that he shouldn't have, through no fault of his own. He now knows what he can and can't have and willingly goes without.

If only I had asked for your help earlier on, I would have avoided the hate and the unrest in the family. I even had to have a course of antidepressants and finally gave up my job as a midwife. But now, life suddenly looks rosy again.

I hope you continue your good work. If only people would recognise that this is a major problem and that hyperactive children can be helped.

Many thanks,

Mrs A.G. Reading, Berks.

Already, I suspected that diet could be a factor with Tom's behaviour. He would be awful if I allowed him to have sweets. A magazine article had highlighted the danger of food additives, especially in fruit juice and fizzy drinks. His thirst was still immense, I wondered whether there was something sinister in the fruit juice he always craved. I started to keep a diary to discover any link between food and drink and his behaviour. If only it had been that straightforward.

I maintained these diaries for several months before concluding that there wasn't any reliable association. Certain things sometimes affected him and at other times, didn't. When particularly affected, his pupils would dilate, and his eyes would literally look like black marbles. I decided to subscribe to the Hyperactive Children's Support Group. I thought it couldn't hurt to follow the dietary advice about colourings, flavourings and foods to avoid. There was tons of advice on parenting techniques, most of which I was doing anyway. It was reassuring though, to realise that other mothers had similar problems with their children. My loneliness eased slightly.

However, I had to admit that his behaviour wasn't just 'over-activeness.' It was an endless daily battle in every sense, and it showed no signs of abating. Previously, I had hoped that armed with the power of speech, Tom might have been more open to being reasoned with and less frustrated as he would be able to communicate his feelings.

If anything, it was all deteriorating. I took him back to the doctor.

As he trashed her surgery, she fired questions at me. "Are you sure he's not just naughty?" She watched as he clambered up onto the examination bed and leapt off it. "Children do typically push their boundaries at his age."

"No." I retrieved him from bouncing up and down on the weighing scales. "He's been like this for a long time."

"Do you think it's worsened since you separated from his dad?" Noticing his interest in her briefcase, she yanked it out of his reach.

I looked at her, bemused as I sank back into my chair. "How could he remember? He was only six months old."

"Do you have a new partner?" She asked. "Sometimes that can be unsettling for a child and their behaviour can suffer."

"Yes, but his presence has no effect on Tom as far as I can see," I replied. I decided not to add Martin's opinion that something was 'wrong' with him.

"Maybe he's just energetic," she suggested. We both watched him as he used the emptied upturned toy box as an aid to climb onto her desk. I sprang up and seized him again.

"Could you be *depressed* Sarah?" She tapped her pen against the side of her face. "That could be why you're finding it tricky to cope."

"I'm definitely not depressed!" I tried to restrain Tom on my knee before he caused any more destruction. "I sometimes get a bit down with it all, like anyone would. I'm finding it difficult to cope because he's such a handful. He still doesn't sleep properly. And as you can see, he never stops moving." Powerless to keep hold of him, I lowered him back to the floor. "He's biting others constantly and his tantrums are horrendous."

"OK," I struggled to hear her above the din he was creating. "I'm going to get a child psychologist to see you both." I wanted to cheer as she typed on her computer. "I'm not sure what they'll be able to do. He's still young. But we can give it a try."

THE CHILD PSYCHOLOGIST

WHEN THE APPOINTMENT TOOK PLACE, I decided to take Martin with me. He had spent enough time around Tom to be able to back me up and seemed pleased that I'd invited his involvement, as well as finally having listened to him. I didn't tell him that his 'opinion' had nothing to do with this referral – I'd always handled Tom myself and would continue to do so.

I also asked Peter and Elizabeth along, hoping that 'en-masse', we might be more forceful, and I would be less likely to be treated as a young, clueless single parent. Peter and Martin seemed to have adapted well to their new roles of being my 'ex' and my 'current' partner. I got on well with Elizabeth too, so woe betide any expert 'professional' who tried to blame relationship breakdown or parental dysfunction for Tom's behaviour.

Tom catapulted around the antiseptic-smelling room, like a sprung ball in a pinball machine. We all introduced ourselves. The psychologist was a middle-aged woman; with a worn face and a brisk voice. She began by reading out the letter from my doctor.

"*I would be grateful if you could advise this lady who has an 'over-active' little boy.*" She glanced at Tom before continuing. "*I believe she would benefit from advice in controlling his angry outbursts, particularly when in public. He is also prone to biting.*" She pulled a face. "*In addition, she has made me aware that she is having toilet-training difficulties with him.*"

"So," began the psychologist, pressing the letter into quarters. "What help would you like in particular?"

"Anything and everything! Whatever you can offer!" I smiled, watching as Tom tipped out a box of bricks. The woman did not smile back.

"I'm really struggling with him. Stop it Tom!" He was hurling the bricks around. "I've brought along my behaviour diaries I've been keeping for a few months." I fished around in my bag. "Can I read you bits of them?"

"Go ahead." The woman relaxed backwards in her chair, a bored expression on her face. "That might be helpful."

I cleared my throat and began reading. *"Just before bed, I caught him smearing poo over his bedroom wall."* The room was silent. I straightened up in my chair.

"Martin took him to the park where he was throwing stones at cars. He tried to wee over another child, but she got away." Martin shook his head at the memory.

"Took him to visit a friend. He bit their dog!"

"He bit *their* dog!" The woman looked flabbergasted and by the look in her eyes, did not believe me either.

I nodded before continuing. *"Put him to bed at eight. Checked on him at nine, he had stripped his bed, emptied his cupboard of clothes and was wedged behind his bed with books piled on top of him. He finally settled at around 11.15pm."*

I peered at the woman.

"Go on."

Taking a deep breath, I flicked forwards several pages. *"Caught him standing on the table, weeing at the TV."*

Peter chuckled but straightened his face in response to my glare.

"Put kitten in freezer," was an entry made by Elizabeth. Another read, *"Shut kitten in dustbin."*

Swapping the diary for another one, I read from a randomly opened page. *"At a friend's house, he took her baby daughter's nappy off and was laughing at her bum!"*

"Using a 'swipe' action, swept all my belongings from my dressing table. After I had picked them up, he did it again."

"And again and again and again," Martin interjected. "Sarah, I don't know why you bother to *try* and keep things on your dressing table."

I ignored him. *"Tantrum on bus. He was screaming and trying to bite me then he bolted into the road as we got off.* He behaves like that every time we use public transport," I added.

"He sounds like a character!" She smiled now, surveying him. He was trying to climb up the back of Peter's chair.

"What Sarah is trying to get across to you," Martin addressed the woman now. "Is that the examples of behaviour she has given are not isolated incidents." He glanced at me as though seeking my approval that it was OK to speak out about my son in this way. "Every minute of every day, she has her hands full with him. He never, ever stops. He seizes every opportunity to do something as out of the ordinary as possible."

"He *is* only three." The woman seemed to be disregarding his comments. "Also, no disrespect to you, Sarah, but you are young." Her eyes washed over me in appraisal. "It's often hard to manage." My face burned with indignation. "I'm twenty-three, not sixteen! And I've been on my own with him since he was six months old! I'm perfectly used to it!"

"It's never easy when you're on your own." Her tone was gentle as she ignored my comments too. I was infuriated.

"She's not on her own anymore," Martin said.

I wish you'd make your bloody mind up, I wanted to reply.

"I think the diaries you've been keeping are a fantastic idea." The woman pointed to the books in my hand. "There may well be a link between his behaviour and what he is eating. I'm going to send you an appointment to see a dietitian to get further advice." Reaching behind, she took a pen and notebook from her desk. "And that's it?" I deflated as I tried to decipher her writing from upside-down. I hadn't really known what I wanted her to do but it was more than just seeing a dietitian. "Will we not have another appointment with you?"

"There's not a lot I can do." She shrugged dismissively as she dropped her pen. "I just need to take a few details from you, so I know where to send the appointment."

I bent to retrieve the pen. Tom had snatched it up. Knowing I wanted it, he screamed and clutched it tighter. When I finally prised it from his grasp, he launched himself to the floor hysterically. I gathered him up and tried to sit him on my knee, which he had never liked. Before gaining the power of movement, I had been able to sit him on my knee and cuddle him. But now he arched his back and flayed his arms wildly.

"Try holding him a little tighter," the woman suggested, noticing his reticence. "That's it. Wrap your arms around him and grip him firmly until his temper subsides."

Tom let me know he did not like this by slinging his head backwards into my face. I jerked it out of his way just in time.

"Hold him as firmly as you can," continued the woman, her face hardening slightly as Tom began booting me. "Place your leg, across his to stop that." In demonstration, she swung one of her legs across the other. After a few moments Tom's anger seemed to ebb out of him.

"That seems to work." She appeared delighted. "If you

restrain him in that way, he will begin to learn that *you're* in charge, not *him*. Whenever he is over-active, hold him securely until the anger goes." She swept her gaze over Martin, Peter and Elizabeth too as if silently advocating this method to them as well. "Once he realises you have got him and he can't do as he wants, he *will* calm down, you'll see."

PERCEPTIONS OF OTHERS (A "SOCIAL WORKER")

MARTIN and I decided to stop for a drink in a beer garden on the way home. It was a gorgeous evening and we both needed to 'de-stress' after the appointment. We'd been getting on a bit better now I'd accepted that I needed outside support with Tom, and Martin had been making noises about properly moving all his belongings in. Much of his stuff was still at his parents' house, where he'd stayed when first separating from his ex-wife.

As soon as we parked, Tom sprang from the car with the enthusiasm of an animal released from captivity. We found a seat but instead of enjoying the play equipment, he kept charging towards the gate. I was up and down, repeatedly dragging him back to the table, terrified he would make it to the gate as there was a road nearby. After a while, he tired of this 'game,' and instead, filled his pocket with stones, finding great amusement in chucking them around. People sat near us peered uncomfortably at him, and us.

Then, in an unguarded moment, he took a swipe at my drink. There was a crash as the glass shattered on the floor, then a titter of disapproval went up. My face blazed as every eye in the beer garden rested upon me.

"I'll get you another and a dustpan and brush." Martin stood, glowering at Tom. "Then we'll get out of here."

"I think we should go now," I protested. But he had already vanished inside.

As I tried to gather the larger shards of glass, Tom tried to bolt towards the pub after Martin. Recalling the advice of the psychologist, I raced after him and hauled him back to our table. Dropping him onto my lap, I endeavoured to firmly hold him in the way she had demonstrated. My arms fastened around his arms and upper body. I pressed him close so that he could not throw his head back. Desperately, he kicked his legs as I prayed he would soon calm down. It was taking all my strength to keep hold of him. His face was contorted with rage as he squealed like a piglet facing slaughter.

"What you are doing is *disgusting*!" hissed a woman, who cannot have been any older than me. She surveyed me with her hands resting on her hips and hatred in her eyes.

"W-what?" I relaxed my hold on Tom. I hadn't planned on interference from onlookers.

"I'm a social worker. That's wrong." Her top lip curled in disgust. "It's child abuse. Let him go." She bent forwards and tried to get hold of his arm. "You're hurting him."

"Of course I'm not!" I stood, balancing Tom on my hip. "I've been shown by a child psychologist how to restrain him actually. So mind your own business!" The air was heavy with silence.

"You want that child taking off you!" She beckoned two other women to join her. "You cruel bitch!" She began tugging at Tom from behind.

"Get off him!" I tried to maintain my hold but suddenly, I was hurled to the ground by the two women. The 'social worker' was booting me in the head. Thud, thud, thud.

Howling in pain, I could hear Tom's wails echoing around and could only pray that he would not use this opportunity to bolt into the road.

"Get off her!" Urgent footsteps stamped towards me. "Get the hell away from her!" Martin dragged them all off me and they dispersed into the gathered crowd. He pulled me to my feet and towards the car, hauling Tom behind him. I was weeping hysterically. Blood drizzled down the side of my face. The pain to my head was agonising but overwhelmingly, I cried with shame.

THE DIETITIAN

I WAS ADVISED by the dietitian to look on the internet for help. The appointment was a waste of time. However, I found a form of use:

It was a shopping list template listing additives to avoid. There were 19 different colours, 9 preservatives, 5 emulsifiers and 6 flavour enhancers.

So as well as having Tom's behaviour to contend with whilst shopping - I would now also have to spend time studying every packet and tin that went into the trolley.

THE GP (AGAIN)

MAY 1997 (AGE 3 YEARS, 5 MONTHS)

"Is Tom not with you?" The GP peered past me as I walked in.

"No, he's at nursery."

"So, Sarah, how can I help you today?" She leant towards me.

"It's Tom, it's not getting any better," I began. "I need something to slow him down!" I clasped my hands together. "He's on the go constantly and I can't afford to take my eyes off him for a moment."

"You know we can't give him anything." She shook her head. "He's still little. It's not as simple as being able to medicate him."

"But he's wrecking everything. My home, in fact everything I've got. He breaks all his own stuff too." I paused as I remembered other information I needed to add. "Then there's the pooing and the biting. I don't know what to do with him – I'm at my wits end!"

"He's still soiling? Have you tried putting him back in nappies?"

"Of course." I laughed incredulously. "He takes them off.

He's *potty trained* when at nursery." I sighed. "He's so naughty; I wish I knew what I was doing wrong!"

"I can refer you to the 0-19 Team again," she suggested.

"But they were useless!" I shuddered at the memory. "There must be someone else who can help!"

"It may be a different person this time. Some of the staff can be more helpful than others." She poised her pen, awaiting my go-ahead. "Obviously they all have expertise in different areas of child development."

"Fine then, I'll give it another go."

I left the surgery feeling anything but optimistic.

DIFFERENT 'EXPERTS' (THE 0-19 TEAM)

SEPTEMBER 1997 (3 YEARS, 9 MONTHS)

THIS TIME I ATTENDED ALONE. Thankfully it was not the same man as the last time we had seen the 0-19 Team. There were *two* assessors this time. A man and a woman. Feeling apprehensive, I sat down.

"How can we help?" The man eventually raised his head from studying a form. I noticed his huge nose and combed over hair.

"My son has severe behaviour problems." My voice was shaky. "I think there could be something wrong with him."

"That's certainly a worrying thing for you to be saying about your son – how old is he – three?" The woman surveyed me in a way that made me feel even more uncomfortable. She looked close to retirement age with tightly curled hair and glasses which hung from a chain and rested upon her bosom. "What makes you think that?"

I reeled off all the usual information. Sleeping, impulsivity, over activity, biting, soiling and smearing, etc, etc. I was beginning to feel like I had been through it so many times.

However, they *seemed* to be paying attention. They were

making the right noises as I spoke. This spurred me on. They *did* seem sympathetic as I reeled it all off.

"Right, let's get a bit of background," the woman announced, pulling a pen from her bag and accepting a form from her colleague. "Is it just you and Tom at home?"

"No, there's my boyfriend, Martin." I flinched as I used the word *boyfriend.* Obviously, *husband* would have sounded more respectable.

"And he's Tom's biological father?"

"Er, no, he's not." I fiddled with my necklace.

"I see." She wrote something. "And how long have you been together?"

"Nearly two years." I leaned against the back of my seat, feeling more confident. Two years was decent. I was not some mother that introduced any random man to her son.

"Does Martin get on with Tom?" Her neck veins protruded as she bobbed her head up and down in time to her questions.

"Of course." For a moment I wished he had accompanied me to this meeting. "But he struggles with Tom's behaviour too."

"How old was Tom when you separated from his real dad?" She turned her form over.

"About six months." It seemed such a long time ago.

"Hmm. Right." Looking thoughtful, she uncrossed her legs. "Parental separation might be a contributory factor here. It often is."

"But he was six months old. *And* it was all amicable. His dad still sees him. I don't think it's that at all!"

The man spoke. "What about your parents Sarah? Do they help out?" He fired questions without waiting for an answer. "Does Tom have a good relationship with them?"

I shook my head. "I don't have contact with my mum, to be honest." Holding my breath, I knew this was probably the vital nugget of information they would have been waiting for.

"Oh." The woman looked taken aback. "Why's that?"

"I used to be in care." My voice was unsteady. "It's a long time ago, but I didn't see my family for eight years." Every time I said the words, sadness tugged within me. "I'm in touch with them now though, apart from my mum, that is."

"*You were in care?* For how long?"

"Why do you want to know?" I sat forward, poised to defend my corner.

"It could be relevant. These things often are."

"Just whilst I was a teenager. But it wasn't my fault," I added quickly. This was what I had fretted about. That they would blame *me* for Tom's behaviour.

"Have you any brothers or sisters?"

"Two sisters. Two brothers. All younger." I pressed my hands together in my lap.

"Were *they* in care with you?" The woman was continuously scribbling notes.

"No. Why?" Butterflies were batting their wings defensively within my stomach. "What does that matter anyway?"

"Why were only *you* in care?"

"Because it was only me that my mum didn't want." I cringed, aware of how pathetic I sounded. "She wasn't well at the time."

"What was the matter?" *Nosy cow!*

"Severe depression." I studied the gaudy floral lamp on the table beside me. "She was in hospital for a while."

"Depression can be hereditary." She stopped writing. "Have *you* ever been assessed for depression yourself, Sarah?"

"I thought we were here to discuss Tom." My composure was starting to slip.

"Yes, but it's fascinating to know what issues parents are bringing from their own childhoods." The man spoke now, clearly preaching from the same handbook. "It can affect how they nurture *their* children." His hesitation indicated his uncertainty of whether to proceed with his next remark. "History *does* have a way of repeating itself."

"What are you implying?" The hairs on the back of my neck stood up.

"Nothing at all, we're familiarising ourselves with the situation and then we can all decide on the best way forward."

"I want help and support for my little boy." My voice was sharp now. "Why are you harping on about my childhood? I'm nothing like my own mum. I'm a caring mother and love my son. Otherwise I wouldn't be here!"

They both looked at me.

"I wonder if parenting classes might help." The man spoke again. "You're young yourself and with little support -."

"Parenting has a huge impact on behaviour -" The woman started.

I jumped to my feet.

"I'm not going to sit here while you blame me." I strode towards the door and yanked at the handle. "You're not going to help me, are you?" Banging the door of the oppressive little room behind me, I hurtled towards the freedom of the car park, vowing to soldier on myself. *What the hell did they know anyway?*

And I did, for a while, as best as I could. But I knew eventually, we would have to be taken seriously. I had finally admitted to myself that there was something behaviourally and emotionally not right with Tom. It was probably something simple to treat too. I needed someone to listen to me.

AN EXIT STRATEGY

Tom was at his worst on a morning. The breakfast throwing and refusals to dress were nothing new. But he had devised a *new* tactic. It was as though he were trying everything in his power to make mornings as problematic as he possibly could.

I repeated the same procedure with him day-after-day as I asked him the same question:

"Do you need the toilet before we go Tom?"

He would shake his head, a devilish grin dancing upon his lips.

"Are you sure? Will you have a little try for me?"

"No! Don't need to go!"

Sometimes I *made* him sit on the loo – promising him a reward of some description if he didn't poo himself.

"Oh Tom!" I would get a whiff of him at the door. "I asked if you needed to go!"

He would stare at me, a mixture of innocence and mirth, as I prepared to remove his soiled clothes and replace them with clean ones. Every single morning.

THE EXTENDED FAMILY

I WOULD SOMETIMES HAVE to implore my brothers not to laugh at Tom when they visited; they'd be amused at his antics, particularly his swearing. To hear such dreadful words emerging from such a little boy was shocking.

It was doubly mortifying when I was out with him. On public transport, I would silently pray that he would behave. To make it worse, he would thrive on the stunned reaction of any audience.

My brothers and my dad visited every Thursday and Tom would grow increasingly manic as the evening wore on. I looked forward to their visits, having not seen them for eight years. My mum had now left their family home – meaning they could all resume a relationship with me – something she had, on threat of repercussions to them, prevented.

Never did one of these family visits occur without a breakage. It might be a cup or a picture. Or something more awkward. Once he swung from the curtains, pulling the whole rail down; and another time, he yanked one of the doors from the TV cabinet.

My family would eventually tire of his behaviour. There is only so long that anyone can endure an overactive three-year-old leaping all over them!

"You *dirty* little git!" One evening, my dad wrenched Tom into the air and held him aloft, as he carted him towards his bedroom. He then vanished into the bathroom.

"What happened?" We all whispered to each other. "Did anyone see?"

It transpired that Tom had clambered onto the sofa, lodged himself behind his Grandad's back and weed over him. Stephen and Chris howled with laughter as they learned what had enraged our dad.

Chris, however, was not laughing later when Tom weed in his coffee.

HUMILIATION

JANUARY 1998 (4 YEARS, 1 MONTH)

One afternoon, I was asked into the office at nursery when I collected Tom. It was a stark room; devoid of any indication that it was linked to a nursery, apart from a child's painting on the back of the door.

"I need to speak to you about Tom's behaviour," stated the officer-in-charge, pointing to a chair in front of her desk. "I've been meaning to speak to you for a while. Normally I finish at five, but I've hung on today to see you."

Sighing, I sat down. *Here we go.*

"Other parents are complaining." She looked at me, her hands clasped together on the table before her.

"What's he done?" I tried to disguise the weariness in my voice.

"He's constantly swearing and bullying others, often smaller children." She paused and seemed to be searching my expression for a reaction. "He doesn't seem to have any concept of sharing at all. He becomes violent when he wants to play with something another child has. Is he like this at home? Does he have any brothers or sisters?"

"No, it's just him." I could feel my face heating up. "I do have friends with children of a similar age that he plays with though. He *is* used to playing with others."

"Does he play considerately with *them*?" She didn't wait for my answer. "Because he seems to be having real difficulty mixing with others *here*. When he does occasionally strike a partnership with another child, he becomes controlling and possessive. He certainly cannot play with more than one child at a time."

"I'll try to speak to him about what you've said to me, if I can get him to listen, that is!"

"Well, if you could *try* to speak to him, we'd be grateful."

"I'll do my best." I rose from my seat, thinking the conversation had concluded. But she continued.

"We're having difficulties when he plays outside too." I sank back onto the chair. "His climbing ability is extraordinary."

I laughed. "I know."

She didn't laugh. She continued. "He keeps trying to scale the exterior fence and today he got onto the roof of the kitchen." She gestured through the window to indicate the roof she was referring to. "He doesn't seem to have any fear of heights. None of us have ever seen anything like it!"

"He's always climbed." I was not shocked when I looked out at the roof. Or when I noticed the height of the fence. "He's climbed since the moment he could move. It's as though he has no sense of the danger."

"Well, it looks like we're going to have to stay vigilant." She stopped, again making me think she had finished. "Do you have any problems at home with mealtimes?"

"Well, yes," I relayed hesitantly. "But he's getting *slightly* better." "Well, you'll have to let us into your secret. It's getting to the point where we may have to separate him from the others at lunchtime. He's a terrible influence. There's more on the floor than he's eating. He's unable to concentrate."

I kept nodding as I listened to her.

"He seems to have an unlimited supply of energy too. We'd expect him to be burning himself out by lunchtime with the level of activity he maintains. Most of our children have a nap after lunch."

"Tom's never needed much sleep. Not even when he was tiny."

The officer-in charge shook her head as she carried on. "I should also mention his tendency to do his toileting outside. He has no qualms about pulling down his pants and weeing wherever the mood takes him. When he needs the toilet, he should be telling one of us." Her expression was grim. "It's unacceptable."

"I agree," I sighed. "It's a phase he's going through. I hope to God it passes." It was time to be honest – there was no other way. Maybe she could help me somehow. "I don't know what to do with him. The doctor and health visitor have seen us on numerous occasions; we've been to the 0-19 Team twice, and seen a dietitian *and* a child psychologist!"

"That information should have been given to us before now. We need to know when children in our care are being assessed for special needs."

"I was worried you wouldn't be able to keep him. I need my job. I need to work."

She did not answer; I accepted her silence as a sign that my initial fears were justified. Our conversation concluded with the agreement that they would collaborate in monitoring Tom and maintain records of his diet and behaviour. Monthly review meetings would be held to discuss his progress.

With a pain in my head beginning to emerge, I scuttled from the office to retrieve him from the construction area.

"No!" He bolted in the direction of the toilets. "Go away!"

My face was on fire. "Don't be silly Tom!" Other parents were watching. "It's time to go home." I dashed after him.

"Get off me! Don't like you!" As I caught him, he tried to pull away. "I'm staying here!"

Tears stabbed behind my eyes, but I kept them fixed on his defiant face. "Come on sweetheart." I could not bear to see anyone else's expression. "You can come back and play tomorrow!"

In the end I had to practically drag him out. In his eyes, home was probably boring; compared to nursery, anyway.

Manoeuvring him in the direction of the bus stop, I could hardly stand to speak to him. I cannot imagine what the staff and other parents must have made of us. This behaviour was repeated on other occasions as I collected him; it was also inflicted on Martin once who then said he would never pick him up again.

On the bus ride home did Tom:

a. Pull my hair?
b. Bite my hand?
c. Scratch the side of my face?
d. Wail and thrash uncontrollably?
e. Throw his shoe at a man four seats in front of us?
Or f. All the above?

(You guessed it!)

SUSPENSION FROM THE DAY NURSERY

SOON AFTER, the officer-in-charge summoned me to her office again. I had been called out of work this time. I was accustomed to regular negative reports, usually relayed from the nursery nurses. This was the second time I had been called into the office.

"I'm not sure what action we're going to take," she said, leaning on her desk. "But Tom has badly bitten a baby."

"Oh no!" I took a sharp intake of breath as I accepted the seat she pointed to. "I don't know what to say! I'm so sorry!"

"She was laid in her carry cot after lunch, and Tom, when no one was watching, bit her thumb as she was falling asleep. Her thumb is black and blue. She's not even a year old."

I was horrified. "Was it definitely him who did it?" My voice trailed off. "It's just you said no one was ..."

"Guilt was written all over his face." Her mouth was set in a thin, hard line. "I think even Tom was taken aback by the baby's screams. Her mother is furious as I'm sure you can appreciate. She's on her way."

"Can you tell her how sorry I am? I really am." I was on the brink of tears.

"I think it would be in everyone's interests if you were to collect Tom and leave the building before the other mother gets chance to confront you." Her eyes were fixed on the office door. "Understandably, she is making all kinds of threats. Tom will have to be kept away from nursery for the remainder of the week. We have to be seen to be taking action."

The door burst open. The entrant needed no introduction.

"Your monster of a son!" She shrieked as she stormed towards me. "Have you seen what he's done to my baby?"

"I'm sorry." I sprang from my chair. "I'm so sorry!"

"His teeth want extracting," she snarled as I crept past her. "What an animal!"

Hardly daring to meet her eyes, I slipped out of the room. I had never felt shame like it in all my life.

STARTING SCHOOL

SEPTEMBER 1998 (4 YEARS, 9 MONTHS)

"Come on Tom. You've got to get some sleep." I twisted my head around Tom's door. It was nearly midnight and I was about to turn in myself. "You've got a big day tomorrow."

"Can't get to sleep," he muttered from beneath his bed. "My brain won't stop thinking."

"It's because you're excited about big school." I reached under his bed to pull him from his hiding place.

"Never can get to sleep," he groaned. "Lots of spiders keep wiggling inside me."

"You'll be fine once you get used to school. It will *make* you tired."

~

Martin gave us a lift to school the next morning. Together we observed as Tom hurtled around the playground. He was so preoccupied with looking around at the other boys that he went flying over a bench, crashing to the ground at the other side.

"Oh my God!" I rushed towards him. Blood was seeping

from his forehead. A crowd gathered, dispersing as a whistle was blown.

"Trust Tom to make an entrance on his first day," I smiled at the teacher, Mrs Henderson, as we walked into the classroom. He clutched a paper towel to his head.

"We'll keep an eye on him," she assured me. "Now Tom, what do you like to do most?"

"Draw," he replied without hesitation. "And climb."

"I don't think there'll be any climbing today." She passed him some paper and a tin of crayons. "But perhaps your mum would like you to draw her a picture. You can give it to her when she comes back later."

That was my cue to leave. I had faith that 'big school', might help solve some of our problems. It would tire him out and offer Tom more structure in his life and further discipline.

~

The first few weeks passed without incident. Then one afternoon, I was waiting beside the clique of mothers for the end-of-day bell. My thoughts were broken into by Mrs Henderson who suddenly appeared beside me.

"I need to chat with you about Tom's behaviour," she began, as she bustled me inside the classroom. Tom seemed settled on a chair with a book. "We're having a few problems. He's not getting on well with other children. When they don't want to be his partner, he hits them."

"And that's not all!" Mrs Armstrong, the head teacher, strode into the classroom and came up behind Mrs Henderson. "Tom is the *only* child I have *ever* had from reception class sent to my office."

Oh no. "Why?"

"Going to the toilet in the playground! The lunchtime assistants are saying he is *always* doing it. We've had to have a chat about it, haven't we Tom?" He skulked in his chair as she addressed him. "You know we don't do that at our school!" She looked at me then.

"I'll speak to him," I promised.

"Are you going to tell your mum what else you did today Tom?" His teacher, in a gentler tone, nodded first towards Tom then the fish tank.

"I wasn't going to hurt them." His voice was small. "I wanted to see what would happen if they weren't in the water."

"We'll have to find somewhere else for you to sit if you can't be trusted near the fish tank," she continued sternly. "Have *you* got any pets Tom?"

"A cat. She's called Lulu."

"And how would you feel if anyone was to hurt Lulu like you nearly did with the fish?"

I refrained from telling them of the constant need to protect Lulu from him. In recent weeks it had been necessary to rescue her from being trapped in the door and more seriously, from being shut in the freezer. Only the previous Sunday, I had stopped Tom as he was lowering her into the bath.

"Sad," Tom replied, without averting his eyes from his book.

THE ENEMY WITHIN

Tom's teacher had asked me for 'a word' after school. "He says he's not got any toys at home," she informed me. "Although that doesn't give him permission to steal them from school."

"Of course he's got toys." My face blazed as I glanced to where Tom was scaling the racks in the cloakroom. " Well, what remains that he hasn't yet destroyed."

Unlike most parents, it was a relief that Christmas was approaching again. For several months, I had been saving to give him another batch of toys.

Martin thought I was crazy. "They'll all be broken within a month." Condescendingly, he watched as I wrapped them a week later. "Then he'll be going around trying to get people to feel sorry for him again."

It wasn't just toys he destroyed. Once, when I collected him from school, he had got hold of some scissors. A chunk of his hair was missing, there was a huge hole in his jumper, and he had unpicked the stitching from one of his shoes. All his clothes, shoes and toys had a restricted shelf life; much less than for kids of a similar age.

Christmas arrived and departed with the usual angst and destruction.

I embraced Tom's first day back at school in the new year with gratitude. At the time, my youngest brother Stephen was staying with us.

"I'm not going," Tom asserted as he observed Stephen playing on the games console. "I'm staying here with Stephen. You can't make me go to school."

"Oh yes I can!" I marched towards Tom and hauled him to his feet.

With challenging eyes, he glared at me as he swore and rammed his fist against the wall. Stephen shook his head.

"I'd have been murdered if I'd carried on like that at his age!" Putting the game controller down, he switched off the TV.

"Get to your room!" I steered Tom towards the door. "Don't you dare come out until Liz gets here!"

Liz was the childminder, I had employed three days a week to collect him from home and take him to school, so I could get to work for nine o'clock. I was working in a different office now, as a PA to the CEO of a large building company. I loved having my own office and was often left to my own devices. It was great to be *Sarah,* rather than just Tom's mum.

Tom slammed the living room door with all his might. I jumped as his bedroom door went next.

"I can't believe how strong he is." Stephen retrieved the controller.

"I know." Dropping into a chair, my heart sank with me as I contemplated the enormity of my day-after-day, week-after-week; month-after-month struggle for survival. I had given up trying to get any professional help for him. I was on my own.

"Oh my God, what have you done?" I peered at Tom as he re-entered the room with scratch marks to his neck.

"He's bleeding! What have you done mate?" Stephen's gaze went from Tom, to me.

"Now I *can't* go to school. Not with my neck like this." He threw himself on the sofa next to Stephen.

A car beeped its horn outside.

"Get your coat on." I hurled it towards him.

"No. Not going!" Folding his arms, he sat as far back on the sofa as he could.

"Now!" I started towards him.

He ripped the hood from his coat then fled back to his bedroom, again slamming the door. I raced outside to where Liz waited, with her other three charges in the back. Tom normally travelled in the front with her so he couldn't bully anyone.

"Where is he?" She wound her window down.

"Having one hell of a tantrum!" My voice trembled with stress. "Because my brother is staying, Tom's refusing to go to school. He's even scratched his neck in temper."

"He hasn't, has he?" Liz climbed out of the car. "I wanted to have a chat with you about his behaviour. There's been a few problems with him at ..."

Stephen appeared, hauling Tom behind him.

"If he goes to school without any more carrying on, I've promised we'll have a game on the PlayStation at home time," Stephen announced, jubilantly.

"What have you done to your neck?" Liz looked astonished.

"She made me!" Tom pointed towards me.

A feeling of liberation swept over me as Liz's car eventually pulled away, leaving me free to set off. But there was a call for me shortly after arriving at work.

"Is that Tom's mum?" It was the head from his school, whose voice I had grown too familiar with.

"Yes." None of my colleagues were around, for which I felt grateful.

"I'm afraid Tom has made a serious allegation against you. He's disclosed to our caretaker that you're responsible for the scratch marks on his neck."

"Of course I'm not. He did them himself! He was carrying on this morning. He didn't want to come to school!"

"*He did them himself?*" I could hear the doubt behind her words.

"Yes, you've got to believe me! Of course it wasn't me!" Jumping from my chair, I checked along the office corridor that no one was listening to the conversation. "He's lying!"

"Did anyone else see him do it?"

"No, not exactly, but my brother was at our flat and *knows* what happened! And my childminder!" I was garbling; terrified. "She'll back me up too." *How could I be getting blamed for this?*

I rang Martin and wept down the phone.

"Get on the phone to the childminder NOW!" There was more anger than worry in his words. "This needs bloody sorting!"

Her number was constantly engaged. Pacing up and down the office, I glanced out of the window. It was a beautiful winters' day and people were going about their business. I was different to them all; burdened and blamed. *Thank God the boss had not been in with any of this going on!* I hit the redial button again.

"Liz, it's Sarah," I announced, feeling weak with gratitude that she had finally picked up.

"I thought I'd hear from you soon."

"I need you to talk to Tom's school for me?" Nervously, I twisted the phone wire within my fingers. "He's told them I scratched his neck!"

"They've already been in touch." Her voice was calm, unlike mine. "Don't worry, I've put them straight."

"What did you say?"

“That you would *never* hurt him, and that he admitted to me how he'd done it *himself*.”

“Thanks Liz.” I sank back into my chair. “I was worried they'd believe him.”

“He's a little so-and-so, isn't he? What a dreadful thing to say.”

“I know.” *What a kick in the teeth.* I felt utterly deflated.

Within days Liz presented me with her notice. She avoided my gaze as she told me. “I'll hang onto him till you sort something else out.”

It was decent of her, considering. He was always hitting and swearing at the other children. The only option left was to hand *my* notice in at work and search for a job nearer home so I could work after school hours had started.

Two days later, Liz had only just collected Tom when she rang.

“Do you know that Tom has got several five pound notes on him?”

“No … where's he got that from?” Then, as I rummaged for my purse, I realised. I tipped it up. Empty.

“It's mine,” I informed her, miserably. “Can you take it off him?”

Six years old and taking money from my purse. If he can do that now; what's he going to be capable of when he's older?

THE BEHAVIOUR CHART

MARCH 2000 (AGE 6 YEARS, 3 MONTHS)

THOUGH I HAD SERIOUS RESERVATIONS, Martin and I decided to buy a house together. Some of the time I was happy with him, but he could be controlling of me. Many of my friends had slipped away. Once when we were having 'words,' I said something about this. Martin said nobody wanted to know me because of my son and reiterated that I would never find another man who would take Tom on. Though he hadn't really 'taken Tom on' but he was very critical of him and my parenting of him. I was desperate to leave the cramped council flat that had been our home for over six years and take this newly refurbished house, with its little yard. It was huge inside.

Tom progressed from having a box bedroom to a large bedroom with a skylight. I bought a loft bed, rugs, cushions and posters. The adjacent 'spare' room housed his TV and my ironing pile. Here, he could watch films and play his games console to his heart's content.

At the time of the move, he became unsettled. The cutting of his clothes and chunks of his hair became more frequent. On hearing the word 'no' he would grit his teeth and nip his own skin until it reddened. When angry, he thumped himself in the face and would lash out at me and my attempts to restrain him. His sleeping deteriorated too. From being asleep by midnight, it became one in the morning or beyond. At the time, I attributed it to the upheaval of the house move.

That month when I got paid, I packed a bag with pocket money sized treats; felt-tips, cars, bouncy balls, balloons, that sort of thing. Then I put a behaviour chart together. He had to get a tick next to each 'criteria' to choose from the 'treat bag' each day:

Getting ready in the morning without fuss; good behaviour at school; eating dinner without misbehaving, etc. If he managed to get six treats in the week then he could choose an outing: swimming, the cinema, bowling, or somewhere else within reason.

For the first few days I tried to overlook bad behaviour so I could give him a tick. When it could not be ignored; he climbed up to the high kitchen shelf and stole his reward.

A 'BREAK' AWAY

"We're going to have a holiday at the Lake District," I informed Tom as we loaded the car up. "We'll be sleeping in a tent."

Martin and I were intending to have a few days there later that year, for our honeymoon, so we wanted to try it out there first.

The journey was eternal.

"Tom, quit doing that!" Martin glanced in his rear-view mirror. Poking his fingers down his throat, Tom was trying to make himself retch.

"That's disgusting! Stop it!" But it was too late. He threw up all over the back seat.

"Maybe it was car sickness," I grimaced as I dabbed at his slimy vomit with kitchen towel. As always, I defended him.

"Like hell it was!" Martin got out of the car. "I saw exactly what he was doing."

When we eventually arrived, Tom vaulted from the car, straight towards the campsite shop.

"Sweets!" He demanded, without pausing for a response.

"You must be joking." I rummaged around my bag for our booking form. "You were sick on the way here."

"I made myself." We were at the entrance of the shop. He surveyed me jubilantly. "I'm not really ill."

"What did I tell you?" Martin's face bore a smug expression as he locked the car. "There's no way he's getting sweets!"

"Yes I am!" Tearing into the shop, Tom grabbed a packet and slammed them on the counter. I marched in behind him.

"Sorry." I snatched them away from the shopkeeper. "He's not allowed them. I'll put them back."

"FUCK OFF!" Tom hurled himself to the ground. I walked away from him and out of the shop. Luckily, he raced after me.

"I want sweets!" He was wailing as though he had never been fed as he booted the sign outside the shop with such force that it fell over. The shopkeeper followed us out. His hands were thrust into his apron pockets, as he shook his head, no doubt denouncing my parenting skills.

Because he was refusing to walk, I half dragged, half carried Tom towards the spot where Martin had begun to pitch our tent. His attention was suddenly diverted towards an adventure playground. Wrenching himself free, he bolted in its direction.

"Not so fast!" Hurtling after him, I caught hold of the hood on his jacket.

"But mum, it looks ace!" His tantrum was apparently forgotten.

"You don't deserve to play in the park." Martin was unloading the car. "Not after the way you've carried on today."

However, I gave in. He was in my vision from the spot where we were setting up, battling against the wind. It was a tougher fight against Tom though when I attempted to retrieve him from the park. By the time we returned to our pitch, Martin had lit a barbecue.

"Here, have a drink." I handed Tom some juice.

Instantaneously, he tipped it over the barbecue, which sizzled; flames becoming smoke. Satisfaction crept across Tom's face at the power he had yielded.

"You little ...!" Martin looked ready to explode alongside the spitting embers. "I don't know why we bothered coming."

WEDDINGS

THE YEAR BEFORE, Tom had been a page boy for Vicky. At the start of the day, he'd looked adorable in his suit. However, he refused to enter the church after the bride. After I'd spent some time bribing him, he'd agreed, only to cause uproar inside.

I had been forced to drag him out, therefore missing the ceremony and instead only able to hear the echo of it from outside. None of their wedding photos had included Tom. Scaling gravestones and climbing trees was a preferable activity. Eventually, he ensnared the other page boy and bridesmaid too. By the reception they looked like they had rolled around in a ditch.

"Why would *anyone* want Tom as a page boy?" Martin had snorted as we sat observing Tom catapult the dance floor.

Though I knew it might be carnage, I would have given my right arm to have Tom as *my* page boy. But we knew that *our* big day would become *his*. I wrestled with the dilemma until eventually Martin took it out of my hands.

"He's not coming." His tone confirmed the matter was not up for discussion. "He'll ruin it if he's there. In fact, if *he's* there, I won't be!"

Eventually we agreed he could be at the reception and allocated people to help keep an eye on him. But for me, his absence gaped like a chasm.

A SIBLING FOR TOM

APRIL 2001 (7 YEARS, 3 MONTHS)

How I will know my second baby is different from my first:

1. It will settle when held.
2. Maybe it will sleep.
3. The baby will only need milk every few hours.
4. His or her cry won't be a highly pitched screech.
5. The baby will be relaxed, not a mass of thrashing arms and legs.
6. It will be soothed when hearing my voice.
7. The baby will be calm when born, not bright red and screaming its lungs out.

I pray, I pray, I pray. No way can I go through it all again. And I'll know within the first couple of hours whether I've had another hyperactive baby.

PARENTS' EVENING

OCTOBER 2001 (7 YEARS, 10 MONTHS)

DESPITE EXTENDING THE INVITATION, nobody wanted to accompany me to parents' evening. I wrestled with the door at the school's entrance against the wind and was comforted by the blast of warm air that greeted me. Immediately, I was taken back in time by the dusty wooden aroma combined with rubbery plimsoll. Raking my fingers through my hair, I tried to tidy it. Then I waited outside the classroom.

Tom's Maths and English books had been left out for me to look at; it was heartening to see that when he had attempted some work, most of it had been ticked. Much of the time, however, he would be lucky to have written the date and title. Sometimes he had answered a question or two or written a sentence. Both books were scrawled over in red pen: *not enough work Tom, must try harder Tom, this is not good enough: please see me.*

As I continued to wait, I spotted his class photo pinned to the classroom door. I scanned the faces for Tom. Displaying a fiendish grin, he had been positioned next to the teacher.

Laughter erupted from within the classroom. A clock ticked above me. *How much longer?* I wanted to get this over with. I searched the corridor walls for Tom's artwork but couldn't find any. The wind, rattling through the crumbly walls, made me shiver. It was eerie being in school so late at night.

The classroom door eventually burst open and two happy parents emerged. It must have been good news for them. I wished Martin had come with me. After all, he was my husband and Tom's stepfather now. Although that seemed to have given him increased licence to criticise us.

"Come in." Mr Murphy held the door for me.

Creeping in like a timid child, I sat down as directed. My eyes struggled to adjust to the fluorescent lighting after the dinginess of the corridor. As I prepared myself for the onslaught, my heart raced.

"Well," he began. "Thanks for coming in. Let's start with some positives." I noticed he was avoiding eye contact with me.

Positives! These I was interested in hearing!

"Firstly, his punctuality and attendance are good," he stated as he referred to a chart. "And he's certainly a lively member of the class. A little *too* lively though."

I laughed nervously.

Mr Murphy did not laugh. Or even smile.

"Are there any problems at home that might be affecting him?" Now he met my eyes. I looked away.

"We've moved to a new house." I shuffled on the tiny chair. It wasn't the most comfortable place to be in my seven-month-pregnant state. "That's not had a good effect on his behaviour."

"I know about that. But he's gone considerably downhill since he joined me in September. Is there anything else?"

"He's having a brother or sister." My hand patted my belly.

"Well that can unsettle children too. How's he feeling about it?"

"OK, I think. He's not really said much."

"Does he get on well with his stepdad?"

"Mostly. He's hard work though. Tom, I mean." I think I

meant Martin as much as Tom though. He'd become distant. We'd found out we were having a boy and was convinced it would be the same as Tom and have similar behaviour problems. My pregnancy had become the loneliest time of my life, with Martin *never* there.

"Tom's behaviour is like nothing I've ever seen." Mr Murphy looked troubled as he continued. "He can be, forgive me for putting it like this, well *wild*."

"I know." My voice was faint. "It's the same for me at home. I can't do a thing with him."

He frowned. "I gather you've had him to one or two specialists."

"One or two," despite my nerves, I chuckled. "And some. Not one of them has been able to help."

"It's not good for him and it's certainly not fair on the rest of the class. No one learns a thing. I've started segregating him and making him work *there*." He gestured towards a small table right in front of his own desk. "But even when he's right under my nose, he still manages to disrupt the class. So, then we shift his table into the corridor." He pointed towards the door. "Meaning my teaching assistant is also leaving the room to supervise him. It can't go on!"

"I'm sorry."

"You *must* speak to him." His voice had an urgent edge. "It's getting to the point where we might have to bring in some help." He took a form out of a folder and put it in front of me. "Do we have your consent for this, if we have to proceed?"

"Of course, I hope you have more success than I have." I accepted the pen he offered. "Where do I sign?"

"Just there. We can try. There's no way we can continue like this though."

"The more he gets to know someone, the worse he behaves. You've probably noticed that yourself." This teacher did not seem to be talking down or blaming me, which helped me relax. "It's been the case with *all* his teachers, childminders and nursery. At first, he's wary, then he learns which buttons to press and what weaknesses people have."

The conversation moved onto the usual tales: fighting, spitting, swearing, stealing, weeing.

A backlog of parents had accrued. I didn't meet anybody's glare as I traipsed past them.

No wonder no one had wanted to come with me to parents evening!

TOM'S GAMES

DECEMBER 2001 (7 YEARS, 11 MONTHS)

One afternoon, Tom wanted to play in the garden, whilst I unloaded the car. Then after I had finished hanging the washing out, I looked to see what it was that was keeping him quiet.

"What are you doing?" I peered at his careful structures in the soil.

"Making a graveyard." He was engrossed in his activity. "Look, those are the graves. That's a car with the body in, this is a coffin."

"Oh." I studied the mounds he had formed. "Do you not want to play a more *cheerful* game?"

His games were bizarre. Boxes became coffins for his soft toys. His pictures depicted guns, graves or violence. I had been vigilant in not allowing him to encounter any violent viewing; however, that did not seem to prevent these 'games.'

I had started to allow him to play outside. He was almost eight and would play on the expanse of grass adjacent to our home. I could keep him in vision from the lounge window. He and a neighbouring boy of a similar age would seek each other out. But Tom would want to play fighting games and the other boy didn't. Tom would try to control the play so inevitably their time together was usually fleeting.

Some older boys once invited him to join their game of football. I remember thinking how positive this might be. However, he attempted to dominate the game and refused to pass the ball to anyone else! He was soon ejected!

"His swearing's getting out of hand," Martin informed me as I returned from my antenatal check-up the following week. "One of the neighbours has complained and decided Tom can't play with her son again. Oh, and he won't be riding his bike for the foreseeable." He nodded towards where it lay, forlornly in the grass outside. "He's wrecked it in temper. It had a puncture and I said I would fix it later. He didn't want to wait so threw it at the wall instead." He continued to stare at it. "I could see him from the window, flattening it. It's buckled now!"

"Why didn't you stop him?"

"He's your son Sarah. You bloody look after him in future."

"I was getting a check up to make sure *our* baby is OK. *Our* baby, Martin." My pregnancy had been the most miserable time of my life. And God help me if I *did* have another baby like Tom. I already sensed that eventually I was going to end up facing single parenthood. However, this baby's activity already seemed different. Whilst pregnant with Tom, it was like I had a football team in there. This one tended to come to life mainly when I was resting – either in the bath or putting my feet up.

~

The next morning, Tom tantrummed because he wanted his bike. After a while, I ordered him to his room. Martin hadn't been home all night and the boiler had stopped working. I was close to my due date and felt as though if I cried, I would never stop.

A short time later, because it was quiet upstairs, I thought

I'd better check on him. He had scrawled all over one of his walls and his duvet cover with felt tip pens. Stuffing from his soft toys was strewn across every surface in his bedroom. Most of them had had their heads torn off and Tom was now busy yanking out the remaining stuffing.

The day before my due date, I was informed that the parents of another boy had been into school to complain about Tom bullying their son.

On my due date itself, he ran away from school, after flying into a rage because he had not got his chosen part in the school play. They had even reported his departure to the police! Luckily, he resurfaced soon after in a nearby park.

At the time I needed him the most, Martin had buggered off somewhere. Luckily Peter and Elizabeth were able to take Tom for me before I became ill with all the stress.

A TIME FOR CALM

I WAS mindful of the fact that children can feel left out when a new baby comes along. I had bought Tom a present and a card saying *'You're a Big Brother Now.'* I had it ready to give to him when Elizabeth brought him to the hospital to meet little Alex.

I studied his face for a reaction. He looked shyly at me as I sat, propped up in the hospital bed. Then he astounded me. "I know how you got a baby ... you did sex." He grinned.

Elizabeth and I exchanged uncomfortable glances as his attention switched to his new brother. "Do you want to hold him?" I offered, as I manoeuvred myself from the bed.

Nodding, he launched himself into the spot from which I had emerged. I gently passed Alex to him. Then watched. I still smile at the photograph capturing that moment. Tom leaned, still as a statue against my pillows, cradling his little brother, protectively resting his hand under his head as though he was the most precious thing in the world. The pride is evident in his expression and I recall the surge of hope that everything was going to turn out fine.

Alex turned out to be the opposite of Tom. I knew he was different as soon as he was born. A contented baby, he adored his sleep and even when awake, would lie in my arms or in his rocking chair, happily watching the world go by. He was so lazy he would fall asleep whilst he was feeding.

However, like Peter, Martin failed to assist with the night feeds, and I was worried that for the second time, my relationship was going to break up whilst I had a tiny baby. I was grateful that this time, I was experiencing normal, 'new-mum' tiredness, rather than the indescribable exhaustion I had suffered the first time around. I was, however, struggling to feel any 'joy' and ended up being prescribed anti-depressants for a while. Martin worked by day and went to the pub at night, so I was operating as a single mum. I slept in the spare room with Alex in his Moses basket at the side of me.

~

As the weeks passed, I started to feel better and more self-sufficient. I enjoyed getting Alex wrapped up and wheeling him out in the early spring sunshine to collect Tom from school. Other mothers, rather than side-lining me, as they always had done because of Tom's reputation, would approach me to look at Alex as he slept, all snug, in his pram. This new-found friendliness cheered me – it was wonderful to feel included in playground conversation rather than be on the edge of it, or the subject of it.

The initial connection which had been forged between Tom and Alex did not progress. I tried to involve Tom in caring for his brother, but he was not interested. I would ask him to entertain him whilst I prepared dinner, but he could not be bothered. When we were out, he refused to hold onto the pram. He sometimes seemed indifferent to Alex; as though he was invisible. I fretted and worried as Tom spent increasing amounts of time in his room. Attempts to coax him out proved futile; he seemed to prefer doing his own thing.

At least his behaviour had improved and we were going through a quieter, calmer phase. Complaints from school had eased. I stopped keeping behaviour diaries. I didn't have the energy to anyway. There were less incidents taking place whilst he was at his dad's. It was as though Alex's birth could have altered him in some way.

For a while, I took my eye off the ball. However, it bounced back at full pelt and smacked me hard, squarely in the face.

HOLIDAY MEMORIES

SEPTEMBER 2002 (8 YEARS, 9 MONTHS)

SOON AFTER, we attempted a week at the coast. I was hoping that the time away might bring Martin and I back together a little bit. I was married to him, had a baby with him and badly wanted to make things work.

The journey to Filey was horrendous. Tom travelled in the middle as he had damaged the seatbelt behind the driver side. But he kept unclipping himself and trying to clamber into the front of the car. Or he would boot us through the backs of the seats.

"Carry on and we're going back home," Martin shouted at him.

Then without warning Tom threw up. After dealing with it, we set off again then Alex suddenly began shrieking, so I pulled back over.

"Tom, Tom!" Was all that was audible between sobs. As I shifted the hand that clutched his back; there was a huge purply patch which appeared to have been nipped and twisted. Other marks on his back indicated that he might have been repeatedly poked.

"You nasty little bully!" Martin's gaze travelled from Alex's back to Tom.

"How could you do that to your little brother?" I added, gathering Alex in my arms to comfort him. I was going to have to step up my vigilance.

When we arrived, I suggested a pub lunch. I was so stressed; I wanted a glass of wine. Tom vanished into the toilet. After ten minutes I sent Martin to investigate.

"He says he won't be a minute." He retook his place at the table. "It bloody stinks in there."

"Well his tummy wasn't good on the journey." I tugged the menu from its holder and began scanning it. "Maybe it's that."

Tom eventually joined us. His shirt sleeves were soaked. I absently observed as a man went into the toilets but reappeared straightaway, visibly gagging, before striding over to the bar. A member of staff then entered the men's toilets. He exited in a similar way; horror etched on his face.

"Martin," I hissed, my appetite waning. "Will you go and see what Tom's done in there?"

Hesitantly he headed for the toilets but immediately emerged, looking grim-faced.

"Let's get out of here." He gestured towards the door. "I'll tell you in the car. Just go." As we got through the door, he snarled at Tom: "You dirty little git!"

"What on earth has he done?" I slid into the car.

"Smeared poo *everywhere*." He slammed himself into the driving seat and rested his head onto the steering wheel. "It's all over the walls, floor, even the door."

In hindsight, Tom should have been frog marched back in there, made to own up and clean it. But I was too ashamed.

Whenever my back was turned that week, Tom delighted in making Alex squeal by nipping, poking or trying to squash him. The constant vigil I had to keep wore me out. Inevitably the time passed with Martin and I alternating who took charge of which child. So much for a family holiday.

Once when I took them together, at a play area beside a river, Tom had eaten his ice cream and was trying to steal Alex's.

"You've had yours Tom," I said. "Let Alex eat his."

"You fuck off," he shouted. "I hate you." He jumped up and ran off.

I ended up crying. God knows what passers-by must have thought as I searched for him in tears. Half an hour elapsed before I discovered him, hiding up a tree in nearby woods.

He wanted *everything!* Sometimes, I indulged him. At other times, if I refused, the tantrums heightened like a hurricane. Swearing at the top of his voice, he would make it known to anyone within earshot how he never got anything, and he would punch or kick whatever was available. He was unstoppable. I was at my wits end!

After the 'holiday,' one of my first ports of call was my GP. Again.

"We don't prescribe it *lightly*," she tried to explain when I begged for Ritalin. "It can cause all sorts of other problems, like stunted growth, developmental problems *and* disturbed sleep."

I laughed. "The fact that he is weeing in corners and smearing poo everywhere would illustrate his already apparent d*evelopmental problems. Twice* whilst we were on holiday! I thought my days of having to rid walls of his excrement were behind me. And *disturbed sleep!*" My voice probably sounded manic. "He doesn't sleep! Never before the early hours. Even when he does drop off, he wakes up continually. Then he's up at the crack of dawn!"

"I can't prescribe Ritalin," she repeated. "It's such a new

drug and I am reluctant to make existing problems even worse. I'm not saying *never* but certainly not now." She paused. "How about I refer you to the 0-19 Team again?"

"The 0-19 Team?" I sniffed, feeling hope fade out of me like air from a punctured tyre.

"I think before we go down a medication route – Tom needs to see someone more specialised." She began typing onto her computer. "The 0-19 can refer you on, which is the route I will recommend."

"To who?"

"A child psychologist or psychiatrist."

"And then what?"

"They would be in a position to make a diagnosis, making medication more of an option."

I was hopeful at this so agreed to the referral.

"There's a bit of a waiting list at the moment," she warned. "Perhaps a few weeks."

"That's fine. As long as I know something's happening." I rose to my feet. "It's only now I've had Alex that I see how serious Tom's behaviour is. And if it was all down to my parenting skills, Alex would be the same, surely!"

"No one's blaming you Sarah."

BULLYING INCIDENT 1

FINALLY, the appointment with the 0-19 Team came around. Elizabeth had agreed to accompany me as I was dreading it. As usual, I was convinced I would be criticised and condemned. First, she came to our house for a preparatory cup of tea.

"Just tell it like it is," she advised as we watched Alex playing with his cars. "And I will too. They *have* to listen this time."

After preparing the children's lunch, I sat them together at the table.

"For God's sake, Tom!" Elizabeth pushed his fork closer to him. "Use your cutlery. Your table manners are getting worse."

He was attempting to eat spaghetti with his fingers. It splattered the floor and table.

"It's like this every mealtime." I ran a face flannel under the tap. "Isn't he like this when you've got him?"

"Yes, he is," she caught the flannel I flung to her. "To be honest, we avoid stuff like spaghetti."

My gaze wandered from his sauce-stained face to Alex, spooning spaghetti from his dish to his mouth. At nearly two years old, he had hardly spilled anything.

Elizabeth rinsed our cups whilst I rummaged around for coats and shoes. Then an ear-splitting scream echoed from the lounge.

Left unattended, Tom had seized the opportunity to hurt Alex. Springing from the room, he raced past me up the stairs. I ran in to investigate, with Elizabeth in hot pursuit. Alex's scream was silent - his face contorted in pain.

"Breathe!" I shouted.

As he gasped, the screams started. As any mother knows, when your child is small, they have different cries for various things. Hunger, tiredness, boredom, pain. This one was awful. Not yet able to talk properly, we could only assume the pain was in his ear. Elizabeth moved his hand.

"Oh my God!"

My eyes travelled to the site of his earlobe, blackening with injury.

"Tom! TOM!"

THE 0-19 TEAM (AGAIN)

JANUARY 2003 (9 YEARS, 1 MONTH)

"Why did you do that to your brother?" The man seemed shocked as he questioned a defiant-looking Tom, who didn't reply. "This is not the first time your doctor has referred you, is it?" He turned towards me.

"No, it's the third." I sat back in the chair, leaning on the armrests. "I hope we can get somewhere this time."

He took a form and pen from his briefcase. "Well, I can promise to listen, but what will happen after, I can't say yet."

Elizabeth took every chance to offer her own opinions and experiences as the conversation progressed. After all, they had him nearly every weekend.

Discussing Tom negatively in front of him made me feel guilty. However, that dissipated each time I glanced at Alex's swollen ear.

I revisited Tom's babyhood; the sleeplessness, breakages, tantrums and soiling; then the more recent urinating, outbursts and bullying of other children.

Alex played in the middle of us all, surrounded by cars. Tom was behind my chair, quiet as he fiddled with something.

"Tom, what're you doing?" Elizabeth went towards him and retrieved some scissors.

His trouser leg was cut up one side and he had cut a hole in his jumper. *Surely, the man had to do something!* I thought.

"I'm going to refer you to the Child and Adolescent Mental Health Team," he announced, writing something on his form. "We will get Tom assessed by a child psychiatrist." I could have punched the air. *At last!*

As we left the building, I knew I should be meting out sanctions for Tom's earlier behaviour, however, a voice sounded within me. *This is not his fault. He didn't choose to be like this. There is something wrong.* And it was seeming as though we may get it sorted out.

MORE HUMILIATION

SEPTEMBER 2003 (9 YEARS, 9 MONTHS)

I HAD BECOME bored of working in an office and wanted to do more with my life than be a secretary and a mother. I was lucky in that I still got respite from Tom each weekend but with Alex, I was pretty much on my own, apart from the crumbs of time and attention that Martin sometimes threw at us.

My marriage was going around and around in circles – it was almost as if Martin had some kind of monthly cycle. For around a week each month, he would be normal, attentive and full of plans. Then for around a week, he would become distant and angry about everything. After that we would have several days of absence whilst he drank and relived his youth. Throughout this time, he'd be nasty when he was at home. I would be on eggshells, trying to keep the children out of his way and forced often, to stay at my dad's or at friend's houses with the boys. Lastly, a 'hangover' week would occur, when he would be jealous and possessive over me and full of remorse for his previous behaviours.

I had decided I wanted to take control of my career which in turn would provide the option for me to set myself free from him. Because I had been in care, I had completely flunked school as a teenager. I had to enrol on an Access to Education course so I could then get on a Teaching and English degree.

I loved studying – it opened my mind, and my horizons, but I was juggling much more than the other trainee teachers on my course.

Tom had reached the age for sex education. As a result, his drawings became more graphic. I worried myself sick about him. My fears were confirmed when my friend Joanne telephoned me one afternoon following our visit to her house.

"Sarah, I'm telling you this because you need to know," she began.

"What's happened?" *Aaargh, what now!*

"It's Tom."

"What's he done?" I balanced the phone in the crook of my neck as I poured drinks for the kids.

"Well," she paused. "He's asked Rebecca to show him her knickers today. He also said he would give her chocolate if she sucked his willy. It was whilst they were in the garden."

"Whaaaat!" I splashed juice everywhere.

"I won't say anything to Paul," she said. "And I've told Rebecca not to either. He would have a go at you."

"I know." Tears stabbed behind my eyes as I sank onto a chair. "Tom's on the list to see a psychiatrist. Hopefully we'll start getting help soon; you know about the problems I've always had with..."

"Of course. I'm not blaming you. I've no idea how you've coped all this time."

Once I allowed him to have a friend to stay. Once was enough.

Just after two in the morning, Tom swore at me when I ordered them to be quiet. When I returned a short time later, he hurled a book at me! Finally, I sent Martin in and he sent Tom's exhausted-looking friend to sleep on the sofa.

"You shouldn't speak to your mum like that." I overheard his friend hiss at Tom once or twice the next morning. "When can I go home?" He kept asking as he waited for his mum. That was the last time he and Tom played.

It was a similar story with all the children he encountered. He would monopolise and try to control potential friends. He would lash out if they tried to exert their wishes. So he was a bit of a loner.

It was heartbreaking. But I was optimistic that this would improve once I had persuaded the experts to give us Ritalin.

I was at a complete loss of what to do. In my teacher training at university, I had been reading about using *positive behaviour strategies*. This meant ignoring anything negative as much as possible and rewarding his positive aspects. I leapt upon episodes of him behaving calmly and praised him to the skies.

I made endless promises of rewards. *If the teacher doesn't speak to me at the end of the school day, we'll spend an hour at the park. If you get through the week without being in trouble at school, you can go bowling. If you settle down and go to sleep, I'll take you swimming tomorrow, etc.*

Maybe I was setting him up to fail though because he did not have the focus to remember what he had to do in order to get his reward. But he would never forget the 'reward' itself and if I refused it, he would lash out at anything around him.

On occasion he turned the anger inwards and beat himself in his face with his fists. It was horrifying. I kept trying to bring forward the appointment to see the child psychiatrist. But we had to wait.

TOM'S TEACHER

A STERN, male teacher may have had a handle on him. So my heart sank when I met his next teacher. She seemed young and barely any taller than Tom. Perhaps I was mistaken to judge her on appearance, but I could not help worrying that he would make mincemeat of her!

Four weeks into term, she admitted she couldn't manage. I listened as she recounted various episodes she had endured in her brief time with him.

"It doesn't matter what warnings I give; he laughs at me."

"The whole class is disrupted. They don't agree with what he's doing, but they all stop to laugh at him. This eggs him on even more!"

"His language is foul. Every colleague I've spoken with can't believe that he's still in mainstream school."

"He bullies, he destroys things."

"There's no point in me trying to teach him if I can't even get him to behave."

"My teaching assistant is refusing to work with him. She can't manage him either."

As we talked in the empty classroom, she seemed near to tears. I felt wretched and tried letting her know that I had been having awful trouble with him since his birth, and that she was one in a long line of people who had struggled with him.

THE HEAD TEACHER

Mrs Armstrong peered at me from behind her desk as though I might have a solution stashed somewhere. "I always suspected we'd get to this point," she said.

"I've told you we're on the list to see a child psychiatrist, haven't I?"

"Yes, several times!"

"I'm sure once he is actually diagnosed with ADHD, he will be prescribed Ritalin, then he will sleep better, calm down and his behaviour will improve and-"

"But that doesn't solve the immediate problem." Standing, she wandered around to the front of her desk and perched herself on the edge of it. "What do we do about him in the meantime?"

His teacher, Miss Thomson dropped her forehead onto her hand. "I can't go on teaching him. Not like he is. My class is out of control with him amongst it. I'm beginning to question whether I'm even cut out for teaching!" Her voice wobbled around the cluttered interior of the head's office.

"What if we get help for him?" Mrs Armstrong spoke again, resting her hand on Miss Thomson's arm.

"I've been trying to get help for years!" *Why now?*

"He'd meet the criteria for funding now," Mrs Armstrong looked thoughtful. "We'd have more hope of getting it for five *half* days. We're unlikely to get full days. Would you say he's worse in the morning or afternoon?" She leaned over me to get a file from her bookshelf.

Miss Thomson's head jerked up. "Afternoons probably. We always do Maths and English in the morning and the whole class are calmer generally. Afternoons tend to be less structured, meaning he's more likely to go off the rails."

"That's settled then. I'll apply for funding for afternoons." Mrs Armstrong slid a sheet of paper from her file.

I watched her, confused. "What does that mean?"

"It's not easy to get." Mrs Armstrong ran her pen along the length of the form. "Normally children have severe learning difficulties. But if we're successful, we'll get a one-to-one mentor for him. Someone to help with his work, give behaviour reminders and hopefully keep him on task." She glanced towards Miss Thomson, who appeared to have cheered slightly. "Then if he gets too much, the mentor can take him from the classroom situation so he can let off steam and calm down."

"That sounds promising." I felt brighter too. "Do you think it will be granted?" We seemed to be running out of other options.

"We've got a strong case. It could make the difference between him making it through this school or having to attend somewhere more specialised."

THE EDUCATIONAL PSYCHOLOGIST

WITHIN TWO WEEKS I attended a meeting with a fierce looking man who was going to pronounce judgement on my son. He had observed him over the course of an English lesson.

I have included his report here:

School Action Plus

Educational Psychologist's Assessment Summary

Basis for this report:

- Initial discussion with school
- Meeting with parents and step parents
- Observation of, and interview with Tom
- Records of behaviour made at school by staff, and school reports

Background Information and current concerns from Parents and Step parents

Mum has been concerned since Tom was a baby: hyperactive behaviour and not sleeping. At the age of eighteen months, Mum sought help from the 0-19 team through the GP. Although parents' concerns are severe, querying ADHD and wanting statementing, Tom can sit as though butter wouldn't melt in his mouth.

Mum is now seeking re-referral. Tom's natural parents have separated; Tom lives with his mum and spends some of the weekend at dad's house. He used to be better behaved for his dad but is now also cheeky and abusive to him.

Behaviours causing concern more recently have included:

- Extensive breakages: (TV, video, ornaments as well as his own toys.) He also recently in temper broke a window.
- The problem with sleeping, which is getting worse. At home Tom won't keep still; he sits upside down on the settee and talks constantly.
- Aggression towards his younger brother, Alex, whom Mum can't leave alone in the same room as Tom: he is jealous and has bullied/bruised him and put his hands around his throat. He lashes out at his stepmum who has had to restrain him from hurting her.
- Wetting and soiling: although Tom is toilet trained, he wees in corners of his bedroom and recently smeared faeces in the toilets on holiday. He admitted this to me saying "*I did it because I don't like myself.*"
- Tom is lonely and unhappy at school. He says he hasn't any friends, that nobody likes him and that it

is boring; he doesn't want to go. He says he is *different* and gets upset. Although he is intelligent, he can't concentrate and so can't do the work. Parents are worried about high school transition, fearing he will truant.

- Endangering himself and getting into trouble when he plays out: climbing on garage roofs, falling out and starting fights with older children. Other parents complain about him. Tom's parents are embarrassed to take him anywhere in public. More and more they have had to try and isolate him and not let him play out. In the summer holidays (2003), on a caravan park, he was terrible, not going to sleep until 2am, demanding money and having tantrums in public.
- They fear he is going to cause himself injury – he sneaks knives into his bedroom, jumps off roofs and he head bangs/hurts himself.
- He is clumsy/not well coordinated, struggles to use a knife and fork and is unable to tie his shoelaces.
- At home parents run behaviour programmes with charts and Tom is interested in the idea of having goals to work towards. But if he doesn't earn his reward, he steals it.

Background from School Staff

Tom was difficult to manage in reception class, for example pulling down his own and others' pants; and he had a difficult year in year 2. He calmed down a little in year 3 with a male teacher. But from the Christmas in year 4 (with another male teacher) he deteriorated again.

. . .

Tom has acquired a name for himself and tends to get blamed by his class even when an incident is not his fault. In school he can be reasoned with; he responds well to 1:1 support. However there are still regular incidents causing concern:

Aggression towards his peers, making threats and hurtful remarks; answering back and shouting at staff, angrily banging doors/furniture; in July he blocked the toilets with toilet rolls. School have maintained diary records of his incidents, so they are not listed more fully here.

In interview and observation in class

A morning lesson I observed in his Year 5 class began calmly. Tom started as he was expected to do with quiet reading, joined in the class prayers appropriately, and raised his hand when he wanted the teacher's attention. It took him longer to settle to a writing task than it had to settle to reading, asking for books/equipment, taking a child's pencil from another table then denying it, talking and singing instead of writing, obviously looking for others attention/approval. At the end of the writing period he threw his book across the table onto the floor but picked it up without comment when told to do so.

He frequently frowned. During an overhead projector presentation of a poem, by the teacher, he was restless in his chair, and yawning, rocking back, slouching down, lifting the group's table up and down with his knees, etc. However, he answered questions well (e.g. suggesting rhyming words for a poem and defining what adjectives were) and when it was his turn to read aloud to the class, he read well. The work was clearly within his ability.

I understand that Tom manages better in more structured/ formal morning teaching sessions but finds afternoon sessions (which I did not see) more difficult.

In the 1:1 interview Tom told me that he liked his current teacher and preferred literacy to maths. However, year 3 was his best year as they had several good school trips. He was reticent in talking about things that went wrong in school or at home but stated there were good and bad moments. He names several friends for me, and staff he liked. Sometimes there were arguments with his friends. Sometimes he was good with his temper; sometimes he couldn't control his anger. He had achieved a certificate the week before I saw him for not fighting and getting into trouble all week.

He said his behaviour at home and school was about the same. He thought the arrangement of living with Mum and seeing Dad at weekends worked fine, although he said he got on better with Dad, as there were sometimes arguments with his Mum. As in class, he was rather frowning but when a smile came it was a nice smile.

Identified needs

Tom's history suggests a high level of emotional need. This may well be linked with an attachment disorder,** but this diagnosis would be better coming from the Child and Adolescent Mental Health Team. Tom's behaviour has a major impact on his family/families at home. In school he is more unsettled in less structured situations.

Recommendations

To provide increased supervision in afternoons and social times and opportunities to work in 1:1 and small group settings on feelings and anger management, I would support schools' request for 'F Band' funding for inclusion.

Educational Psychologist 24.11.2003

This report is based on one hour of observing Tom.

*** Attachment Disorder is most common in fostered and adopted children but is found in other so-called "normal" families as well - due to divorce, illness or separations. It happens when a child is not properly nurtured in the first few months and years of life. The child, left to cry in hunger, pain or need for cuddling, learns that adults will not help him or her.* (Source: Behaviour for Learning)

Clearly the definition of *attachment disorder* demonstrates how easy it was to blame me. I was livid when I looked it up! I immediately complained in writing but never received a reply. However, funding was granted for a learning mentor.

THE LEARNING MENTOR

To my disappointment it was a lady, nice enough, *too* nice in fact. I had hoped a male would have been appointed; someone Tom might be wary of. However, for several weeks, Miss Thomson's complaints lessened. Tom was given frequent breaks, distracting activities and opportunities to let off steam in the playground. For a while things worked and I relaxed.

But before long, he had worked out the learning mentor's fallible traits and which buttons to press. I was summoned into school for yet another meeting.

THE CHAIR OF GOVERNORS

NOVEMBER 2003 (9 YEARS, 11 MONTHS)

"I'M MR PHILLIPS." The man gestured to a seat in front of the desk. "Chair of Governors."

"Oh, erm, nice to meet you." *Was it?*

"We're here to discuss your son, Tom." Pausing, he shuffled through a file. "As you're aware, this school has persevered with all his problems."

"I know, and I'm grateful." I leaned forward.

"The thing is, we're reaching the end of the line." Halting his paper shuffling, he linked his hands together on Mrs Armstrong's mahogany desk. "Complaints from other parents are mounting and the next school year is important. We've SATS to consider, not to mention the transition to high school."

"Yes." *Oh God, what was he saying to me?*

"We *have* to consider the needs and welfare of *all* our pupils in school, not just Tom."

"I know." I was defenceless against this important man who seemed to be finally writing off my son.

"This meeting is the first step towards Tom being permanently excluded from this school." His voice had become sterner. "It is a verbal warning that his behaviour *has* to improve, most considerably, with immediate effect."

"But what if it doesn't?" My heart was doing somersaults. *Shit! Surely he wasn't going to end up expelled. Not from primary school!* "I'll try talking to him, obviously, but I've tried everything already and-"

"The next step will be a written warning." His face displayed no emotion. "After that if there is still no improvement, I'm afraid you will receive a letter telling you to withdraw Tom."

"But then what would I do?"

"You could apply for a place at other schools in the area – if they have places. They would be reluctant to accept him if he'd been excluded from here though. You might be looking at a pupil referral unit."

"What's that?" I felt deflated. "A secure unit where staff are specifically trained to deal with severe behaviour issues; there are appropriate facilities and smaller class sizes." By his tone of voice, I could tell that he deemed it an appropriate environment for Tom.

"But surely he would only get worse if spending his days with other like-minded kids?"

He shrugged. Like he had indicated, his priority was the rest of the children at his school. It was abundantly clear to me that the school wanted Tom out. They'd had enough.

THE CHILD PSYCHIATRIST

EVENTUALLY, hope arrived in the form of an appointment. All of us, including Elizabeth, Peter and even Tom, had to fill in an array of questionnaires regarding relationships, concentration, sleep and so on prior to the meeting.

I helped Tom with his. One question was *do you have enjoyable time with your friends?* The responses to choose from were *often, sometimes, rarely and never.* After ticking *never*, he turned to me.

"No one wants to play with me cos I'm bad." His blue eyes emitted a sadness that sliced straight into my heart.

"You're not bad, you daft thing!" I tried to hug him. His body went rigid and I could sense him squirming. He had *never* done hugs. I remembered the Educational Psychologist's 'diagnosis' of attachment disorder. What he didn't know was what a *wanted* child Tom was.

"Right Tom." We were hunched together at the kitchen table. "What answer shall we give for this question? *Do you feel you have someone you can talk to?*"

Again, he answered *never*.

"But you know you can always talk to me." My voice echoed

around the kitchen competing with the din of the washer's spin cycle. "Or Martin, your dad or Elizabeth."

~

We had to attend the first meeting without Tom. We waited in a shiny clinical room, squinting at each other as the sharp sunlight bounced off the gleaming white walls. The only reassuring touches in this room were a box of tissues and a basket of potpourri. Feeling jittery, I leaned forward to inhale its scent. It was lavender-ish, an improvement on the surrounding 'dettolly' smell.

Peter shot me a peculiar look. "I don't know what you expect to achieve by this Sarah." Elizabeth glared at him. "Why should this person be any different from the others?"

"Look, it's worth a try. Just back me up, will you."

A demure, dark-haired woman entered the room.

"I'm Victoria Harris." She closed the door with great care as though she was trying not to disturb something. "Nice to meet you all." As she shook each of our hands, we introduced ourselves. She was quietly spoken, and her voice had a 'posh' edge. Although expensively dressed, she looked young, perhaps a recent graduate; first impressions made me feel dubious as to whether she would be able to help.

"Right I need to get some background." She nodded towards me. "I'll begin with you Sarah. Family, medical history, that sort of thing." For a moment I tussled with the notion of omitting the fact that I had been in care in my teens. Then I decided not to. *What would be the point?* In any case, she hardly flinched when I mentioned it. Maybe, she was not of the *'abused people become abusers'* brigade. Then the questions were directed to the others whilst she scribbled notes on her notepad.

"I'm sure you're tired of going over it all, but we do need to go right back to the beginning. To put a clear picture together, I have to learn *everything.*"

"How long's this appointment?" I joked, starting to relax a little.

She smiled. "Don't worry; we'll get through what we can." Taking her diary from her bag, she began leafing through it as she spoke. "At the next appointment, I'd like to meet Tom as well, so I can observe his behaviour and interactions with all of you."

Her questioning probed my pregnancy and the birth, my early days with Tom and his sleeping patterns. *Had he been a planned baby? Was I well after birth? Any depression? What support had I had? How did he sleep? How did we bond?*

There was no point in being anything other than honest. Support from anyone had been in short supply back then. It had been a struggle, but we had got by. Tom was my only child then - I had not worked for the first eighteen months, so he was my entire life; we were inseparable. It had not been until he was approaching two, that I had been forced to accept there was something not right and had sought support. It had been painful for me to admit there was a problem with my own child, but it was something that I would have always had to face up to eventually.

Not all the questions were directed at me, which I was pleased about. Everybody else was included in the discussion. Her thoroughness gave me confidence and I was disappointed when the ninety-minute appointment came to an end.

THE FOLLOW-UP APPOINTMENT

JANUARY 2004 (10 YEARS, 1 MONTH)

THE SUBSEQUENT MEETING INCLUDED TOM. There was an air of expectation as we convened in the same room as before. Tom shifted in his seat, avoiding Victoria's eye as he fiddled with everything.

"Have you got a car?" He asked, when she asked him about how he was getting on at school. His gaze wandered about the room; he seemed to be having trouble concentrating on her questions.

"I've heard you've a talent for drawing." She offered him paper and pencils. "Perhaps you could draw whilst we talk."

As he drew, Victoria continued to try and hold his attention. His answers were given as a shrug or in one word. Not once did he smile, but he seemed calm. Part of me wanted him to display his destructive behaviour, if only to quantify our claims.

True to form though, he drew one of his shooting pictures.

"Can you tell me about your picture?" Victoria got up and studied it over his shoulder, without portraying any other reaction.

"He's the baddie, he's the baddie as well and he's shot him in the head."

"Oh." She sat back down. "What other pictures can you draw?"

"I can't be bothered!" He slung the paper and pencil to the floor.

"Tom, pick them up."

"No, you pick them up." He flung himself back in his seat.

"You threw it down." Peter frowned towards him.

Elizabeth bent down and retrieved the items from the floor.

Tom jumped up, throwing his chair back with a scrape that made me jump, then ran towards the door.

"Get back here!" However, I was secretly glad he was playing up. She needed to be able to see this.

"Get lost." The door slammed behind him with Victoria in pursuit. The four of us stared at each other.

Hallelujah!

I am finally being listened to!

GETTING SOMEWHERE

MAY 2004 (10 YEARS, 5 MONTHS)

WEEK AFTER WEEK WE ATTENDED. Sometimes with Tom; sometimes without. The four of us would go, or Martin and I, or Peter and Elizabeth. Tom, as he became more familiar with Victoria and the stifling consulting room, was starting to let his guard slip and display more 'Tom-like' behaviour!

Eventually Victoria announced that she could make a diagnosis. I shifted in my seat. *ADHD, Ritalin...please!*

"Although traits of his behaviour are consistent with ADHD, I don't believe that is the underlying problem."

"So, you *don't* think it's ADHD?" Leaning forward, I was disappointed that she disagreed with me.

"No."

"But he's got *every* symptom of it in abundance. I've been with him every single day of his life and know him better than *anyone*."

"I'm not disputing your opinion," she insisted. "Just that his symptoms point more to a conduct disorder."

"Conduct disorder," I echoed. Finally, a name! A condition! Something! Anything! But what did it mean?

"It's an 'umbrella' term," she explained, shaping her hands

in the air like an umbrella. "It embodies all sorts of different problems and behaviours that Tom is demonstrating.

"Is it treatable?"

"I'm afraid not, however it *can* be managed."

"How?" I was happy to clutch at anything.

In the weeks that followed, we considered all sorts of scenarios and ways of dealing with them. In her calm manner, she helped me (and the others to a lesser extent) realise that Tom was, well Tom. A magic wand was not available.

But we could change ourselves, hence, I had to watch my reactions to his behaviour. Nagging, exasperated, shouting responses and use alternative warnings, then a sanction, then following things through. Calmly.

I was the adult, he the child. If I stayed composed, then I may have some hope of keeping him calm. This also applied to the others. *Fat chance,* I thought, with Martin in mind.

Victoria stressed the importance of me spending time with Tom, without Alex or Martin there for at least an hour each week. Doing something of *his* choosing, so he would feel he had me to himself. I knew this was worth a try. From having had me to himself for eight years, he now had to 'share' me with Alex. It was something I had not considered before.

We discussed boundaries, consequences and distractions. All of this went over several appointments. I became empowered and more in control. Suddenly I had a better understanding of what I was dealing with.

I was going to give it everything I had to get his behaviour straightened out. Every scrap of advice Victoria had offered would be implemented, particularly the firming up of boundaries and being vigilant over additives in his diet.

A fresh start would be the way forward; a brand-new school and a more tolerant mother. No way would I ever give up on him!

CONDUCT DISORDER

Conduct Disorder (CD) is a disruptive type of behavioural disorder in which a child routinely violates the personal rights of others and shows no care for others' property. CD is more diagnosed in boys than girls and affects approximately five percent of the population under 15 years of age in the United Kingdom.

Signs/Symptoms of Conduct Disorder

There are a variety of signs/symptoms of conduct disorder, though for a formal diagnosis, there must be at least one shown, and it must be shown for a period of more than six months. Common signs/symptoms of CD include aggressive behaviours toward others or animals, destructive behaviours towards the property of others including harming or destroying items (including cars and homes), lying to others, stealing from others and playing truant from school. Older children and teens may also engage in behaviours harmful to themselves such as smoking and tobacco use, alcohol use, substance abuse and engaging in unprotected sexual activities.

Diagnosing Conduct Disorder

A diagnosis of Conduct Disorder must be made by a professional in child psychology. There are two types of conduct disorder and the distinction is marked by age. Child-Onset Type CD is diagnosed when at least one sign or symptom is shown, for at least 6 months, prior to the age of 10 years. Adolescent-Onset Type CD is diagnosed when at least one sign or symptom is shown, for at least 6 months, after the age of 10 years but no signs or symptoms were shown prior to the age of 10 years. CD may also be described as mild, moderate or severe. Children with mild CD will exhibit few signs/symptoms and cause little harm to others. Children with moderate CD will exhibit multiple signs/symptoms and cause harm to others. Children with severe CD will exhibit signs/symptoms and will cause much harm to others through their actions or the consequences of their actions.

Treating Conduct Disorder

The method of treatment selected for a child with Conduct Disorder will be determined by the child's age, signs/symptoms, and tolerance for or comfort with medications and/or therapies. Main approaches to treatment include cognitive-behavioural therapy which helps to improve a child's problem-solving, communication, impulse control and anger management skills, family therapy/counselling and possibly medication to treat the signs/symptoms of CD.

Living with Conduct Disorder

It is imperative that a child diagnosed with Conduct Disorder has a supportive family and home environment. Not only is this important for following whatever treatment programme is devised, but it helps the child realise that they are still loved and appreciated despite their behaviours. A healthy diet and plenty of exercise is also essential for children being treated for CD. Notifying teachers of a diagnosis of CD is also significant as it will help the child feel supported at school.

Source: www.kidsbehaviour.co.uk

ANOTHER BULLYING INCIDENT

NOVEMBER 2004 (10 YEARS, 11 MONTHS)

After Tom was diagnosed with CD, Alex was diagnosed with asthma. Luckily, Elizabeth and Peter lived close by and would collect Tom at short notice, enabling me to get Alex to hospital. His condition would deteriorate quickly if he was not given steroids and a nebuliser. Twice he ended up in resus. It was terrifying and I subsequently became neurotic with ensuring his room was dust-free; and keeping him away from traffic fumes and cigarette smoke. Tom resented the attention I was 'lavishing' on him.

"I love you both the same," I would assure him, when he whinged that I only cared about Alex.

"I don't see why you have to *sleep* at hospital with him," he pouted. "It's not like he'd care if you went home." I had left Alex with Martin at the hospital, in order to return home for some things, then to drop Tom off with Elizabeth and Peter.

"Tom, if you were ill or hurt in hospital, I'd stay with you too," I draped my arm around his shoulder. "Hopefully it's just for a night or two."

"I hate you!" He yanked himself from me and stormed

through the front door towards the car. "And I hate *him* even more!"

Sadly, he seemed to mean it. Worryingly, he often emptied Alex's asthma inhalers. Alex's medication was being trialled and his asthma was still out of control. I ordered extra inhalers and hid them everywhere.

His fifth asthma attack, when he was nearly four years old was by far the most severe one. Our hospital stay lasted five days.

"We're going to try him on Seretide," said the consultant before he discharged him. "It's not normally given to children under twelve, but Alex is a big lad for his age. I think he'll tolerate it. It's been successful; it's a preventer *and* reliever in one."

On leaving the hospital I went directly to collect Tom, promising to treat him to a takeaway supper and a DVD. Alex seemed worn out so I decided to give him an early night, promising Tom that I would be back downstairs soon to watch the film with him.

It was a chilly November night, so I got Alex into his fleecy pyjamas, with a vest underneath. Giving him a blast of his new inhaler, I turned back his bedclothes so he could climb in.

"Mum, it's wet!" Springing straight back out of bed, he shivered.

"It can't be." But as I touched his sheet, I realised it was soaked with cold water. The bedroom heater had been switched off and his window opened as far as it would go, with the curtain pulled back across it. I called Martin up.

"This is bloody serious!" Martin was grim faced. "If Alex had fallen asleep downstairs, we'd have carried him up and put him into bed in the dark, maybe without realising."

"He'd have had icy air wafting on him all night too," I added, pointing to the window.

"He only got out of hospital a few hours ago," Martin went on. "You do realise this is Tom trying to hurt him."

I nodded miserably. "It's probably my fault too Martin." I hung my head as I scooped Alex up. "I've been too wrapped up with this one - I haven't given Tom enough time."

"Don't be ridiculous, he's four!" He pointed towards where Alex was snuggled into my chest. "He's been in bloody hospital! What did Tom expect you to do?"

"He's still a kid himself." I nestled into Alex's hair, breathing in his innocent scent.

"And a nasty one at that!" He leaned towards the bedroom door. "Tom get up these stairs NOW!"

"Why have you soaked Alex's bed?" Martin stood, hands on hips, glaring at Tom as he appeared in the doorway.

"I spilt summat, so what."

PLAYING WITH FIRE 1

ONE MORNING I AWOKE, unusually at 7 am, to a silent, still house. Tom was usually awake from about six o'clock. I tiptoed up to his room. Pushing his door open, I was greeted by the stench of smouldering rubber and a missing square of carpet in the centre of the room. His bed had been shifted from its usual spot and he was busily hacking a similar sized square from the area under his bed with a lethal-looking kitchen knife.

"What do you think you're doing?" I stared in horror at his activity from the doorway.

He jumped. "Nowt!"

I noticed a box of matches on his windowsill with a large square of charred carpet beside them. *That's what he was doing!* Replacing burnt carpet with a square from beneath his bed. *Did he think I wouldn't notice?* As my gaze travelled from his windowsill back towards him, I noticed several scorch marks along his wall. He appeared to have held a flame to it. *It was a miracle the house was still standing!*

"You stupid boy!" Marching to the window, I snatched up the matches.

"I was only messing about."

"You could have burnt the bloody house down!" Striding towards him, I thrust my hand out for the knife.

"Take a chill pill Mum." Thankfully he placed the knife in my hand without argument.

"Where did you get the matches?"

"I dunno."

"Right you can stay up here all morning." I swiped at the piece of carpet he had chopped out. "I can't believe you could be so stupid."

In addition to the scorch damage, there was litter everywhere, the usual whiff of wee and a stereo that lay in bits.

"Are you going to give me some breakfast or are you going to STARVE me? I hate you, you stupid COW!"

TINSEL AND TANTRUMS

DECEMBER 2004 (NEARLY 11 YEARS)

BEFORE WE KNEW IT, it was Christmas. Tom was up at five and went to wake Alex. Exasperated, I knew any possibility of sleep had gone and made my way downstairs with them.

"Has he been?" I nudged an excited Alex as we neared the foot of the stairs.

"There's no such thing as..."

"Ssssh," I said to Tom. "Don't spoil it for him."

Alex gasped when he noticed that Santa had drunk his glass of Baileys and eaten the mince pie.

"Look Mum," he reached for the stump of carrot that Rudolf had left.

"You're dumb." Tom burst into the living room.

Then they noticed the presents under the tree. Tom skidded across the carpet and began tearing into them.

"No, that pile's yours," I redirected Tom to the other mound beside the tree.

"But that's smaller," he wailed. "That's not fair. He's got more presents than me!"

"You've both had exactly the same spent on you," I sighed.

"But he's got more. *Why* has he got more?"

"Oh, for God's sake Tom. The stuff you've got is more expensive."

Within several minutes, Tom had ripped his presents open.

"Oh." He unearthed a parcel containing new clothes. Then *"what have you bought me books for?"* Then *"crap,"* as he opened a game for his console from my sister.

He was delighted however, with his portable DVD player.

"How much did it cost?" He asked, waving it in the air.

"Tom, don't ask how much things cost. It's rude."

"Is that it?" He rummaged amongst the discarded wrapping paper. "Is that all I get?"

I felt deflated, having struggled for two months to ensure presents for my boys. They had been carefully planned and like lots of parents, had left me short of money, with only enough left aside for Tom's eleventh birthday which was a week away.

The portable DVD player did not last long. In a rage over something, Tom slammed it shut, breaking its fragile screen. I wanted to weep at the wasted money, but what really affected me was the fact that he had robbed himself of his main Christmas present. When I refused to replace it, he vented his temper elsewhere in his bedroom. He tore down his curtains and broke the glass in his window by launching his handheld games console towards it. This now lay in pieces on the carpet. It was one of his most long-standing possessions, having survived an entire year before meeting its demise.

For anyone with a destructive child, I would heartily recommend the durable 'Gameboy' console. But even that was not ultimately Tom-proof!

So, there it was, Christmas 2004. Tinsel and tantrums. Trying to pacify an impossible child!

HIS LAST YEAR AT PRIMARY SCHOOL

TOM SPENT his final primary school year at a different school. I hoped he would reach high school without being excluded. It was a matter of me keeping a firm rein on him and continuing to persevere. I had faith that everything would ultimately work out.

When we visited the new school, my insides were rattling with anxiety. I had given him a pep talk (well, read him the riot act), and he had been promised a treat if he managed a tour of the school without causing any kind of scene!

It was closer to our home and miraculously the school agreed a space for him with an immediate start. They would send for his old school records. I had to complete several forms but found myself skirting around the 'further information' section.

History of Conduct Disorder. I wrote in small writing. *Currently under specialist and making improvement. Please telephone if you require any more information.*

It was not long before his new teacher did. When I had been introduced to him on Tom's first day, I had been delighted. An older teacher; he was probably approaching retirement, and seemed strict. He lurked behind a beard, filling me with belief that Tom would be unable to master him.

Six weeks elapsed before I received the call.

"This is Mr Brown."

"Has Tom settled in OK?" I stammered.

"A little *too* well, I'm afraid! He drew a slow breath. "Thomas has joined this school at a late stage in his primary career and one would expect such a child to be, how shall we put it, a tad reserved in his dealings with new teachers and other pupils."

"But?"

"We appear to be wrestling for one-upmanship. Evidently, he is an intelligent boy but seems to be channelling that intelligence into activities that have little to do with schoolwork. In other words, he's causing mayhem and I *won't* tolerate it!"

"I agree with you." Suddenly, I felt guilty for not giving him warning. But maybe if I had, an immediate opinion would have been formed of Tom without giving him a chance to settle in first.

"Do we have your blessing to deal with Tom as we see fit?"

"Of course. But what do you mean?" *Do what you want with him!*

"Segregation, detentions; lunchtime and after school." He paused and breathed deeply again. "Doing work whilst others are enjoying art, missing the school trip, being banned from the school disco, being left out of cycle training; in other words, all the things that I know will get to him."

This teacher meant business.

"Yes, do all that, you have my complete blessing. I'm surprised you needed to ask!"

"Just don't be upset if he comes home moaning about me. My bark is worse than my bite!"

I laughed, relieved I had moved him. For the rest of the year, Tom was miraculously in hand at school.

AFTER-SCHOOL CLUB

FEBRUARY 2005 (11 YEARS, 2 MONTHS)

SADLY, it was a different tale at the after-school club, linked to the school, where I paid for him to be supervised when I had late finishes at university. Looking back, I do not know how I juggled teacher training, an English degree, an eleven-year-old with Conduct Disorder and a four-year-old. Especially with the unsupportive husband I had.

The school club was run by several young mums. Tom soon made his presence felt, meaning that week after week I was dragged into the office to hear endless accounts of his behaviour. Most of it was bullying of other children or cheek to the staff. It was low-level stuff at first, but they were becoming fed up.

"He's the only year six child we have in the club," remarked the lady in charge one afternoon after she had asked me into the office. "All the other children of working parents go home on their own at that age."

"You don't understand. He'd burn my house down! There's no way he could be trusted!"

"Well you need to have a strong word with him. Because if

things don't improve drastically, you're going to have to make other arrangements."

"I understand; I'll speak to him. I need this school club place. It wouldn't be safe for him to go home alone, he's not responsible enough."

They persevered a bit longer but inevitably, his behaviour deteriorated to the point where parents were complaining about his bullying. Things came to a head when he stole money from the handbag of one of the staff.

I didn't try to change their minds when I was told of their decision to ban him from the club.

THE TRANSITION TO HIGH SCHOOL

I INSISTED on accompanying Tom on his first day at what Alex had dubbed *'big, big school.'* Tom looked grown up in his uniform. I had huge hopes that high school would provide a turning point. The lump in my throat was enormous as I attempted to hug him.

"Gerroff Mum!" He wriggled away. Like I have mentioned before, Tom did not *do* hugs.

I gave him the first in a long succession of house keys, hoping that a bit of trust and responsibility would be a positive step forward. I bought him neck cords and key rings to keep them safe. By the third key I stipulated they must remain in his coat's zip-up compartment. Or his bag. But in quick succession he lost his coat *and* his bag. Both containing our house keys. Bus passes were lucky to last more than a couple of days before being mislaid.

. . .

For Christmas that year, I gave him his first mobile phone. It was amazing to see him grateful for a change and I prayed that it would not meet the same fate as his present from the previous year. But within four weeks he had lost it and vented his frustration by thumping and kicking walls and doors in the house. Then he trashed his bedroom. Aghast, I listened to the commotion, powerless to intervene.

Replacing missing school jumpers was a pain. Some parents might have taught him a lesson by not continually replacing them. But it was a cold winter and I worried what school would make of me if he did not wear adequate jumpers and coats. Within two terms, he had three different school coats. He was costing me a fortune.

However, that first year at high school passed without major incident. I kept a vigil over his school 'planner,' which contained details of homework, punctuality and behaviour. Points were awarded or taken away. Negative comments in the planner resulted in detentions. Tom was not short of these, but never was I telephoned, nor asked into school that year.

Maybe we had finally turned a corner?

HAPPY HOLIDAY

MAY 2006 (12 YEARS, 5 MONTHS)

To attempt another holiday with Tom in tow was possibly daft, in hindsight. But it had been nearly two years since we had tried.

On arrival at Butlins I gave him £10; this was the amount of spending money he would get on each day of the holiday. It lasted ten minutes in the arcades! He asked for more and thumped the wall upon being refused. He was only thwarted by an approaching security guard.

Throughout our 'break,' Tom's constant demands for entertainment, food and drink were relentless. With a thirst as immense as always, he would gulp his own drink like he had spent the day in a desert and then guzzle down Alex's.

I spent the week being shouted and sworn at, and having vile names slung at me whenever I said 'no' to him. As the week wore on, I questioned why I had ever bothered to organise a 'holiday' for us. It was anything but. Martin spent most of it doing his own thing.

On our second to last day Tom announced he was going swimming. It was an amazing pool; one of the main attractions of the holiday park, with water chutes, wave machines and rapids. We arranged to join him there. But within half an hour he reappeared with bloodshot eyes, reeking of chlorine.

"How come you're back?" I clattered around the chalet, chucking swimming things into a bag. "We were getting ready to come down."

"I'm not going." He flung himself onto the sofa.

"You look like you've already been." I touched his hair. "How come your hair's wet?"

"I dunno." He licked his lips. "I've been sick."

"Sick? Have you?" I felt his forehead. "You were fine this morning."

"I drank loads of pop, had some sweets then went on some rides."

"Well you'd better go and have a lie down for a bit." I poured him a drink before passing him the bucket from under the sink. "I'm not ill." He sprang up. "I'm alright now."

"Well, you might be feeling a bit better but if you've been sick, you certainly can't go swimming."

He agreed to stay at the chalet in front of the TV. However, when we arrived at the pool, it had been closed.

"Why have they shut it?" A woman emerged from the building. From her damp hair and flushed cheeks, she'd managed to have a swim.

"Some bloody kid who didn't even bother to get himself out of the water. "Grimacing, she explained what had happened. "He stood there and barfed. Dirty little sod! The place is shut for two days now whilst they filter all the water."

Martin and I looked at each other. I hoped the woman didn't notice the shamed expression upon my face. *Oh Tom!*

EXPENSIVE TRAINERS

JUNE 2006 (12 YEARS, 6 MONTHS)

Tom was becoming 'label-conscious.' The clothes I bought him did not match up to what he was sure he deserved.

"But I need them Mum!" Some £90 trainers were consuming him, and he had been whining all morning!

"They're too expensive." I stacked plates onto the draining board. "If they're what you want, you'll have to get some of the money together yourself."

"Yeah and how am I bloody supposed to do that?" Leaning over me, he filled a glass with water.

"Get a paper round or something." I wiped my hands on a towel. "That's what I had to do at your age."

"Yeah right," he began stomping out of the kitchen. "I'm really gonna do a stupid paper round."

"Well if you were to get half of the money together yourself," I called after him, "I'd help you with the rest."

But that was not good enough. The argument rumbled on for days, during which time he became madder about them. Undoubtedly his heart was set on these trainers and he expected me to pay for them.

"Either you buy them, or I'll smash up the house!" He

eventually screamed before barricading himself in the bathroom. I hammered on the door, worried about the damage he was doing as he banged and crashed around.

Slumping onto the top step of the staircase, I glumly observed the front door that I hoped Martin would suddenly appear through. Tom was not usually as bad if Martin was in the house. An odd sensation was prickling at the nape of my neck. Fear.

Finally, Tom emerged, before trying to barge past me. Racing into the bathroom, I then exhaled with relief as I assessed the damage. *Just a couple of squashed shampoo bottles!* That, I could deal with. Their floral scent drifted up my nose and briefly composed me. But then I swung around and groaned at the three holes he had booted in the door.

My descent down the stairs passed in a blaze of fury. I found Tom in the kitchen, calmly making a sandwich.

"You little…" Somehow, I refrained from throttling him. "We'll be charged for that door. How can you carry on like this?" His sandwich making paused as he calmly peered at me, his eyes flashing a piercing sliver of hatred. Then grabbing the kettle, he hurled it at my feet, before slamming out of the house.

It was evening before he returned home, wearing one trainer. I tried to ignore him.

"You'll have to buy me them trainers now," he stated with an air of victory as he pursued me upstairs.*

*Don't worry. I didn't.

EDUCATION WELFARE

SEPTEMBER 2006 (12 YEARS, 9 MONTHS)

For the Attention ***of the Parent or Carer of Thomas Clifford***

The school attendance of the above named has dropped below 75%. Your son usually does not arrive at school at all or else leaves the school premises shortly after registration.

I am aware that this matter has been brought to your attention on several occasions but as it does not appear to have improved, we are left with no alternative other than to issue you with a formal warning.

It is your duty, as someone having parental responsibility, to ensure that your child attends school regularly. Failure to do this will result in further action being taken against you which could include prosecution or a fixed penalty of £50.*

Yours faithfully

. . .

Education Welfare Officer

*I was incensed by this letter. I drove him to school each day, dropping him at the main entrance and waiting until he went inside. Short of remaining with him for the entire school day, I am unsure what else I could have done.

MORE BULLYING – AT SCHOOL THIS TIME

OCTOBER 2006 (12 YEARS, 10 MONTHS)

"WE'RE RINGING with regards to an ongoing bullying problem." It had to be serious if one of Tom's teachers was calling me in the middle of his lunch break. Perhaps things were about to slot into place. His behaviour at home had deteriorated. If he was being bullied at school, that would also explain the truanting. There would be a few words coming their way if that was the case. No way was I prepared to allow my son to suffer bullying.

"We have a boy in Tom's class, Duane, with Asperger's Syndrome," he continued. "Unfortunately, this makes him an easy target. He has fallen victim to low-level abuse from Tom for several weeks; name calling, snide remarks, that sort of thing."

My heart sank, along with the words of defence I had prepared. Tom was not the victim – he was the bully.

"Duane's parents have put a formal complaint in. He doesn't want to come to school. There are witnesses to it all, mainly other class members, who have seen many occasions of Tom's behaviour."

“I don’t know what to say...” I clenched my eyes as though I could block out the shame.

“It’s getting worse too. Tom has apparently been threatening to hit him - the poor lad’s beside himself. We’re going to have to isolate Tom from class for the rest of the week.”

“OK. I understand.”

“We’d be grateful if you could talk to him about his behaviour.”

“Of course.” My eyes remained closed as the conversation concluded. “I’m so ashamed of him.”

“He’s a weirdo,” was Tom’s explanation for how he had treated him.

“Tom!” As he sat beside me in the car, I was gutted at his response.

“He is! In fact, he’s a freak.”

“You nasty boy,” I was struggling to concentrate on the road, unable to bear the spite in his face. “Where did all this hate come from? You weren’t brought up like this!”

PLAYING WITH FIRE 2, EXCLUSION 1

NOVEMBER 2006 (12 YEARS, 11 MONTHS)

EVEN IN THE school's isolation unit, Tom was evidently unable to behave. "This is Tom's head of year," boomed a male voice down the phone. "Is that his mother?"

"Yes?" I glanced around as life progressed normally in the supermarket.

"I left him unattended in the unit. I had something to deal with." His voice wobbled in anger. Or maybe stress. Or both. "Not even for ten minutes."

"And?" Amidst the beeping of checkouts, I dared not hear what Tom had done this time.

"Lucky I came back when I did! I caught him holding a lighter flame up to a pile of folders." His words were garbled as though he couldn't get them out fast enough. "One or two had already caught fire."

"I can't believe he would be so stupid!" I was forgetting where I was as several other shoppers peered at me. "It's one thing after another!"

"I managed to put them out without the fire alarms being set off, so at least the school didn't have to be evacuated." His voice had evened out a little now. "But it's so serious that we'll be placing him on a three-day fixed-term exclusion. The entire school could have been burnt down."

"But I'm at university most of the time. I've no one to supervise him."

"I'm afraid there's nothing we can do about that."

Bowing my head, I contemplated having him at home for three days. "Are you able to set work for him to do at home?"

"Yes. I'll get something organised. But he needs to be off the school premises as soon as possible. Can you collect him?"

By the time I got there he had run off. The receptionist stared at me as though I was something she had trodden in. She was obviously a member of the *blame the parents* club!

Hastily, I retreated to my car, half-relieved that I could prolong the inevitable confrontation with Tom until later.

When he made it home that evening, he was clearly under the influence of something. As he brushed past me, I caught the whiff of a chemically, herby smell.

"He's stoned," Martin stated flatly as Tom headed for the kitchen. "That's weed."

"Give over." I shook my head, refusing to consider it. "No way."

Martin nodded to where Tom was eating his way through a packet of biscuits while he waited for his dinner to reheat in the microwave. "Munchies. You'll see."

The three days of him being off school were hell. After the first day, I gave up attempting to get him to do the work they had set; it wasn't worth the abuse.

The relief I felt when he returned to school was immense! However, within days they were back on the phone.

EXCLUSION 2

"I'M SORRY." It was his head of year on the phone. "We're excluding him again. We've had two incidents today."

"Oh great!" M*ore* time off university. "Now what?"

"He's damaged a computer after looking at inappropriate material on the internet. After being caught, he slammed his fist down onto the keypad. It won't switch on now."

"Will I be billed?" I felt drained.

"There's a possibility that the school's insurance will cover it. The repair bill could be hefty, we'll have to let you know on that."

"What's the other thing?" I enquired, slumping onto a bench in the sunshine. All around me, other trainee teachers were going about their business – their only worries perhaps being assignment deadlines and where their next school placement might be.

"He's stolen a bag from another pupil. Luckily, we got it back. Eventually, he led us to where he had hidden it in the school grounds. Several people saw him take it – I think he realised he was cornered."

"Was anything missing?" My friend Jane sat beside me, and

patted my arm, knowing the situation that I was currently discussing would be centred around Tom.

"No, thankfully. We would have had to involve the police if that had been the case. I have to say though he's lucky we haven't informed them. Next time we will."

EXCLUSION 3

APRIL 2007 (13 YEARS, 4 MONTHS)

"I'M sorry to be the bearer of bad news but we're going to have to send Tom home," stated his head of year, without even introducing himself as I answered the phone. Tom hadn't managed to last until morning break!

"Why?"

"He's been smoking cannabis on school premises." Mr Wharton sounded more bemused than usual. "Evidently, he's still under the influence."

"I'm unable to collect him for at least an hour." I glanced towards the clock in the refectory.

"He needs to be off the premises right away. We can't be having drugs flying around." Pages rustled. "Can we contact his father?"

"Be my guest."

~

Peter looked furious when I arrived at his house that evening.

"How long's he been smoking cannabis?" He rose from his chair.

"*I don't know.*" I shrank beneath his glare. "What do I know? I don't bloody give him it."

"I'm not having it." His finger wagged in the air. "I want to know where he's getting it from! He's thirteen, for God's sake!"

"The little swine has pinched twenty quid off me!" Martin slapped his wallet down like a prized fish on the kitchen worktop. I had only just walked in.

"Are you sure?" My stress levels soared again.

"Sarah, it was all I had in it." He thumped his hand onto the soft leather of his wallet as though the action reiterated his point.

"Maybe you've made a mistake." I yanked a cup from the draining board. Despite all we were going through, I never wanted to admit the worst about Tom until I had to.

"It was only last night when I checked it to make sure I didn't have to go to the bank. I was in the shop, paying for something, and found it empty." Snatching it up again, he thrust it in front of my face. "It was bloody embarrassing. So unless *you've* taken it, it must be Tom."

"I don't think he'd steal off you." I walked away from him, desperate not to argue. I'd had enough.

"Oh come on!" He could not conceal his exasperation. "It wouldn't be the first time, would it?"

Unfortunately, he was right. Martin prised the truth out of him later that evening by pretending the wallet had been fingerprinted. I ignored the smug look he gave me after Tom had flounced from the room.

Consequently, we attempted to ground him. He roared with laughter before storming from the house.

THE FIRST ARREST

AUGUST 2007 (13 YEARS, 8 MONTHS)

"TOM'S BEEN ARRESTED," Martin informed me flatly.

"What?" I gasped down the telephone, hoping I was dreaming the conversation.

"He's thieved a crate of beer from a shop. The stupid idiot thought he could pick it up and stroll off with it." He laughed then, which irked me. "His mates did a runner and left him to face the music."

After making my excuses at university, I began my reluctant journey to the police station. I was becoming increasingly upset with Martin. Whilst I wanted to get Tom help and support, it was like Martin enjoyed the drama and watching his behaviour deteriorate. We weren't on the same page with anything.

"You've got my son in custody," I announced to the desk sergeant. "Thomas Clifford."

"Ah yes." He scanned the 'admissions' board. "I must say, they're getting younger."

I was led to the airless "custody suite." It was grim. The police staff looked at me as though I had committed a crime myself. Shuffling uncomfortably, I was unsure where to look. I tried to close off my sense of smell to the stench of odorous feet.

I could see it wafted from several pairs of trainers that waited outside cell doors.

An officer unlocked one of these doors. Out crept my bleary-eyed son, appearing as though he had been crying. As he avoided eye contact, I was amazed to notice what could have been shame crossing his face. I overcame the compulsion to hug him and glared at him instead.

"You stupid boy, what were you thinking of?" I demanded. I looked up into his face, suddenly realising he now towered above me.

"I know." His gaze remained at his feet. "I won't do it again."

"I hope it's taught you a lesson, being locked up in there." I gestured in the direction of the cell from which he had emerged.

"Not nice places, the cells, are they Tom?" The officer grunted as he bashed information into a computer behind the green desk.

Tom shook his head. "I won't do it again. I'm sorry Mum."

"We're going to let you go with a caution this time," announced the officer. "But we never, ever want to see you in here again. Do you understand?"

"You won't!" I led him towards the door by the arm. "I'll make damn sure of that."

"What in God's name were you doing?" I reversed out of the car park.

"I fancied a drink." His smirk said it all.

"You're thirteen years old. You shouldn't be anywhere *near* alcohol, let alone pinching it!"

"Yeah right." Clearly his meekness in the police station had all been an act.

"Well, you're grounded all week and don't ask me for a single penny either. Any pocket money is well and truly stopped."

He did stay in the following evening, but the one after, he

strode out whilst I had my hands in the washing up bowl. I resisted the urge to chase after him. If I had captured him, I would not have been responsible for my actions.

It was approaching midnight when he fell in through the door. Anxiously, I had waited up for him.

"You're drunk!" I shrieked.

"So what!" Slurring his words, he knocked into the banister.

"Where did you get it from?" Grabbing his jacket, I tried to get him to face me.

"Me mates." Placing his foot on the first step of the stairs was a challenge for him.

"Look at the bloody state of you. You can barely walk! We'll discuss this in the morning!"

Laughing raucously, he lurched upstairs. Soon after, I peeked into his room, relieved to find him sleeping. Placing a bucket beside him, I watched him sleep for a moment, making sure he was breathing OK. Just like I had when he was tiny. Still he looked the picture of innocence. My boy. The cause of constant angst and torment. When was it going to end?

HIS 'FRIENDS'

SEPTEMBER 2007 (13 YEARS, 9 MONTHS)

Tom had acquainted himself with an undesirable bunch of friends. They would all hang about near our home, turning the air blue with their language. It was easy to see how Tom's behaviour had found itself in freefall again.

There seemed to be a lot of in-fighting between them. Once Tom surged through the front door as though he had the devil after him. Locking it, he then bolted upstairs. Within moments, a thumping at the door pursued him.

"Where is he?" Demanded a pock-marked lad, as I threw the door open.

"Upstairs." I counted five of them.

"I want him down here!" A lad at the back barged to the front and squared up to me.

"I think you'd better calm down." I stepped back.

"Get him down here!" Another lad demanded.

"Don't talk to me like that!"

"And you're going to stop us, are you?" Another grinned around at his friends.

"Get away from my door!" I grappled for the handle. "Now!" As one tried to jam it open with his foot, I had to force it shut. I locked the door and raced upstairs, a hammering echoing after me.

"Whore!" One of them yelled.

I felt scared. *Thank God Alex was asleep! Where was Martin when I needed him?*

"What's going on?" I demanded of Tom, who was observing his 'friends' from behind his curtain. They were hurling stones and clumps of mud at our house.

"One of em smacked me." Turning away from the window, he looked at me. "For no reason. They were filming it on a phone."

Taking hold of his chin, I studied his face. "Well you don't look as though you've been smacked."

"I got away, didn't I?" He jerked his chin away.

"Slut."

I winced. "Have you heard what they're calling me?"

"It's not my fault." He returned to his curtained surveillance.

"They're *your* bloody friends."

I went to check on Alex, who miraculously slept. Then rang Martin. Whilst awaiting his answer, the front door clicked shut. Shooting to the window, I had not been fast enough to see which way Tom had headed.

"Martin, I need you to get home." Lifting my hand to my forehead was not going to ease my headache. "Alex's in bed and I need to find Tom; these lads might beat him up."

"He's a big boy now. He's probably brought it on himself. You know what he's like."

For ten minutes, I fretted as I paced the lounge, before deciding that I must do something. Locking Alex in, I left the house to search for Tom. I'd only walked ten yards before I spotted him, striding towards me, thankfully unscathed.

"They'll regret it if they come at me again." Tom looked defiant as he squatted and patted his sock.

"What're you on about?" I grabbed hold of his shoulder as he sprang back up.

"They'll really get it."

"What have you got down your sock?"

"Nothing."

"Show me. Now."

"I wasn't going to do owt with it." Bending down, he produced my vegetable knife which glinted in the early evening sunshine. Dread crawled over me.

"What if you'd fallen?"

"Well I wouldn't have done, would I?"

"Tom, you're stupid sometimes! What would've happened if the police caught you with it?" Shedding my cardigan, I wrapped it around the knife. "You know about knives! I don't understand. What were you going to do with it?"

"Just scare em."

"And what if they'd turned it on you! I can't believe it, I just can't." I was ranting but I didn't care.

The next evening his 'friends' returned. Rather than knock on the door, they rhythmically thumped upon it.

Flinging the door open, I counted four of them this time.

"Where is he?" One of them demanded.

"Look lads." Perhaps I might have more success if I addressed them levelly. "What's the problem? You were all mates a couple of days ago, there's no need for all this trouble."

"He's a liar." An angry finger jabbed towards me.

"Look, I'm sure it can be sorted out."

"We don't wanna talk to *you*. We wanna talk to *him*." He tried to peer beyond me.

"Tom's not here."

"Don't believe you." He pushed at the door.

"He's at his dad's."

"Well I wanna check his room." He took a step towards me.

I put my hand up. "You're not getting one foot in here. I've tried to be reasonable, but you just want trouble." I began closing the door. "I don't know what Tom has done to upset you but you've no right to come banging on *my* door, giving *me* grief. I've a five-year-old in here."

I shut the door on their mocking laughter, praying they would go away. Martin was in the bath this time, so I did not feel so vulnerable.

To assure myself of their complete departure, I glanced through the window. I was horrified to find them spitting at my car and bombarding it with mud. Without thinking, I darted out towards them.

"Get away from my car or I'm calling the police," I screeched. They scattered like birds.

One of them screamed their favourite word at me; "whore," as I approached them. They all started running. Why they ran, I'm not sure, but I was relieved they did. If they hadn't, I have no clue how I might have dealt with it.

They ended up behind a fence. I wasn't afraid, just furious.

"Do you not have any different words in your vocabulary?" I jeered as one of them shouted *whore* again. "That one's getting boring."

"Sarah!" Martin roared as he strode towards me, with a face like thunder. The gang dispersed in all directions.

"What were you thinking?" He caught up to where I stood. "They have knives, and all sorts these days."

"My car," I panted. We both looked towards it where it languished, coated in disgusting spit and clumps of mud. "And a fat lot of use you were."

"Look, we'll sort it tomorrow," he promised as he steered me back towards the house.

BITTERSWEET

Elizabeth and Peter had news when I collected Tom that weekend.

"Tom's going to have a brother or sister!" Elizabeth patted her belly.

"Congratulations!" I threw my arms around her. They had been together for years and I knew how badly she wanted a baby of her own. But, try as I might, I could not quell the nagging, and some might say; selfish thoughts.

What if they stop having Tom as often?

What if he wants to live with them full-time when they become a 'proper' family?

What if he bullies his new sibling as much as he's bullied Alex?

What if he dotes on his new sibling? How will Alex feel then?

Will Elizabeth still be as supportive when she has got a baby of her own?

. . .

Niggling, conflicting questions. A deep-seated suspicion that the worst might be yet to come with Tom. A knowledge that of course their priorities would lie with their unborn baby. A resentment that Peter was possibly going to side-line his eldest child in favour of his new one. A worry that I would soon be grappling for survival on my own.

FORTNIGHTLY

BEFORE LONG, Peter and Elizabeth reduced Tom's weekly visits to fortnightly ones. It was hardly fair on Elizabeth to be expected to cope with his angst as her pregnancy went on. One evening she rang me.

"Tom's been using my bank card to credit his phone."

"Are you sure?" I wanted to scream.

"Positive. I've been in touch with my bank. It's credited his number five times in the last few weeks."

"Are you sure it wasn't Peter doing it for him?" *There I was, refusing again to believe the worst of him.*

"I've already checked that. That was the first thing I did. No. Tom's taken it upon himself to thieve money from me." Her voice rose up an octave. "At a time when I have everything to buy for the baby."

"I'm sorry. I really am. What do you want me to do with him?"

"Well. I've passed his details to the bank. They may involve the police; I don't know. But we should let him think they will." I could hear the anger in her voice. "He can pay it back."

We never discussed how this 'payback' might manifest

itself. Perhaps I was expected to deduct it from his pocket money, subsequently taking the flak from him. Or maybe they were planning to reduce my maintenance payments. This episode spelt the beginning of the end for the respite that had been a necessity for me over the years.

MONTHLY

DECEMBER 2007 (13 YEARS, 11 MONTHS)

"HE'S ASKED what would happen to the baby if he was to boot me in the stomach!" Elizabeth shrieked at me. "He wanted to know if it would die!"

"Oh God! Where's Peter?"

"Working. I can't cope. *I just can't cope!*" She was hysterical.

"I'll come and get him." Wrenching mine and Alex's coats from their hooks, I snatched up my car keys. "I'll be there in ten minutes."

"If I lose this baby because of him."

I felt desolate as I made the brief drive. *How could he say such a thing?* I glanced at Alex, sat beside me, nearly six years old, calm and amenable. Every time I looked at him, I thanked my lucky stars. As for Tom, I'd be fortunate if they ever had him to stay again.

"Do you think I'm going to let you do to my baby what you've done to HIM?" Elizabeth screamed at Tom, gesturing towards Alex.

"Calm down Elizabeth. Please!" I steered her towards her sofa. "You shouldn't be getting into this state! I'll take him home and sort him out. You get your feet up." I moved the footstool towards her. "This'll never happen again."

"Damn right it won't."

Later that day I received a text to say they were reducing his visits to monthly. Slumping onto the sofa, I contemplated the reality of *never* having a break from his antics. I was truly out of my depth.

"Mum, I can smell smoke!" Alex screwed up his nose. So could I. Smoking was banned in our house. Mainly because of Alex's asthma but I hated the smell too.

He was smoking in his bedroom. Taking the stairs two at a time, I burst through his door.

"YOU DO NOT SMOKE IN MY HOUSE!"

"It's my room. I'll do what I like," he tapped his ash onto the carpet.

"You won't!"

As I lunged towards him, he blew smoke into my face. "Slag!" He shouted.

The hairs stood up on my neck, but I backed away. There would be nothing to gain from losing it. Besides I was in shock at the level of venom spewing from his every pore towards me.

All I had ever done was love and take care of him. *How could he despise me so much?*

The next time I went upstairs, I paused as I heard money jangling. He was in Alex's bedroom, emptying his money box. I caught him in time, saving the money Alex had put in there for his next batch of cars.

"Morning," smiled my neighbour as we both left our homes the next morning.

I fished around in my handbag for keys as we wandered together to our cars. "Morning, how are you?"

"OK thanks, has your week got off to a good start?"

"Not really." I was so upset that something I would not normally divulge to my neighbour came tumbling out. "I've caught my eldest trying to steal from my purse."

"Oh no!" She screwed her face up.

"He seems to be going through another horrendous phase. I'm gonna have to start keeping everything out of his way."

"It sounds like you ought to fix locks on your doors."

"That might not be a bad idea."

Before long, that was how we lived. Valuables were locked away and my handbag was always on my shoulder. It became our normality. My friends were amused when I kept my bag on me when I visited *their* homes. My 'bag attachment' was becoming ingrained!

~

When Alex came to open his cards on his sixth birthday, he discovered the task had already been done. Tom had stolen all the money from them. After ringing around to find out who had put what in the cards, we discovered that his theft totalled £40. The people concerned promised they would give Tom's birthday money, which was also approaching, to Alex instead.

"How could you do that?" I waved the torn envelopes in Tom's face.

"What does *he* need money for anyway?" Tom snatched them from me. "He's only six!"

"How dare you open other people's cards?" Wrenching a cup from the cupboard, I slammed it on the kitchen worktop. "You disgust me!"

"Shut up, you stupid fucking div!"

You may or may not agree with my actions, but I swung a

slap at him. However, he was quicker than me and managed to dodge it.

~

Within days, he helped himself to the TV satellite box.

"What did you get for it?" I made no attempt to hide the sarcasm in my voice.

He ignored me.

"Where did you sell it?"

He shrugged his shoulders. We also discovered Martin's wedding ring had vanished from the bedroom. But Tom was admitting to nothing. We vowed that we could no longer afford lapses of forgetting to secure the bedroom door. Everything of value *had* to go in there. To have a thief living within our midst was devastating.

THE BEHAVIOUR CONTRACT

JANUARY 2008 (14 YEARS, 1 MONTH)

As the school term recommenced, a meeting with Tom's head of year, Mr Wharton, was thrust upon me.

"I felt it was important to get something in place before Tom returns to lessons." He explained.

"Like what?" My voice echoed around the empty science lab with the whiff of potassium permanganate, sulphur and bunsen burners.

"Well, we know that things are tricky for you when we exclude him." He rummaged around in a file, "so we're going to try some other methods."

I was all ears. It was a relief that school were acknowledging my predicament.

"We're going to put him on a behaviour contract," he announced, taking some paper from his file. "I will be *closely* monitoring him."

"How will you do that?" I leaned forwards on the high stool to study the sheet of paper. "I've been trying all his life!"

"He'll have to come to me at the start of every morning *and* afternoon." He took out another sheet, which showed Tom's attendance record. "Obviously I need to verify that he's actually in school."

I nodded, trying not to gasp at the 56% figure which blared out from it. "You do know I'm doing all I can to get him here."

"Of course. I've seen you dropping him off on several mornings."

"I bring him to the door," I added. "But I can't control what happens after."

"I know. I agree."

"So why do I keep getting letters from Education Welfare, threatening me with action?"

"I wouldn't worry. They're standard. If anything comes of them, we'll sort it. Anyway, back to this contract." He pointed at his sheet. "We're going to give him clear rules about the conduct expected in each lesson. His teachers will fill this form in at the end of every lesson to show whether he has achieved each target." He slid it over the workbench for me to inspect.

Arrive on time for lesson.

Stay in lesson.

Complete work set.

Display respectful and appropriate behaviour.

"But that's what he can't understand!" I stated as I gestured to the bottom 'target.' "*Respectful and appropriate behaviour.* It needs to be more specific."

"We're going to do work with him around that. Miss Hussain, head of his *next* year group, also leads pastoral care." He gestured with his hands as he spoke. "She'll work on a one-to-one basis for at least two hours each week with him, to look at aspects of his behaviour and how it affects others."

"And when he breaks the contract?"

"He'll be dealt with using an *internal exclusion*. This is an effective deterrent for many pupils. Come with me, I'll show you the room." Rising from his stool, he replaced the sheets in the folder and grabbed his bag.

Obediently, I followed him to a room containing several wooden, graffiti-covered booths, not dissimilar to a polling station. It was airless and musty with an overwhelming smell of stale chewing gum.

"They hate it in here." Smiling, he swept his gaze over the room. "But if he can't work in class, he'll be working in here more often, supervised of course."

"And if that doesn't work?"

"We'll cross that bridge when we come to it."

My first contact with Miss Hussain did not begin on a good note. One morning, she was waiting for me when I dropped Tom off at school. She was a tiny lady with a brisk manner and a stern voice.

"A mobile phone's been stolen from another pupil." She led me to her office.

"And it's Tom?" I glanced back at Tom before following her in, hoping that he would remain in the reception area as Miss Hussain had instructed. If left unattended, he had a habit of running off.

"There's no actual evidence, but his name *is* being bandied about. Can you keep a look out for it?" Her voice was highly pitched, and she was dressed in garish colours. "Maybe you could check his room?"

"Of course. I certainly wouldn't put it past him. He's light fingered enough at home. I can't even leave my handbag around anymore."

"I've been told about it," her voice seemed to soften. "It sounds like you're having a tough time."

"I always have."

"I've been reading a bit of the background. But I think we

can sort him out." I was surprised at the change in her face as it broke into a smile. "He's not a bad lad deep down."

Even though I remained silent, my expression must have spoken volumes.

"I haven't failed *yet* with a pupil that's been allocated to me," she added, with an air of authority. "We need to bring out the best in him; give him opportunities to engage in things he's good at."

"Whatever you think." *Good luck,* I yearned to add.

"There's no such thing as 'bad' children." She seemed to be appraising me. "And Tom's certainly not one."

"How well do you know him?" Surely, *she must have been kept up to speed with his antics.*

"Well...we've had one or two encounters." She smiled, clearly the memory of these 'encounters' had provided her with some amusement. "But he's always been polite."

"Well, I wish the same could be said of him at home." That morning's expletives were still echoing around in my head. "He speaks to me like I'm something he's stepped in."

KEEP YOUR HANDBAG ON YOUR SHOULDER!

One morning, I left my bag in the kitchen. Tom was in there, like a rocket-fuelled turbo. I think I sensed, rather than heard the abrupt movement. Anyway, I caught him in time.

"Well I needed some money." As I snuck into the kitchen, he snatched his hand away from my bag.

"Why didn't you ask for some?" Glaring at him, I waited for his answer.

He scowled. "Cos you're a tight cow!"

"You can't speak to me like that!"

"I just did. You're a tight-arsed fucking stupid bitch." He stamped up the stairs.

My anger dissipated beneath a wave of sadness. *How can he speak to me like he does? I'm his bloody mum!*

Within moments, my thoughts were disturbed by Alex's screeches.

I raced upstairs to find Alex clutching his face.

"What have you done?" Screaming at Tom, I hurtled towards Alex. Pushing past me, Tom tore down the stairs. I could smell Martin's aftershave.

"I hate the lot of you!" Tom banged the front door on his way out.

"He squirted me!" Alex clutched his eyes.

Steering him towards the bathroom, I noticed a bottle of aftershave in Tom's bedroom doorway. *He'd squirted Alex with it.*

I filled the sink and bathed his eyes. He squirmed as I dabbed at them. "You poor little thing. There, let's keep doing this. They'll soon stop stinging."

MISSING

FEBRUARY 2008 (14 YEARS, 2 MONTHS)

Although only fourteen years old; it was not out of character for Tom to stay out until all hours of the night.

On the first few occasions, I reported him missing if it got beyond midnight. The police would arrive; usually treating me with an air of disgust before studying his photograph. They would scribble down a description and leave, informing me that an eye would be kept out for him as they were out and about. He would always turn up though.

Once he returned whilst the police were taking his details, which pleased me. I listened as they described the more important jobs they should be doing, rather than wasting their time and energy on a boy who didn't have the respect for his mother to return home when he was supposed to.

Eventually I stopped reporting him missing when he was late. Deep down I knew he was alright. I knew I would sense if he wasn't.

. . .

One Saturday morning I awoke with a start.

"Have you let Tom in during the night?" I nudged Martin.

"No. Don't start fussing about bloody Tom."

I leapt out of bed and towards his room, in case he had got in through a window or something. He didn't have a key, having lost so many. Usually we hid the key outside for him if he was likely to be home before us.

His bed had not been slept in. Forcing myself to stay calm, I reasoned that the selfish toad would be at a friend's house. He would come back later, as always.

Only when it was getting dark again, did I start to panic. I rang his dad, two of his friend's mobile numbers that I found in his room and finally, the police.

"Why are you only *just* reporting him missing?" The policewoman, when she arrived, looked at me as though I was the most inadequate mother on the planet.

There was no sign of him that night either. By morning, I was worn out from pacing the house. I was bent double with worry about what might have happened to him.

"All he has to do is ring," I wailed to Martin, staring through the window for the millionth time. "Just to let me know he's alright! I think something's happened." I stopped as this realisation crept over me. "He's never stayed out for this long before!"

"Well he's ruined my fucking weekend." Martin looked right through me, his face as hard as stone. "I'm off to the pub."

It was difficult, but I had to act normally, for Alex's sake. By lunchtime I decided it was time to go looking myself. Driving round every nook and cranny of the neighbourhood, I tried to pause alongside gangs of youths so I could scan their groups.

From the back, they all looked like Tom, even the girls in their hooded 'uniforms.'

As dark fell again, a blanket-like depression wrapped itself around me. No way could I go home without him. Filling my car with more petrol, I forced myself to eat some crisps before widening my search.

The groups were more formidable in the dark. However, I began to stop and question them as to whether they knew Tom or had seen him over the weekend.

Most of them stared as though I was an alien species. My questioning produced a mixture of giggles and sarcastic responses. Nevertheless, one or two, mainly girls, seemed mildly sympathetic. But no one admitted to knowing him.

Eventually, I struck lucky. "Yeah I saw him last night." A girl glanced at her friends as she spoke, as though seeking their approval. "He stopped at Meddy's gaff."

"Would you mind telling me where he, or is it a she, lives?" I wrenched my phone from my bag, ready to type an address in.

She looked at me. "You say you're his mum, right?"

"Yes. I've been looking for him all day. I've even reported him missing. I need to know he's OK."

Eventually she provided a street name but claimed not to know the number. Within five minutes, I was there after punching it into my sat nav. After driving up and down several times, I spotted him with two others.

"Tom!" I wound down the window.

"Oh no, it's me mum." His companions sniggered. Tom tried to bolt behind a gate but swiftly realised there was no escaping me. "I'll be home later, right?"

"No, it's not alright. Get in this car. NOW!"

"Fuck off." He reddened as his friends laughed louder. "Do one!"

"Do you know?" I said in a loud voice. "He hasn't been

home since Friday. Probably not even washed or changed his underpants."

Tom marched over and slung himself into the passenger seat.

"You make a show of me like that again and I'll fucking -"

"What Tom. What will you do?"

"You'll see."

He gave no explanation and offered no apology, other than he *"couldn't be bothered"* coming home. Noises of regret were shown to the police though, when they came to speak to him.

"Bloody filth," he said as soon as they left.

I rang Elizabeth and Peter to inform them of his return. They had been concerned but not to the extent I had.

"He's really putting himself at risk," said Elizabeth.

"I know. He thinks he's older than he is." I closed the living room door so he could not hear our conversation. "The cannabis smoking, the truanting, everything - it can't go on. I'm so worried about him - I've no control - he won't listen."

After further discussion we decided that Elizabeth would make a referral to social services, asking for help again. After all, by virtue of his own behaviour, he was making *himself* vulnerable. Having grown up in care, social services were the last people I wanted to involve but I was out of ideas and eager to grasp at any hope of help with him.

How could I keep him safe if I had no idea where he was half the time?

PLAYING WITH FIRE 3

MR WHARTON HAD RUNG ME, yet again. "I know we said we wouldn't, but we're going to *have* to exclude him."

"Why. What's he done this time?" I was becoming convinced that Tom was acting up on purpose; obviously exclusion was preferable to school.

"He set fire to a bin," he sighed. "The whole school had to be evacuated."

"Oh, for God's sake! But what happened to the internal exclusions?" I was in the university library and had too much work to be collecting and babysitting Tom.

"This is too serious. He's going to have to remain at home for the rest of the week."

"Great." I gathered my books together.

"Can I ask," asked the school receptionist the following week, "why Tom isn't in uniform?" Her manner was as patronising on the telephone as in person.

"He was wearing it earlier." I had to think for a moment but yes. We'd rowed about it!

"Well he isn't now. And it's happening too often. One of his teachers has asked me to mention it."

"He must have put a change in his bag." I wasn't going to react to her superior tone of voice; I could not be bothered. "I'll check his bag in future"

"If you could."

Mornings had become a daily battle.

"I'm not putting that on," he would protest with exacting regularity.

"Tom, every other pupil in your school has to wear uniform. Why should *you* be any different?

"I'm not wearing it. Alright?"

Sometimes he concealed a change of clothes *beneath* his uniform. Or he would try to sneak clothes out. Within days, I knew what and where to check. So he devised craftier methods, such as hiding his bag outside. He *was* wearing what *he* wanted for school. For this and a multitude of other reasons, I detested mornings.

Neither of us were 'morning people' and would clash like cage fighters. As he was growing, so was the severity of his attitude. The abuse I got from him broke my heart. When he was angry enough, he would punch holes in walls or trash crockery.

Then came the straw that threatened to break the camel's back.

WHAT MIGHT YOU GET WHEN MOTHER'S DAY FALLS ON YOUR BIRTHDAY?

(i) flowers
(ii) chocolates
(iii) perfume
(iv) breakfast in bed
(v) a lazy day
(vi) a police hunt for your son after he burgles your next-door neighbour

As we drove up our street, anxiety mounted. Police officers were all around our home. Parking quickly, I raced over.

"What's happened?" I reached a policewoman. "I live here!"

"Burglary. We're looking for the occupants of 164. Two lads. They've got into number 166 through the back door. They've taken quite a bit."

Adrenaline coursed through me like a flooded river.

"YOU!!" Cried the girl from next door suddenly as she hurtled towards us. "Your son! I was barricaded inside my own room." Hysterical, she continued to yell accusations at me. "What sort of parent brings up a monster like him?"

"That's enough." The police officer caught hold of her

by the arms that were flailing ever more in my direction. "Let's get you inside. We'll catch him, don't you worry. It's not his mother's fault. I'll be with you in a moment," she nodded towards me before vanishing into next door with the girl.

What on earth had been going through his head? Unlocking our door, I leaned wearily against the outside wall. Moments later, the policewoman's voice pierced my desolate thoughts.

"Your neighbour wants to say sorry," she announced, steering me into my house. "She was upset. It's all been a dreadful shock, but she's aware that blaming you isn't the answer."

"*She* hasn't done anything to apologise for." I held the living room door ajar.

"The forensics will be along shortly." She followed me. "There are cars out searching for him and his mate."

It didn't feel real.

"Do you have a recent photo?" She scanned her eyes over our living room. I gestured towards the one that had been taken the previous year at school.

"Handsome young man, isn't he?" She commented as I took it from the wall. "Any idea why he'd want to burgle your neighbour? He doesn't look the sort."

"It's nothing to do with how he's been brought up." I took the picture back from her. "I've done everything I can. He's a nightmare."

"I can vouch for that." The father of the girl next door had returned and came up behind the policewoman.

"Sarah, we're not blaming you." He brushed past the policewoman and into our living room. "Not one bit. We just want our stuff back. And obviously for him to be punished."

"What did they take?" I was hugely relieved about his attitude.

"Two laptops, a camera, a mobile phone, a purse and a

games console." His voice was calm. There was no blame in his eyes. I could detect something else though; pity.

"I'm sorry…"

"It's *him* who should be sorry. *You* didn't burgle us."

Just then his daughter emerged behind him. "I shouldn't have yelled at you like that. It's just the whole thing shit me up." Her dad draped an arm around her. "I don't know how many lads were in the house. I was on my own - they could've done anything."

"He'll get what's coming. I'll see to it." Never in my life had I felt so guilty.

Several hours later, Tom returned. "Where've you been?" I couldn't look at him.

He slung himself into a chair. "Nowhere."

"Do you want some dinner?" I stood up.

"Yeah, I'm starving." I left him channel hopping, blissfully ignorant that I knew anything.

His plate spun around in the microwave. The smell of chicken made me feel even more churned up than I already did. After leaving him to eat, I made the call, speaking to the police from the kitchen. They arrived within minutes, just as Tom had finished eating.

"I'm arresting you on suspicion of burglary and false imprisonment." I listened as he was given his rights and led away. My eyes could not meet his.

~

"We're ready to interview now," asserted a male voice over the telephone. "Can you make your way to the station?"

"Why?" That was the last place I wanted to be.

"As his appropriate adult." His tone suggested I should be aware of this. "It's procedure."

"So Tom has *my reassuring presence*? I don't think so." No

way could I sit at his side after what he had done. They called the Youth Offending Team instead. It was hours before I heard anything else.

Eventually they telephoned me. "We're releasing him. Your neighbour didn't physically see him; she just believes she recognised his voice amongst the others. There's no evidence to actually place him at the crime scene."

"But there must be fingerprints..." I could hardly face my neighbour as it was. But if he was to get away with this...

"None."

"You're joking!" My voice rose up. "But he did it!"

"We know that. However, there's no proof to charge him. Only if he confesses."

"Right." I snatched my car keys from the table. "Keep him there. I'm on my way."

"Just do the right thing," I urged Tom in the sweltering interview room. The officers had left us alone. He looked dishevelled and unbelievably young. Being locked up for several hours had done him in.

"I want them to let me go Mum. This place is awful." His bottom lip wobbled. For a moment I thought he was going to cry.

"Why did you do it?"

"We didn't plan it." Regret seeped into his expression. "The door was open and we both kind of egged each other on."

"But you locked her in her room." I shuddered to imagine what must have been going through the poor girl's mind whilst this was going on.

"I'm not proud of myself you know." He stared down at his hands.

Tom was unaware that the police did not have adequate evidence to charge him. At his still young age, he would not have understood the technicalities anyway.

"If you're honest, you'll be in less trouble." I studied his face.

"But they'll lock me up."

"Not if you tell the truth." I rested my hand on his arm. "You'll be punished, yes, but they'll go easier on you if you own up."

"Then they'll let me go?" His eyes glimmered hopefully.

"Yes. I'll stay with you whilst they interview you."

The police got a taped confession for which they thanked me. He and his friend were charged and released on bail, with a curfew, to be in at home between seven at night and seven in the morning.

Some mums might have felt bad for 'shopping' their son, but there was no way I would have wanted him to get away with it; I was sure of what I had done. The looming punishment would act as a future warning. No sanction I ever meted out improved his behaviour. Maybe the courts would succeed where I couldn't?

THE THIRD ARREST

I CLOSED my eyes as Tom was marched from our house by the police two days later. "We're arresting you for criminal damage," the officer had said before handcuffing him.

There was no denying his actions that had been caught on CCTV. This time I agreed to act as his 'appropriate adult' at the station. I knew that I did not have a lot of choice!

They also asked him about a break-in that had happened near to us but didn't have enough evidence to charge him.

After the interview, I had to wait whilst the Crown Prosecution Service decided on what was to happen next.

I slumped onto the freezing metal seat that was screwed to the floor. Whilst observing my bleak surroundings, I avoided meeting anyone's eye. Thirty minutes were passed texting and Googling.

Just as I wished I had brought something to read, a voice made me jump.

"We need you to be present whilst we search him." The officer's head popped around the door in the waiting room.

"Search who? Tom?" I jumped up, my backside numb. "But haven't you already done that?"

"I'm afraid we need to *strip search* him this time?" Looking sheepish, he led me back to the custody area. "He's stowed smoking paraphernalia where the sun doesn't shine. We need to ensure he hasn't got anything else concealed in the same place."

For the first time, I saw the inside of a cell. I didn't know where to look as they did the necessary. Although I was supposed to be present, I did my best to stay outside the cell door.

"Are you queer or summat, you?" I cringed at Tom's words. He wasn't doing himself any favours.

"We'll give these to you for safekeeping," The officer showed me back to the waiting room, thrusting the lighter at me.

"Ugh! You must be joking!" I clasped my hands behind my back. "Throw them away!"

They decided to tie the criminal damage case in with the burglary, to be dealt with together at court. I would receive a call when I could return to collect him. It had been decided to keep him locked up a bit longer because of his attitude.

NOTICE TO QUIT

When I got home there was a letter waiting.

4th March 2008

Dear Tenant,

We refer to the incident perpetrated by your son on 2 March, which has been brought to our attention.

In the interests of all concerned, we would ask that you make suitable arrangements for your family to vacate the property at your earliest convenience.

We would ask that you contact this office to discuss a timescale in which this can take place.

Yours faithfully

Housing Officer

DUTY OF CARE

IT WAS ABOUT five hours later, nearly eleven in the evening, when I got the call from the police station.

"The CPS has allocated a court date," announced a male voice. "Tom will be on a seven o'clock curfew at your property until after then. You can come and collect him now."

"I'm not collecting him." After the letter I'd had, I didn't want to be anywhere near him. After the turbulent childhood I'd had, homelessness had always been my greatest fear. And now we were all facing it.

"You're his appropriate adult," his voice grew stern. "You *must* collect him."

"I don't want him here."

"Well, I'm not being funny, but we don't want him here either. He's taking up a cell."

"I'm going to lose my home because of him." Tears were dripping down my face. I tasted their salt as I spoke. "I've had enough."

"Look, love," his voice softened. "Is there anyone else who could pick him up?"

I shook my head, forgetting I was on the phone.

"What about his father?"

"He and his girlfriend have just had a baby. *He* won't come."

"Look love..."

"Stop calling me love!" I must have sounded unhinged.

"He's your son, your responsibility; you *have to* collect him."

"You might as well ring social services. I've had enough. I can't cope with him anymore." I shook as I spoke. Either with exhilaration at the thought of Tom not coming back. Or exhaustion. Or both.

"Are you saying you won't have him back?" "That's exactly what I'm saying." Suddenly, I felt empowered.

"You can't do that."

"Watch me."

"Well I've never come across anything like this. I'll have to speak to someone."

I really *did not* want him back. Weeping, I awaited the outcome of our conversation. Within ten minutes the phone sprang back into life. I ignored it. Then I ignored it again. All was calm for about twenty minutes.

They would have rung social services by now. A social worker would be on their way to pick him up; maybe they would put him in a care home, or perhaps with foster parents. Whichever, they would have their work cut out with him.

My thoughts were disturbed by a banging at the door before it opened. Tom stood in the doorway; a mix of defiance and tiredness.

"We made a call to social services." The police officer nudged Tom towards me. "We were told to return him here. *You* have a duty of care." He pointed at me. "If you try to pull that stunt again, we'll prosecute. Do you understand?"

I nodded dismally; my gaze fastened to the floor.

"Somebody from social services will be out to see you," he

continued, backing away. "But they won't be taking him into care. You can forget that." He seemed to laugh, or perhaps it was a sniff. "He's all yours."

Didn't I know it?

EXCLUSION 4

THE COURT DATE was a month away. In the meantime, he was excluded from school again; this time he had been *caught* stealing someone's phone.

"We're not sure if the girl's parents are going to involve the police," the school receptionist informed me in icy tones over the telephone. "Not now it's been found."

"Could you *ask* them to inform the police?" I leaned against a wall. "I want him punished – it might stop him." I was on my break from a university lecture. Several people peered towards me when they heard me say *police*. I know it was judgmental and you can never know what's really going on in someone's life but at times, I yearned to be able to swap places with some of the girls on my teacher training course. Their lives seemed simple and enjoyable - compared to mine.

"Right, I'll pass your wishes on." She paused. "I've also been asked to tell you about yesterday. Tom's head of year meant to call you but hasn't had chance."

"Yesterday?" I moved away from my 'audience.'

"Yes, someone deliberately set the fire alarms off. The

school had to be evacuated. During this time the deputy head had his phone stolen from the jacket he had left in his office."

"And Tom's taken that too? How can you know that?"

"Well that's it. We've no proof yet. Several people saw him loitering around the deputy's office and that's where the fire alarm originated from but -"

"I'll go through his bedroom before he comes back. But I have to say - I don't think he'd be daft enough to leave it anywhere where I'd find it."

The phone never surfaced.

Within days, we realised Martin's mobile from his expired contract had vanished from beneath our bed. We blamed each other for leaving the door unlocked; then confronted Tom.

"It wasn't me." His eyes met mine and held my gaze. "I'm not going to pinch from anyone anymore. Especially from you Mum. I'm going to sort myself out, I promise." His face looked so earnest I almost believed him.

"Do you know I've rigged a camera up in there." Martin's expression dared me not to give the game away. "We're going to pass it to the police."

"No! I can't be banged up again!"

"Well you should've thought about that." Martin edged closer to him. "What've you done with it?"

"I've sold it."

"To who?"

"To a shop."

"What shop?"

"I can't remember." His eyes stayed fixed on his feet.

"Well we'll see if you can remember when the police ask you."

"Fuck you, you cunt."

After Tom had stomped from the house, I plucked my phone from my bag. I knew if I postponed reporting him, I would talk myself out of it.

"I want to report a theft," I announced shakily.

As I gave the details, the operator seemed interested until it came about that the culprit was my fourteen-year-old son.

"Well it won't be put on as a priority," she said. "You'll get a visit within two to three days."

It was four days, and the 'mighty' CPS decided not to pursue my complaint, anyway.

Tom was on a roll of 'getting away' with things. Soon after, Martin took a phone call from an irate neighbour, also a mother of one of Tom's friends. She had disturbed Tom and another lad breaking into her house.

Having been told by his friend that they were away, Tom had taken the 'opportunity' but had been misinformed of their return date.

They had scarpered as though their lives depended on it when they were caught in the garden. The woman said that she couldn't be bothered with the hassle of involving the police; however, she wanted *us* to deal with him, and to make sure he stayed away from *her* son in future.

I confiscated his computer, knowing it would punish him. It was the only thing that seemed to occupy his time whilst he was at home. It had the desired effect.

SOCIAL SERVICES

I WAS TAKEN ABACK by the arrival of not one, but *three* social workers at our house. Perhaps this quantity of them was indicative of imminent support.

"We've received the referral from Tom's stepmum," announced the youngest looking of the three. And when I say young, I mean young. They perched on the sofa, in a line. "I gather you're concerned about him being *vulnerable* when he's out."

"Things have moved on since then," I informed her, balancing on the edge of an armchair. "He's now in trouble with the police."

"Yes, we've been made aware of that." Her voice was bird-like and she looked as though she's spent at least an hour putting her make up on. "It sounds as though he's putting you through it." The other two laughed. I glared at them.

"I've been to hell and back with him actually." Unsure who I should be addressing, my gaze flickered between them. "And I'm on my way back there again." They could no doubt detect the hostility in my voice, so I consciously tried to load a bit of friendliness into it. "I need some help."

"We've got his history on file," one of them said. "And we've contacted school. I'm unsure as to what help *we* could offer though." Typical. *What you mean is you can't be bothered!*

"Anything! I can't cope with him. He's bullying me *and* my younger son. I admit I've no control over him. Surely this is where social services can step in?" My voice was cracking as I spoke.

"Only with children at risk, *not* children with behaviour problems." The other social worker, glanced at her colleagues, perhaps for approval.

"But he *is* at risk. He's putting *himself* at risk. He's fourteen years old and he's using cannabis for God's sake. And not long ago, he did not even come home for three days." My arms were flailing about with my words, as if they could add support to my plight. "I never know where he is!"

"Have you ever been offered a parenting course?" *Bravo! The magical parenting course. The answer to all my problems.*

I laughed. "I'd try anything if I thought it'd help. It's not me with the problem though."

"Could you give me a moment to speak with my colleagues please?"

Evidently, I was expected to leave the room. The uselessness of it all made me want to scream.

I strained to decipher the low hum of conversation for several minutes. Feeling utterly deflated, I accepted they weren't going to help us. *A bloody parenting course!* Then one of their heads popped around the door.

"You can come back in now." She was all lipstick and perfume.

"Oh thanks." *Whose house was it?*

"We're going to give you a number." Reclining between her colleagues, she rummaged in her bag. I noticed it was Radley. If I had a Radley bag, I thought to myself, Tom would pinch it.

"You can ring anytime you need to." It was a parenting

helpline number. "There'll always be someone there to listen whatever time of day it is."

"And that's it?" In disbelief, I stared at her.

"The help line's staffed by trained volunteers."

"I don't need that kind of help! I need a break from him."

"Look, we'll have a think, back at the office as to whether there is anything further, we can offer you." As if they were tuned into one another, they all rose simultaneously. "We'll be back in touch after we've spoken with our supervisor."

Useless!
Useless!
Useless!

THE FIRST COURT APPEARANCE

I PERSUADED Tom to wear trousers for court.

"It'll show respect," I assured him, ignoring his arguments against wearing a 'gay' pair of trousers.

Outside court, I noticed he was the only boy in trousers and 'proper' shoes. The other boys all looked older. It seemed surreal that Tom was now one of them. It was as though there was a dress code imposed: trainers, baggy tracksuit bottoms and hooded tops.

Disgrace shone from me whilst forced to stand beside Tom, in front of three magistrates and give my name. His crimes of burglary, false imprisonment and criminal damage were to be dealt with together.

When we were eventually dismissed, he punched the air as we got back out into the corridor. His '*punishment*' was reparation - a weekly appointment with the Youth Offending Team.

I, on the other hand, was ordered to compensate our

neighbour with £600. The criminal damage cost me £430. I was also 'awarded' court costs.

For the first time, I regretted my role in persuading him to own up. It was *me* being punished. I had envisaged him receiving a stern amount of community service and some sort of victim awareness intervention.

Before we could leave court, we had to meet with a court liaison officer from the Youth Offending Team. The side room we were shown into contained a poisonous looking, middle-aged woman. Her hair was lacquered to perfection and she had red lipstick all over her teeth. Had the circumstances been different, I would have alerted her to this make-up malfunction. After all, that's what women do for each other. Usually.

"Take a seat," she said.

I dropped into the seat at her command. Cameras were in every corner of the room, yet people had still dared draw graffiti or carve their names into the table.

"So, let's have a look at you then." She peered at Tom as though he were an insect. "Think you're a big man, do you? Burglary, criminal damage, truancy making your poor mother's life HELL!" I jumped as she emphasised her last word.

Tom, for once, remained silent. "Do you know where you're going to end up?"

Recoiling, I observed congealed spit escaping from the corner of her mouth.

"I'll tell you, shall I? A young offenders' institution. Where all no-hopers like you finish up."

"I'm not a no-hoper." Glowering, Tom avoided her gaze.

Go on, lose your temper. She'll make mincemeat of you!

"Oh yes you are." She prodded at the table with a manicured fingernail. "I can see it in your eyes. You're like all the others. Thinking you can do what the hell you want. Well I've got news for you. You can't."

"I know I can't." Slouching back in his chair, Tom folded his arms. *Yeah, course you do!*

"Sit up straight when I'm talking to you!" She sucked up the drool. "Do you know how fortunate you are to be sat in front of me?"

Tom shook his head.

"Very fortunate." She slapped her palm against the table, causing him to jump. "You should've left that courtroom by the other door and now be locked in a prison van. Next time, you will be." She gave him a knowing look.

"There won't be a next time." Tom's voice was softer than I'd ever heard. He sat bolt upright, seemingly not daring to move a muscle.

"There will be if you miss one of these appointments." She thrust two cards at him, which he started to pass to me. "No, they're *your* cards. *Your* appointments." She poked an angry finger towards him. "Your responsibility. That one's a weekly appointment with your youth offending worker; the other is for your reparation."

"What's that?"

"You'll be doing unpaid work to show how sorry you are. Twenty hours." *Whoopee,* I thought, *is that it?*

He dropped the cards into his pocket.

"Bye love," he muttered as we left. I cringed. She would not be happy with that.

"Don't *ever* call me love! Do you hear me?"

"Stupid bloody cow!" We closed the door behind us.

"Always the big man, aren't you Tom?" I half hoped she had heard him. "You wouldn't dare call her that to her face."

THE ANTI-SOCIAL BEHAVIOUR CONTRACT

We had been summoned to the police station, where I had to once again, act in an 'appropriate adult' capacity for the implementation of his anti-social behaviour contract. The officer had a sheet of paper in front of him, which I tried to read, upside-down.

"This is the first step towards you receiving an anti-social behaviour order," stated the police officer.

"You mean an *ASBO*?" Tom sounded almost happy at the prospect.

"You're incredibly young to have two convictions!" he remarked. "And, if you breach the terms of this order, you're risking your parent's tenancy and increasing the likelihood of fines they'll be responsible for."

"When does *Tom* get punished?"

"We expect *you* to take care of that." His glare was piercing, leaving me in no doubt as to his view of me as a mother.

"I've tried everything." I didn't want the police officer having this opinion. I was fed up with being blamed. "If I ground him, he climbs out of windows. If I stop his money, he steals. If I try to stop him from doing something, he does it anyway."

"Not our problem." Leaning back, he clasped his hands behind his balding head, revealing two stale sweat patches under his arms.

"It's not as if I'm a parent who doesn't 'give a monkeys.' I'm here aren't I? I want to sort him out. But I can't." But my words were falling on deaf ears. It was pointless trying to convince this man. "I've tried asking for help. No one is interested."

"Shut the fuck up Mum!" Tom slammed his elbows onto the table.

"You can hear how he talks to me. What am I supposed to do?"

"We're going around in circles here, love." The policeman looked at his watch. "Let's concentrate on the contract. I'll read it out."

ACCEPTABLE BEHAVIOUR CONTRACT

THIS CONTRACT is made on the 9th April 2008

BETWEEN YORKSHIRE POLICE AND THOMAS CLIFFORD

THOMAS AGREES the following in respect of future conduct

1. I will not graffiti or damage property in the Kirkwood area.
2. I will not take any property that does not belong to me.
3. I will not climb on rooftops, lift shafts or other prohibited areas.
4. I will not abuse residents or passers-by. This includes swearing.
5. I will attend school.

FURTHER, THOMAS enters into a commitment with WEST YORKSHIRE POLICE not to act in a manner that causes or is likely to cause harassment, alarm or distress to one or more persons not in the same household.

BREACH

If THOMAS does anything which he has agreed not to do under this contract which WEST YORKSHIRE POLICE considers to amount to anti-social behaviour, an application may be made to the magistrates' court for an ANTI-SOCIAL BEHAVIOUR ORDER to prohibit THOMAS from acting in a manner likely to cause harassment, alarm or distress to one or more persons not of the same household.

DECLARATION

I confirm that I understand the meaning of this contract and that the consequences of breach of the contract have been explained to me.

SIGNED Tom Clifford (Individual)
[Signature of individual]
DATE 9th April 2008

SIGNED Sarah Pearson (Parent)
[Signature of parent or guardian]
DATE 9th April 2008

SIGNED PC 4112 McIntyre (Police Officer) WITNESS
[Signature of police officer]
DATE 9th April 2008

THE ENEMY WITHIN

Cannabis usage was evidently driving Tom. He funded it by stealing. We could no longer keep money boxes or change jars; he had emptied them all. Every day, he hunted around the house for more. His lack of success provoked frustration and anger. We learned to stop leaving anything valuable about.

I became surgically attached to my handbag as Tom would be straight in for my purse if I left it anywhere. Once I fell asleep on the sofa and woke to find £12 and my phone missing.

"You should report it the police," Martin said. "I can't believe we have to live like this. You know most stepdads would be long gone. They wouldn't stand for it."

"I'm not reporting it. It's a waste of time."

"And you wonder why I don't come home in the evening." He didn't look at me as he walked to the fridge. "I only stay because of Alex."

"Don't bother," I replied. Martin and I mainly co-existed and I knew our days were numbered. But I worried that Tom would be able to physically overpower me without the threat of Martin - his presence was a bit of a deterrent for Tom; However, I knew, deep down, that things might be better if he left.

"Well next time he robs off me, I'll be dealing with it myself," he opened his bottle of beer, throwing the lid onto the work surface. "I'll chop his fucking hands off."

"I'll deal with him," I replied. "I'm going to stop his money for a while."

His pocket money never lasted long anyway and he was awful when it ran out.

One morning, Martin realised he had left his wallet in his coat pocket.

"Sarah, get my wallet, will you," he hissed from the bath as I helped Alex brush his teeth. "I've heard Tom get up. If he pinches it, that's all I've got."

I discovered Tom had beaten me to it.

"Give it here." I held out my hand as I spoke in a hushed tone. "Give it to me and we'll say no more about it." My heart was hammering in my chest. I couldn't let Martin know what was going on.

"No." He fastened his fingers around it. "Fuck off!"

Flying at him, I tried to prise the wallet from his grasp. *God, he was getting strong.*

"Get off, you piece of shit!" Then his voice hardened. "Do you want a fucking slap?" His words stung me far more than a slap ever could.

Recoiling, shock washed over me as I saw the hate in his face. Martin's angry footsteps bounded down the stairs. He grabbed Tom by the scruff.

"You ever try to pinch off me again and you will regret it." Steam curled from his shoulders. "I'm already thinking that you should be living with your dad."

Tom smirked, his upright middle finger conveying his thoughts. Martin flew back upstairs, slamming around as he dressed. Minutes later, he stormed from the house with a door slam better than Tom's.

"Where's he gone – I wanted a cig." Tom's face twisted with rage.

"Just get a move on Tom." Snatching my keys, I dropped Alex's coat into his lap. "I'll drop you off at the bus stop." The day had barely begun, and I felt as though I'd done a day's work.

"Oh yeah - how am I supposed to have a smoke." He barged from the room.

"Hurry up Tom, we've got to go." I called up the stairs a few minutes later, trying to quell the stress in my voice.

"Shut up, div."

I blinked back tears that were needling at my eyes. Once I'd dropped Alex off, I let them go.

"I can't take it anymore!" Howling in the silence of the car, I punched the steering wheel. "I've had enough!"

BROUGHT HOME BY THE POLICE 1

MAY 2008 (14 YEARS, 5 MONTHS)

"Is this your son?" The policeman relaxed his grip from Tom as I opened the door.

"You should be at school! Oh my God!" Tom collapsed through the doorway. "Look at the state of you!"

"We found him vomiting in the street. He's clearly under the influence of something but won't say what. "Rubbing his hands as though he'd let go of a decaying bird, he stepped back. "In view of his age, we had a duty to pick him up."

"Thanks," Tom began an attempt to ascend the stairs. I knew exactly what the 'substance' was and suspected the policeman did too. He stunk of it.

"Get yourself to bed Tom," he called after him. "Good luck," he nodded at me. "I trust you'll speak to him about this."

"Of course."

ANOTHER BULLYING INCIDENT, SCHOOL EXCLUSION 5

JUNE 2008 (14 YEARS, 6 MONTHS)

"SARAH, IT'S MISS HUSSAIN," announced the voice." You need to collect Tom right away. We're going to have to say he can't return till after half term."

"But that's nearly three weeks away." I quickly processed the implications of this exclusion in my mind. "What on earth's he done now?" I moved away from the friends I was having lunch with in the university canteen, not knowing them well enough to allow my son's behaviour to be laid bare.

"He, along with his *girlfriend**, attacked another pupil."

"I didn't know he had a girlfriend." Shuffling over to the window, I observed a huddle of students as they sat about in the sunshine.

"I shouldn't say this, but between you and me, she's not the nicest character, foul-mouthed, often in trouble."

"No wonder he's hooked up with her then."

"I've been a teacher for nearly fifteen years. Never have I witnessed such a nasty assault on a fellow pupil. The two of them were booting her in the head. She was in agony. It took several members of staff to get them off her."

"She?" I forgot where I was. Glancing around, I lowered my voice. "He's hurt a *girl*?"

"I'm afraid so. Her parents are in with the head right now. I'm not sure what their course of action will be."

"Can you give them a message?"

"I'm not sure that's the best-"

"Just tell them how sorry I am." I slumped onto a chair. "Not just sorry. Gutted. Ashamed." *The poor girl!* "Tell them to report him and his *girlfriend* to the police." Several of my friends were peering across at me, no doubt wondering what my conversation was about. "He should be punished properly for this."

"I'll tell them."

"I just want what's right." I rested my head onto my hand. "I can't believe it to be honest! How's the girl?"

"I'm not sure. She was hysterical and in a lot of pain. We're all in shock." Mrs Hussain sounded more subdued than usual. "Like I say, I've never witnessed such an awful incident within school. We've no idea what provoked it."

After our conversation had ended, I rang Peter. "If I set eyes on him, I won't be responsible for my actions." I noticed my friends were moving, ahead of our next lecture. "Please will you collect him? I can't take anymore!"

"OK," he agreed flatly. "Though I don't know what you expect *me* to do with him. I'm only going to put him in his room and ignore him."

"Just make sure you remove his TV and games console first." I returned to the table and gulped a final swig of my now-cold tea.

"Too right."

. . .

The girl's parents were satisfied with his exclusion and decided not to prosecute. I went to collect him from his dad's, not wanting to, but obviously having to.

"He's gone. Peter didn't take his gaze from the TV.

"What do you mean, gone?" I swung Tom's door open and saw his curtains ballooning through the open window.

"Great, he's escaped. Now what do we do?"

"Not a lot we can do." Peter's face sagged with anger. "Just wait for him to come back, I suppose."

~

*I never got to meet the 'girlfriend,' however in the two weeks she and him were in touch, he stole my perfume, a gift from my sister, to give to her.

ALL THE PROFESSIONALS

THE COMMON ASSESSMENT FRAMEWORK APPROACH (CAF)

List Of Agencies Currently Involved With Young Person

1. Youth Offending Team
2. Social Services
3. Positive Activities for Young People
4. Kirkwood Medical Centre
5. Child and Adolescent Mental Health Service
6. Fielding Park High School
7. Education Welfare

General Health

Tom is physically fit. He smokes cigarettes and cannabis. Mum has concerns about this drug use and the impact this could be having on his mental health. She says he suffered from ADHD when he was younger and still exhibits symptoms, i.e. lack of concentration, difficulty sleeping and destructive behaviour. Tom has admitted he does smoke cannabis a few times a week (mainly at weekends) however he feels that he does not need help. He has had two sessions with 'Base 10 Drugs Information Service,' but then decided to withdraw from these sessions.

Personal Development

Mum says Tom responds better to male adults and demonstrates a lack of respect towards females. He has friends (usually older than himself, aged 16/17) and hangs around the streets with them. Mum suspects these friends also smoke cannabis. She knows that she appears to be *'always getting on at him'* which must have a negative impact on his confidence at times. Dad and step-mum, Elizabeth have recently had a baby and have restricted contact and visits due to his offending behaviour. Mum says that Tom has a real lack of self-control. He has been excluded on several occasions from school. His drug taking has led to offending behaviour and he is on a twelve-month referral order with the Youth Offending Team.

Enjoying and Achieving

Tom continues to truant and is receiving one-to-one support from the parental support officer and head of year. He will go off site and not return from lunch. He is brought into school each morning by Mum. He is on a 'behaviour contract' at school; however, he continues to display challenging behaviour. Mum states this behaviour can be physical at home and he will 'smash things up' and 'punch the doors and walls.' Whilst he will apologise for this, Mum says there is no emotion behind the apology. She is concerned he does not show remorse for his actions, e.g. towards the victim after the recent break in of their next-door neighbour. Tom disagreed with this. He said he does feel guilty about their impending eviction.

Parenting Examples

Mum is caring and consistent, however she feels 'out of her depth.' She sets boundaries and gives encouragement to Tom but feels powerless to make a difference. Tom has been known to run out of the house and has gone missing on occasions. Mum says she has provided a stable home life for him; however, his recent offending is resulting in the family being evicted from their current home. Mum says that Tom takes more notice of his stepdad Martin, than her, though he does not get on with him.

Family and Environment

Tom no longer stays overnight with Dad and Elizabeth. Efforts on their part to maintain contact with him through meeting him in town have been rejected. Mum must lock everything away in the house otherwise Tom will take it. She says he sells these items to fund his drug addiction. He also sells his clothes and his brother's PlayStation games. Mum senses the cannabis is a 'daily addiction.' She says he has no desire to stop these drugs and feels that this is linked to his criminal behaviour. Tom has recently only narrowly missed out on a custodial sentence.

. . .

Working Together To Name WHAT Changes People Want To See

- Increased attendance at school
- Stop criminal/antisocial behaviour
- Face up to drug use/problem
- To see a positive change in Tom's mood
- Tom to follow rules at home and come in at night

Tom's comments when consulted were 'He would like a motorbike.'

Record Ideas On HOW To Make This Happen

- YOTS – work to be undertaken on drugs, anger management, victim awareness, community service
- PAYP – to invite Tom to positive activities
- CAMHS – Mum awaiting first appointment
- Social Services – feel there is no role for them currently
- School – invite Tom, Mum & stepdad to family fun day
- Dad to be invited to attend next meeting. (this meeting to be arranged asap)
- 1 to 1 mentoring support
- GP to be invited to next meeting

Views

- Tom is OK with the Common Assessment Framework Approach but may not engage with professionals

- Mum is relieved she will receive additional support
- Tom is a young man with many problems and multi-agency input is the way forward.

THE GP (AGAIN)

She probably already knew but, "It's about Tom." I said. As I wearily sat in front of her yet again.

She smiled. "No improvement, I take it?" She had never judged me and had always empathised. But short of referring us on, I knew there was little she could do.

Shaking my head, I sighed. "He's moving onto bigger things now. You know, stealing, truanting, criminal damage, cannabis, alcohol, that sort of thing."

Her expression drooped. "I hoped he'd grow out of it all."

"No chance." I clasped my hands together in my lap. "I'm not convinced about this Conduct Disorder thing, you know. I think it's something else. If we could get a diagnosis, then maybe he could get treatment and maybe-"

"It's not as simple as that, Sarah," she rested her hand on my arm. "It never has been."

"I know, but I can't give up on him. I've got to keep trying."

"I think you've done an amazing job coping and dealing with it, all these years."

"Thanks." It meant a lot, being acknowledged by her, like that.

"The 0-19 Team might be able to reassess him?" She took a pen from her desk.

I groaned. "Isn't there anywhere else?"

"With these sorts of problems, they always have to be the first port of call. Hopefully, they'll be able to refer you on though."

"Here we go again."

This time the 'assessment' was to occur over three sessions, due to his now advanced age.

I, with Elizabeth's backing, placed every problem we were experiencing at the man's, polished feet. By now, going over and over the same information was tedious.

"I want a diagnosis and medication for him," I informed him, scanning his face for a flicker of sympathy. "There *is* something wrong with him. There always has been."

"We'll have to get him reassessed by a child psychiatrist," stated the man, suddenly seeming to jerk into life. "I gather he's seen one before."

I sat up straight. It *had* helped last time. He must have noticed my downtrodden body language give way to a sudden optimism.

"I'm not promising they'll find anything." He wagged a finger in the air. "Mental health problems in adolescents are difficult to establish."

"I know. But I want them to try."

"He'd also have to be willing to co-operate." His pen hovered over the form he was hopefully, intending to complete.

"That could be a problem," Elizabeth looked at me. The words *Tom* and *co-operate* would not usually find themselves side-by-side in a sentence.

"We can try though, can't we?" My gaze swung from one of them to the other and back again. "We've got to get him sorted."

HOW DID TOM REACT WHEN REFUSED MONEY?

JULY 2008 (14 YEARS, 7 MONTHS)

DID HE?

1. Accept this decision without question?
2. Threaten to smash up the house?
3. Steal some?
4. Threaten to wreck my car?
5. Think about getting a weekend job?
6. Inform me he is not going to school until he receives some?
7. Try to break into someone's house?
8. Steal something that he could sell?
9. Tell me that he will be beaten up unless he repays a debt?
10. Lose his coat?
11. Threaten to 'stove' my face in?
12. Lose one shoe?
13. Call me every derogatory name in his repertoire?

Over the course of July, all outcomes apart from 1 and 5 occurred.

E-MAIL TO HIS DAD

Dear Peter and Elizabeth,

Sorry for doing this by email but the following needs to be said. I have done everything in my power for Tom and I think it is your turn. I freely admit I have failed - maybe you can do a better job.

I can no longer cope with him and have got Alex's wellbeing to consider. The situation is making me poorly and for these reasons, I would like us to swap roles: for him to live with you during the week and I will have him at weekends. I have no qualms about changing his school as I think, given his reputation where he is, it would be a positive move.

If you agree to my suggestion, I will also transfer all the child benefits over to you and pay some maintenance.

I am sorry to land this on you, but this might be Tom's only hope of not ending up in care or a young offenders unit. Can you discuss and let me know your decision?

. . .

Sarah

PS If you don't take him then I really am putting him into care. I have had enough.

Days passed ... no reply.

THE CHILD AND ADOLESCENT MENTAL HEALTH TEAM

ONE OF THE two women sat in front of us, beaming, announced. "There are people behind the screen, Tom."

From the letter they had sent, I knew that one of the two was a child psychologist and the other, a child psychiatrist. The smiling one looked fresh out of university; her colleague was probably in her forties. "They're listening to our conversation."

"Why would they want to do that?" Tom yawned from his chair.

"I know it must seem a bit strange," chuckled the other woman. "But it's so they can help us decide how to support your mum with things."

The 'screen' consisted of a window with a blind behind it. I wondered how many people it concealed and became defensive at the prospect of being 'judged' by unseen eyes.

The room we were in was less 'clinical' than on our previous visits, five years earlier. It had been carpeted and 'arty' pictures had been hung. Comfy chairs had replaced stiff plastic ones, though the 'medical' smell lingered. A tissue box on the low table divided us all. It would be likely only me that would have a use for tissues, once we got going!

Tom remained slumped, repeatedly sketching a cartoon of SpongeBob SquarePants. "I'm not saying owt if a load of weirdo's are listening."

"They're not weirdo's, honestly." One of the women rose and offered her arm to him. "Come on, I'll take you to meet them." As she led him behind the screen, I listened as several introductions were made. They returned moments later; all smiles.

Nervously, I waited for the women to proceed.

"Right," began the older one. "Firstly, might I say how nice it is to meet you Tom, and mum." She nodded towards me. "We've been doing a little reading from a few years ago when you worked with Victoria Harris." Pausing, she smiled as she peered towards Tom. "Do you remember her Tom?"

He shook his head.

"He can barely remember what he ate for breakfast," I teased him. "Let alone someone he met five years ago!"

"I gather things have moved on a bit since then," she went on. "According to your GP and Tom's school, you've been having a few more problems."

My mouth opened in readiness to reply but the younger woman got there first.

"We want *you* to be part of this discussion Tom." She spoke as though she was trying to load sincerity into her voice. "No meetings are going to happen without *you* being here. You're a big lad now and it's only fair you hear what's being talked about and let us know what's going on for you."

"Not a right lot." He scowled.

Smiling again at him, she continued. "We're going to be looking carefully at your relationship with your mum and seeing what improvements might be made." She turned to me. "Sarah, I gather from the file that you had problems *yourself* as a child; particularly issues with your *own* mother. I think it's important that we begin by looking at that."

"I don't see how it's relevant." I was irritated they deemed my own background as the starting point.

"I'm not saying it is." Her face oozed insincere sympathy. "Sometimes, though, it's inevitable that patterns from childhood are repeated. We need to explore that." Her gaze flicked from me to Tom and back again. "Perhaps we could arrange that discussion without Tom being present if that makes it easier to talk about such personal matters."

"I thought I was invited to *all* these meetings." Tom said.

"Well, maybe not the ones where we're talking to your mum about *her* stuff."

"It's all a waste of time anyway." Yawning, Tom stretched his arms and legs. "There's nowt wrong with me."

"Really?" I wanted the focus to be shifted away from me. "So why do you carry on like you do?"

"Shut up Mum. You don't know what you're on about. As usual."

The two women watched us; something about the way they looked at us and then at each other made me uneasy.

"We're going to be focusing on the interaction between the two of you." The older woman said. "It will give us a lot to go on at this stage."

"And what about the rest of the family? His dad? Stepdad? Stepmum? Brother? Surely their input is important?"

"To start with we'll stick with the relationship between the two of you. In these situations, it can provide the crux of the problem, and the starting point for putting it right."

So that was it. The initial assessment. They were looking within *me* for answers to Tom's problems. Blaming me. Already, I was disillusioned. They didn't have a clue.

ANOTHER ATTEMPT AT A HOLIDAY

THE LEAST I could do was send a postcard of gratitude.

Dear Elizabeth and Peter,

Firstly, thanks for agreeing to take Tom at such short notice. It would have been awful to have to return home only three days into the holiday. Alex would have been heartbroken. The park manager has said Tom is barred so we won't be coming back here in a hurry. Breaking into fruit machines. It's not as though he didn't have any money to spend. Having said that, I can never give him enough.

We're all a lot more relaxed now; it's amazing how the atmosphere improves when he's not around. The names he called me over the first couple of days here were disgusting. Alex, especially, is relieved at a reprieve from being bullied. He had a terrible scare when Tom held his head underwater at Waterworld. Lovely way to treat your little brother! Anyway, I hope he's behaving for you; we'll collect him from you on our way home.

Thanks again. Sarah x

THE YOUTH WORKER (PAYP – POSITIVE ACTIVITIES FOR YOUNG PEOPLE)

What We Do

PAYP AIMS to prevent crime and reduce anti-social behaviour. PAYP staff have experience of working with individual children and young people aged 11—19 and their families. PAYP works in partnership with other professionals to access the needs of individual children and young people and develop individually tailored support packages aimed at preventing offending behaviour, supporting the transition from primary to secondary school, supporting children, young people and their families to build relationships and providing access to high quality opportunities for positive activities.

Who We Work with

Vulnerable children and young people aged 11—19 who are at risk of becoming engaged in crime and anti-social behaviour. Schools, Social Services, YOT, Education Services, Police and other staff can refer individual children and young people to the PAYP Project.

Tom's delinquent behaviour was rewarded with the following opportunities:

- Days out at theme parks
- Football tickets
- Go-carting
- Cinema trips
- 10-pin bowling
- Quad biking
- Activity days
- Museum visits

Quote from Alex

"How come Tom is naughty but gets to do nice things?"

Answers on a postcard, please.

PLAYING WITH FIRE 4 – EXCLUSION 6

SEPTEMBER 2008 (14 YEARS, 9 MONTHS)

"Is that Sarah?" It was Tom's head of year. Again. I recognised the voice and shuffled away from the eavesdropping ears of other parents at Alex's sports day.

"It is."

"Do you want the good or the bad news?"

"I think I'll go for the good. There's not too much of that where Tom's concerned!"

"Well, he's eventually arrived at school. He got here at 10:25; but isn't in uniform and appears to be under the influence of something. But he's actually *here*!"

I leaned against a wall. "That's the *good* news? I dread to think what the bad news is!"

"I'm afraid we've had to evacuate the entire school yet again. He set off the fire alarms."

"Oh for God's sake! How?" I had raised my voice without realising. Several people in my vicinity glanced over.

"By holding a lighter against the camera in the boy's cloakroom. The front of it melted, causing it to smoke and-"

"Oh no! I'm so sorry." I moved further away from the mothers who were watching me and tried to lower my voice.

"Don't *you* be sorry. It's Tom who should be sorry. I'm aware that he'll be delighted to be excluded. But there's nothing else we can do."

"How long?"

"Until the end of next week." The apology was evident in his voice. "The head's insisted."

"And the cost of the damage?"

"I'll have to let you know."

THE ELECTRONIC TAGGING DEVICE

After the burglary and criminal damage incident, he was in no fresh bother with the police that year. But we were still in and out of court for breach of orders.

As he was proving unable to comply with his reparation order; the courts kept adding further hours of unpaid work onto it. He was not attending his appointments with the Youth Offending Team. After four 'breaches,' the court decided to impose a forced home curfew.

Initially, I was relieved that I would know his whereabouts between 7 pm and 7 am for three months. This quickly turned to despair! We were all pushed to breaking point for the duration, forced to be constantly in his company and at the mercy of his foul moods!

The security team came to install the tag around his ankle and equip our home to monitor his comings and goings. A sense of hopelessness enveloped me. *Was this what it had come to?*

. . .

Tom, of course, tried every ploy he could conjure up to outsmart the tag:

1. Unplug unit from power source and blame me.
2. Snip it off ankle and pretend it snapped as result of a trip on staircase.
3. Use butter to slide it off foot.
4. Stretch it over foot.

The security firm became regular visitors, not caring what hour of the night it was. His repeated breaches meant more court appearances. Swiftly, I learnt to take plenty of reading matter to wile away the endless hours in the public waiting area, surrounded by foul-mouthed, unrepentant adolescents. It was torture otherwise.

GOOD NEWS!

A NEW HOUSE!

A new area!
A fresh start!
We are all praying that Tom does not spoil it!

BROUGHT HOME BY THE POLICE 2

OCTOBER 2008 (14 YEARS, 10 MONTHS)

FATIGUE WAS OVERTAKING the battle with worry. I had stared so long into the darkness that my eyes were stinging. There was no sign of him, and it was nearly 2 am. He had started to catch the bus back to our former neighbourhood as he was struggling to acclimatise to where we had moved to.

By now, we were on first name terms with most of the security team as he repeatedly breached his curfew. The doorbell and what sounded like a police radio jostled me into complete consciousness. I shot out of bed and down towards the front door. My initial panic at seeing a police hat through the window of the door was quelled by a familiar blond head beside it. I flung the door open.

"Where've you been?" I raked my hand through my hair. "I've been worried sick about you!"

"A bit of communication between you both might not go amiss in future," said the stony-faced policeman as he nudged Tom towards me. "We're not a taxi service, neither are we responsible for getting your son home safely. You are." His finger wagged in my direction.

"We've only just moved here." I was aware of how feeble my

argument must have sounded. "My son not coming home is not out of character. I can't get hold of him either. He's sold his phone."

"Do you realise he rang 999 to get a lift? Obviously, he's fourteen and vulnerable, which is why we've brought him back on this occasion." He backed away from me, then added, "if it happens again, he'll be done for wasting police time. And invoiced for the expense involved in taking advantage of police resources. Do you understand?"

"There won't be a next time," I stammered. "I'm sorry."

Sorry had to be the most-used word in my vocabulary. I was sick of saying it!

REASONS HE CAN NO LONGER GO TO HIS DAD'S HOUSE

1. Constant stealing of other people's belongings.
2. Helping himself to money out of money boxes and birthday cards.
3. Smoking cannabis in same bedroom as sleeping baby brother.
4. They don't want him there. (Wish I could use that one.)
5. He can't be bothered going anyway.

EXCLUSION NUMBER 7

(Another letter to add to my collection)

Dear Mrs Pearson,

I am writing to inform you of my decision to exclude your son for a fixed period of four days. The exclusion begins on Friday 4th October and ends on Wednesday 9th October. This means that he will not be allowed in school for this period.

I realise that this exclusion may be upsetting but the decision has not been taken lightly. Thomas was removed from class this morning for displaying defiance and causing disruption. The supply teacher* who was taking his class was distressed after the incident. Furthermore, when he was sent to the isolation unit, he continued to ignore instructions. This amounts to a breakdown of discipline and will not be tolerated.

. . .

You have the right to make representations to the school governing body. If you wish to do this, please contact Mrs G Lynch at the school office. You also have the right to see Thomas's school record. Should you wish to do so, please notify me in writing. There may be a charge for photocopying.

The school has set work for Thomas during the period of his exclusion. Please ensure that this is completed and returned to us promptly for marking. We expect him to be back in school on Thursday 10th October at 08:50 am, where he will report to reception before completing one day in the Isolation Unit.

Yours sincerely

Mr W T Wharton

Head of Year

*I discovered that the supply teacher originated from Poland and had been upset by Tom drawing a swastika on the classroom floor and doing a 'Hitler style' salute whenever she tried to reprimand him.

ANOTHER YEAR; ANOTHER LIST OF:

Tom's thefts

- 2 bikes
- 2 PlayStation games and DVDs belonging to Alex
- Alex's binoculars
- Money (from wallets, purses, money boxes)
- Elizabeth's ring, left to her in her aunt's will
- Numerous mobile phones
- Xbox games belonging to his dad
- Beer and wine from fridge

Tom's breakages

- Remote control
- Microwave

- His computer monitor, mouse, keyboard then hard drive
- His trainers, so he could get new ones
- Crockery and glasses
- His bike, trashed in temper because it had a puncture
- Security camera and laptop at school
- Criminal damage to lift and communal area in block of flats
- His portable DVD player

ONE FOOT IN THE DOOR

DECEMBER 2008 (14 YEARS 11 MONTHS)

AFTER A MEETING, the local Grammar School had decided that to accept him, with his *colourful* history, was setting Tom up for more failure. So Tom had started at a pupil referral unit, which was a bus ride away.

Although still 'tagged,' he had also managed to acquaint himself with the 'undesirables' in our new neighbourhood. The moment his curfew began at seven each evening, he would hang out of his bedroom window, laughing with them as they loitered on our driveway. The jerking of neighbouring curtains worried me, and I begged him not to have them all hanging around.

One evening, as we watched TV, a herby waft drifted into the house. I went to investigate this all-too-familiar smell. Tom's tagged foot held the front door ajar whilst the remainder of him smoked a joint on the other side. Wrenching the door open, I was horrified to see around twelve shadowy youths, all in my drive, passing joints between themselves.

"Get away from my house! Now! The lot of you!"

Several of them sniggered. Hairs of rage prickled at the back of my neck.

"Fuck off silly cow!"

"I'll call the police!"

"You're making a show of yourself Mum," Tom hissed. "Sort yourself out!"

At that, I shoved him from the doorstep.

"You stupid fucking cow!" He turned and squared up to me. "The tagging people will be round now."

"Get lost, all of you!" I stood in my doorway, hands on hips. "That includes you." I gestured towards Tom.

Martin was now behind me. He pushed beyond me, towards Tom. "Get this sorted now, you little shit!" He grabbed him by the scruff. "We're not having this on our doorstep!"

I threw Tom's coat and shoes after him before closing the door.

"You'd better watch your cars." and "We'll be putting your fucking windows through." Echoed through the door as Martin and I stared at each other. I waited for his onslaught.

ARREST NUMBER 4, ANOTHER COURT APPEARANCE

MARCH 2009 (15 YEARS, 3 MONTHS)

"WELL THAT'S MY EVENING RUINED." I let out a long sigh. "I've got to be the appropriate adult. He's been arrested again!" An eternal night at the police station loomed.

"What's he done now?" Martin did not raise his eyes from the newspaper.

"The idiot has drawn graffiti on a bus." Marching into the kitchen, I slammed pots into the dishwasher. "They've got him on CCTV. So he'll definitely be done for it."

"You mean *you* will," Martin said. His smug attitude and lack of support made me want to scream. I knew that as soon as I was less vulnerable with Tom, Martin would be history.

As soon as I arrived at the station, I knew I would be in for a wait. The reception area was crammed. For nearly an hour, I had to stand before finally being taken to the custody area. I gagged at the stench of stale sweat. Because of Tom's age, I had to be with him whilst they 'booked him in.'

"We'll be with you in a few moments," the desk sergeant didn't glance up from his paper shuffling.

Feeling insignificant, I absorbed my now-not-so-unfamiliar surroundings. The 'admissions' board showed that every cell was occupied. I berated Tom for getting arrested on a Friday. I scanned the board for his name. *Cell 7.* There, outside, were his trainers. The heat was stifling, and I longed for fresh air. I had been stood for so long that I felt light-headed.

"Do you mind if I sit down? I don't feel so good."

One of the officers took pity on me, gave me some water, and showed me into the interview room which was a bit cooler.

Several minutes later, Tom appeared in socks and paper trousers. (There had been a cord in his tracksuit bottoms.) His eyes met mine.

"You idiot." I said.

I listened as his rights were read. He was fingerprinted, photographed, swabbed, then taken back to his cell.

"Don't make me go back in there!" A couple of feet before the doorway, he brought himself to a halt.

"You should've thought about that *before*." The officer tried to shove Tom forwards.

"I can't stand it in there." Tom's imploring eyes sought mine. "Please don't make me."

"Look Tom. It's just for a while. Stop making a fuss." The officer slammed the door after him. I looked on, obviously powerless to intervene.

"If I give you my number, can you let me know when you are ready to interview?" I fished around in my bag to check I had my phone. "I'm off to read in my car. I can't stand it in the waiting room."

"You can see how busy we are." He watched as I scribbled my number onto a scrap of paper. "But we'll give you a call when we're ready."

. . .

Two hours went by before they called. By then I had got through two magazines, a newspaper and begun reading a novel. Tom looked desperate as he was brought back into the interview room.

"Can I go home after this?"

"Let's wait and see, shall we?" The officer unwrapped two tapes as he spoke to me. "Have you been an appropriate adult before?"

"I'm afraid so." I sat and draped my cardigan over the back of the chair.

"Right you know the drill then. OK Tom," he announced briskly, "I'm going to go through your rights again, and then I'll check you understand them."

He asked a series of questions. *Did the bus belong to you? The seats you drew on, did they belong to you? Were you intending to clean your graffiti off?*

"For the benefit of the tape I am showing the accused *exhibit A*," he said, placing a bag on the graffiti daubed table.

As I looked, I struggled not to laugh. There, in a clear polythene bag, was a solitary permanent marker.

"Is this the implement you used to deface the bus?" He went on, oblivious to the humour I was trying to quell. Luckily Tom was unaware of it too. Clearly, it was a serious situation, but his line of questioning was so ridiculous that I was relieved to escape back to the sanctuary of my car. In the meantime, Tom was placed back in his cell whilst they decided what to do with him.

Three weeks later we were back in court. Happily, this time, *Tom* was punished and given fifteen hours of reparation. Cleaning buses!

FAMILY LIFE

WHILST AT COURT, I withdrew permission for the tagging equipment to remain in our house. We were living on a knife's edge, waiting for him to surface at seven each evening and enduring the visit of the security firm when he *didn't* return.

Twice, I had been back in court as a result of 'the three strikes and you're out' system. Basically, Tom had got wise to the fact that it was only on his *third* non-appearance, that he would be hauled back to court. There the magistrate would bestow a 'stern reprimand,' and Tom could return to 'strike one' again.

It had been 'hell on earth' having him among us from seven each evening; the whole atmosphere would deteriorate as soon as he walked in. Either he would be stoned, or in a mood so foul, (sometimes both), that we would feel like running for cover.

The neighbours now shunned us; evidently, judging our entire family by the endless presence of hoods, gathered like ghouls, at the front of my house. Even the neighbours next door no longer allowed their daughter to play with Alex.

Tom rejoiced at the tag's removal.

"Don't think it means you can do whatever you want," I warned, shaking my finger at him. "If you're not home by half past ten, the door will be locked from now on."

It was impossible to adhere to this, no matter how much I wished I'd had the strength to. At two, three or four o'clock in the morning, he would beat on the door and repeatedly ring the bell until I responded. He only came home to eat and sleep. Oh, and to steal and bully me for money.

~

"What am I supposed to do with a fucking fiver!" He snatched at a note I had left on the kitchen worktop.

"It's all I've got."

"You're a lying bitch! Show me your purse."

"I'll do no such thing!" I thrust the note back into my bag. "How dare you speak to me like that!"

I listened from my bedroom as he slammed around. Then, with one final bang of the door, I heaved a sigh at the realisation he had gone out. Returning downstairs, I decided that a chamomile tea might calm me down a bit.

"Mum, two of my best games have gone?" Alex appeared in the kitchen doorway, worry written across his face.

"Gone?" My heckles rose. "Are you sure?"

"I left them next to my PlayStation." He pointed back up the stairs. "They were there before. *Little Big Planet* and *FIFA 09.*"

Following him to his room, I hoped to find them myself. They had cost me sixty pounds. As I *had* feared, they *had* gone.

Alex slumped onto his bed. "It probably serves me right for not hiding them better."

I wanted to weep for him. All he possessed that was saleable was at Tom's mercy. It had been a long time since he had given up attempting to save in his piggy bank.

. . .

Tom startled me that evening when he lurched through the door. It wasn't even midnight. This was virtually unheard of on a Friday evening. I was poised to 'let rip' about Alex's missing games but my attention was distracted by the state he was in.

"Oh my God! What's happened?" Spotting his swollen jaw, I gasped. He was also clutching his leg. His torn tracksuit bottoms laid bare an angry gash. "You're going to need stitches!"

"It's nowt Mum. Stop panicking. I got into a fight that's all. The cut's not as bad as it looks." He flinched as I inspected it. "I'm more bothered about me trackies. Can you sew em?"

CHANGING STORIES

APRIL 2009, (15 YEARS, 4 MONTHS)

"Who were you fighting with?" By the next evening his leg thankfully, due to the hassle it would cause to get him to the hospital, looked as though it did not need stitches.

"This lad." He winced as I peeled the dressing back. "No one you know."

"What was it about?" I dabbed at the wound with antiseptic.

"Look Mum. Leave it." He tried to pull his leg away. "I don't wanna talk about it. Alright?"

"Well I do." I put a new dressing on him.

"OK. I'll tell you what happened. Me mates were carrying on over who'd paid for what with a crate of beer and it got out of hand. I tried to break it up. A bottle got trashed and a piece of glass bounced up and cut my leg."

I stared at him. "That's impossible Tom. Glass bouncing from the ground would not cause that." I cut the bandage.

"Don't believe me then. Do I look bothered?"

"Have you heard about the woman attacked at the bus station?"

"Yeah, what about it?" His voice hardened.

"What do *you* know about it?" I could not meet his eyes.

"Nowt really. Didn't see much of it. Was around the corner having a smoke. What are you accusing me of now?"

"But you were there?"

"It wasn't me. Honest Mum. "Searching his face, I detected panic. "In fact, I stopped with her till the ambulance got there."

"It says in the paper that the police got there first." I pointed to the paper.

"It's in the paper?" He snatched it up.

"Of course it is. She was badly hurt." I tried to keep my voice steady. *God he was there!*

"Not by me, she wasn't." Having found the article, he shook the paper out. "I tried to help her get up."

"Was it your mates?"

"No. Well, kind of. Some of em. Not the ones that hurt her."

"Was that where you hurt your leg?" Having re-bandaged his wound, I stuck a plaster on it.

"I've already told you what happened. Someone chucked a bottle and it cut through me trackies."

"Who threw it then?"

"I dunno!" He slapped the newspaper back onto the table. "Will you stop going on! You're blagging my head?"

"A moment ago, you told me it was your mate who smashed the bottle." I remained on my knees upon the floor.

He stormed out. I sat, studying the sun reflecting onto the living room table. My daffodils looked well in the window.

Breathing slowly, in through the nose and out through the mouth, like I had learned at yoga, I tried to calm myself down.

My conscience would not have let me rest if I had not done something. I rang the police station and told them about Tom's leg and the fact that he had admitted to being around the attack.

I hated myself for doing it.

ARREST NUMBER 5

It took two days for the police to come round. In the meantime, I could barely look at Tom. I was convinced he had been involved in the attack of this poor woman.

"It'll be some time before we interview him," advised the arresting officer as he handcuffed him. "We've another two of them to pick up yet."

Later that evening I got a call to say they were ready for me. Again, I waited in the sweltering custody area, scanning for the trainers that would show which cell he was in. Not that it made much difference to anything that was going on.

"We've had a few problems with your son," the desk sergeant said coolly from behind the towering, green desk. Below his sweat-soaked forehead, was a disapproval in his eyes. "Evidently he doesn't appreciate being locked up. He's demonstrated this by head butting the wall. Claims he's trying to knock himself out."

"Is he OK?" Panic soared in me like bile. Memories of him

head banging in his bedroom as a toddler resurfaced. "Have you checked on him?"

"The first aider's been keeping an eye on him. He's not done himself any favours mind. We'll be interviewing him *last*."

I retreated to the refuge of my car to read. Not that I could concentrate on anything.

Dusk was falling, casting a shadow over the police station. The 'windows' of the cells were visible, above ground level. They were dimly lit compared to the other windows. I imagined my son behind one of them and tried to bury the misplaced guilt that was consuming me.

After what seemed like an eternity, they were ready to interview him. Tom's head was raw with injury as they took him to the green desk to read out the charge.

I shook my head. "What the hell possessed you to do that to yourself?"

He ignored me. Then refused a solicitor when asked. "I'm not waiting for one of them to get here. I want to get on with it."

Before starting the interview, they photographed the injury on his leg. It did not dawn on him to question how they knew about this. If he had, my telephone call to the police might have come to light.

He gave the same story he had told me, about having been there, helping the woman, and waiting with her for the ambulance.

"And you were present whilst she was being beaten?"

"I was nearby."

"You could see what was happening? And you didn't help her?" He frowned.

"I did help her. After they had stopped."

"Who's they?"

He shrugged. "I dunno."

"We've got the whole thing on CCTV. Are you aware of that?" The officer's eyes widened as he studied Tom.

"No."

"So when we examine it, we'll see you, *watching*? Then *helping?* We won't see you contributing to her injuries?"

"No. I don't care whether you believe me or not!" His half-broken voice bounced around the room. "I didn't hurt no-one!"

Eventually, he was released on bail, pending enquiries. We were to return the following week. Over the next few days it all felt like a hurricane cloud was hovering above me. I hardly told anyone what was going on but wore the shame like an ill-fitting cardigan. Bail answering day came. I was triumphant that I managed to get him back to the station at the right time. He had put up a fight.

"I'm not getting done for summat I've not done!" He said as I drove us there.

"If that's true then you've nothing to worry about." Clenching the steering wheel, I prayed he was telling the truth, but I could not help suspecting the worst.

"But what if someone who isn't me, looks like me on the cameras?"

"Tom, I don't know. We'll see when we get there." By now, I was desperate to get it over with.

"I'm not going in no cell," he announced as we parked in the station car park. "I'll head-butt the copper this time if he tries putting me in there."

"Don't be ridiculous." Locking the car, I sighed as we headed towards the entrance.

"I will." He dragged himself behind me. "Just watch me."

They *did* lock him up. But he went into the cell like a lamb, despite his previous bravado. The officer closed the heavy cell door and there was a loud clunk as he turned the key. I looked at Tom's trainers in dismay.

"At least I know where he is tonight," I joked, fishing in my bag for my book whilst trying to find light in the darkness of the situation.

"Take a seat in the waiting area love," the desk sergeant nodded from behind the desk. "We'll try not to keep you too long."

Again, I killed time by trying to read. Before long, my backside was deadened from sitting on the metal bench. My head ached in the glare of the fluorescent strip-lights. The automatic doors responded to every bird or whisper of a breeze and continually startled me.

Occasionally someone would come in. They would state their business in hushed tones through the intercom and I would eavesdrop. One man tried making conversation with me. He stunk of drink and I wished he would leave me alone with my book. Finally, a policeman's voice sliced into my boredom.

"Can I have a word?" Snapping my book shut, I dutifully followed him into a side room.

"We're going to have to let him go." He shook his head. "We've not enough evidence to charge him."

"But the CCTV..."

"It's too grainy. They all look the same. They're dressed almost identically. The CPS won't let us charge any one unless we've a lot more than what we've got."

"Do you not recognise anyone on the CCTV?"

He shook his head again sadly. "Unless any of them admit anything, we've got nothing."

"They've got away with it. I don't believe it. That poor woman!"

Tom was euphoric upon leaving the police station.

BROUGHT BACK BY THE POLICE 3

TOM SLOPPED, like custard skin, onto the pavement.

"We found him in an inebriated state and vomiting in the middle of town," announced the policeman, ripping back the sliding door of the police van. "So, we're returning him to you." Hauling him to his feet, he led him towards me. "Miraculously, he remembered where he lived! May I suggest that you get him inside and put him to bed?"

"Look at the state of you! You're a bloody disgrace!" Yanking him inside, I gagged at the stench of regurgitated lager that clung to him.

The policeman turned on his heel, and retreated towards his van, shaking his head all the time.

BROUGHT BACK BY THE POLICE 4

A WEEK later a police van pulled up outside once again. Its formidable form shadowed the house.

Oh for God's sake! What now? I walked to the door.

"Is this your son?" The policeman looked at me as though I were an insect.

"I'm afraid so."

"The next time we find him in this state, we'll lock him up for the night. Is that clear?"

"Lock him up now if you want."

"We shouldn't have to. You should keep him under control." His finger wagged at me.

"I'm trying to. You've no idea what it's like!" My hand flew to my forehead as I tried to sweep my anxiety away. "He's out of windows if we try to keep him in!"

"Well, we've better things to be doing with our resources than to be fishing reprobates like your son off the streets!" Muttering still, he turned and returned to his van.

. . .

Tom had slithered past me and got himself to bed. I fumed as I went upstairs and put a bucket beside him. Backing away, I was grateful to reach the air on the landing where I could take a breath of normal smelling air.

ON HIS OWN DOORSTEP 1

We had lived on the new housing estate for several months. Only a few of the other houses were occupied - the ones that, like ours, had been bought and let by the housing association. Typically, the inhabited homes were all within hearing and seeing distance from ours, so Tom's conduct had been witnessed in full glory.

The site manager had made us aware that prospective buyers were put off by the youths hanging around.

"Bloody hell!" Exclaimed Martin one night, letting a slow whistle out. We were walking the dog in the street around the corner from ours, therefore it was out of our view usually.

My gaze travelled from one house to the next then the next. The yet-to-be-loved homes drooped in the spring sunshine. Lanterns and drainpipes had been ripped from walls. There were two smashed windows and a warped garage door.

"Oh no! That will cost a fortune to put right." A bin cupboard door in one of the porches swayed on one hinge instead of three and someone had lit a fire inside. A bowed garage door was peppered with scorch marks; as though somebody had held a burning object against it. Litter was everywhere and mud splodges had pelted the houses. Then I noticed the graffiti; the same 'signature' had been repeated over and over. As had numerous sketchings of SpongeBob SquarePants.

"Have a look at this Martin"

"Yep, it's definitely him. It's the same signature he's drawn all over his bedroom wall. He calls it his 'tag.'"

"Talk about crapping on your own doorstep."

"It's this kind of thing that could get us kicked out." Yanking hold of the dog's lead, Martin began to walk away. "If I end up homeless because of your fucking son ..."

Later that evening, we all sat in the garden. I was already on edge as Martin had only just got back from the pub and seemed to be in the same mood he had left in. The usual din erupted outside, indicating that again, the teenagers had landed. There would be a restricted view of the 'action' available from the landing window. Martin sped upstairs, tailed by Alex, then me.

"They're at it again." Martin leaned onto the windowsill. "There's a few of them!"

"Is Tom with them?"

"I can't see him."

There was a deafening bang then something smashed.

"I think you should call the police Mum!" Alex stood on tiptoes at the window.

"If you come now, you'll catch them all in action." I told the operator. "They must be costing the building company a fortune."

. . .

For several minutes we waited, expecting a police van to screech up and sling them all in the back. Instead, after half an hour, a lone police officer came trundling down the street on a bicycle.

I went outside, laughing at the idiocy of it all.

The teenagers disbanded as the officer pointed his bike in their direction.

"If the information I gave had been acted on properly;" I called out, "you would've caught them all."

"I know," he scratched his head. "I just go where I'm sent."

The building company employed a 'security guard' to patrol the housing estate each night. He spent most of his shift 'holed up' in one of the empty apartments. Most of the neighbours had reservations about what this middle-aged, portly man in a security uniform would be able to achieve against the might of the local hoods anyway.

MAGISTRATES WARNINGS

JULY 2009, (15 YEARS, 7 MONTHS)

As a result of Tom's frequent court order breaches, I became a 'regular,' at court. Having my handbag checked and being searched using a handheld body scanner became second nature. It became amusing to listen to the various warnings and reprimands given to him:

1. "If you return to this court, you'd better bring your toothbrush."
2. "I'll be dealing with you personally in future."
3. "If I see you in this court again, you'll be leaving by this door, not from that one."
4. "If you end up back here, you might as well bring your pyjamas."
5. "You will be finding out how hard life can be in a young offender's institution if you are brought before me again."
6. "Any more breaches and we'll have a prison van waiting."

7. "I've made a note on your file. If I see you again, your mother will be getting a nice long break from you."
8. "You'll be needing to bring your slippers if you return here."

I wanted to laugh each time I heard one of these 'harsh' warnings. Tom would nod earnestly as though he took them seriously.

FULL CIRCLE

In terms of sleep, we went right back to the beginning. If we were not woken every night by revving engines or stones being thrown at Tom's window, we were woken by Tom himself. It would then take forever to get back to sleep. I would lie awake, awaiting the next interruption, continually turning the problems around in my head.

One night I heard voices on our landing. I froze.

"There's someone in the house!" I hissed at Martin, elbowing him. "Didn't you lock the door?"

"I left it open for Tom. I'm sick of being woken at all hours." There was a knock on the bedroom door. Martin leapt out of bed.

"What the hell do you think you're doing?" Two teenagers, slightly younger than Tom, cowered before him.

"Tom's got my bag," stammered one, backing away. "He nicked it."

"So you just stroll into my house?"

"I need the bag."

"Get out of here now!" He started towards the boys who sprinted down the stairs and away into the darkness.

Tom stayed out all night. I lay awake, staring at the ceiling; consumed with anxiety about the 'bag situation,' and for Tom's whereabouts. Eventually, I must have drifted off as I was awoken to a thumping at the door. I tugged my dressing gown on and peered through the blinds. Martin didn't move. Whoever was at the door was out of my vision, either hidden by the porch or perhaps trying round the rear of the house. I prayed it was Tom.

I was worn out with never having any idea of who he was with or what he was up to. His last mobile phone had lasted eleven days before he had sold it, so it wasn't as if I could contact him.

The banging became more urgent. Through the small windows at the top of the door, I saw two heads, two hats, two police officers. In horror, I realised, that at 6.20 am, this was no social call. It *must* be bad news. Maybe the unspeakable dread I lived and stayed awake with each night had been realised. *Tom.* Trembling, I turned the key. The police must have sensed my terror as they surveyed me. The female officer smiled.

"It's OK. He's in custody."

Heaving a sigh of relief, I leaned against the doorframe. "Thank God. For a moment..."

"I know. Don't worry." She stretched her arm out towards me. "Can we come in?"

I opened the door wider. At least at this hour, net curtains would not be twitching. There won't be many mothers who would be relieved at the news of an incarcerated son, but the alternatives were beyond contemplation.

"What's he done this time?"

"Possession with intent to supply," stated the male officer, matter of fact.

"Oh no!" I sank onto a chair.

"We caught him coasting around in a car with two others at around three this morning."

A car! Now I was even more worried. I had heard about several tragic accidents that had happened in the night of teenagers who had got hold of cars!

"We found over £200 in cash in the car, weighing scales and a substantial quantity of cannabis."

"If you've had him since three, how come you've only just let me know?" I glanced at the clock again.

"We need to search your house." The policewoman's eyes skimmed the room. "So to preserve everything, we've been unable to have informed you of his arrest."

"I wouldn't have moved anything."

"I'm not suggesting *you* would. But some parents might."

"You won't find anything, you know. Do I look like the sort of person who would have anything to do with drugs?" Although who knows what I looked like at that hour of the day.

I was mildly offended as she plucked two pairs of rubber gloves from her pocket, what did she expect to be contaminated with?

"Can I wake my husband?" Springing from the chair, I tightened the cord of my dressing gown. "He'll get a shock if two police officers burst into the bedroom!"

"OK, we'll start searching down here first." She offered a pair of the gloves to her colleague.

Martin had already emerged from bed and was swiftly dressing as I opened our bedroom door.

"It's one thing after another," he hissed. "I can't put up with much more of this."

"Then don't," I replied.

"Is it OK if we come up?" The policewoman called up the stairs.

They searched Tom's room quickly. Other than his clothes, his possessions were of meagre proportions, which made me desperately sad when I allowed myself to consider it. Most of what he had owned had been sold to fund his cannabis addiction.

They moved towards Alex's door.

"You don't have to ransack my seven-year-old's room surely?" They looked at each other.

"I'm afraid we're obliged to search the entire house." The policeman pushed his door ajar and I dashed in front of him.

"You won't find anything in here." I glanced over to Alex where his dark hair was poking out from under his duvet. Whilst he slept, he always burrowed right under it. "He's still asleep for God's sake."

Thankfully they agreed to leave his room alone. Back downstairs we needed to complete paperwork to state that they had searched our home but had not seized anything.

"What's your occupation?" The policewoman waited; her pen poised.

"Trainee teacher." My voice was barely audible.

"You're a teacher?" She shrieked. "And you can't even control your own son?"

I stared at my feet.

"That's not fair," I was stunned that Martin was jumping to my defence. "You don't know his background or what we've been through with him."

Without offering an apology, she continued with her form, passing no further judgement. I was aware that she had voiced what most people thought. *No, I couldn't control him.* I could have scoured every corner of the country and been lucky to find anybody who could.

I subsequently spent nearly four hours at the police station whilst he and his two friends were interviewed and re-interviewed. The police had the cheek to ask that I act as appropriate adult to one of his friends as their own parent had refused to attend. All three of them denied any knowledge of the cannabis, cash or scales, each blaming the others.

The CPS concluded the crime could not be reliably pinned on any one individual, so they were released without charge. I'd have charged the bloody lot of them!

I COULD HAVE PAPERED THE WALLS WITH THESE

Teaching and Learning Centre
Easton Drive
Yorkshire
YD16 6NE

9TH JULY 2009

Dear Parent/Carer,

Re: Tom Clifford

I am writing to inform you of my decision to exclude Tom for a fixed period of one afternoon. This means that he will not be allowed in school for this period. The exclusion is for the afternoon, 9th July 2009.

I realise that this exclusion may be upsetting for you and your family, but the decision to exclude Tom has not been taken lightly. Tom has been excluded for this fixed period because he absconded from the centre and is suspected of being under the influence of an illegal substance.

You have the right to make representations to the education authority about this decision. These representations will be considered by Inclusion Services. If you think this exclusion related to a disability your child has, and you think disability discrimination has occurred, you may raise this issue with the governing body. You also have a right to see a copy of Tom's school record. Due to confidentiality restrictions, you will need to notify me in writing if you wish to be supplied with a copy. There may be a charge for photocopying.

Tom's exclusion expires on Thursday 9th July 2009 and we expect him to be back in school on Friday 10th July 2009. Should you have any queries, please contact me.

Yours sincerely

Head of Centre

PARENTS' EVENING

I BRACED myself as I pressed the intercom of the pupil referral unit. Unlike mainstream secondary schools, the exits were kept locked. Not that this stopped Tom. Regular phone calls kept me informed of his escapes. Through windows, over walls; once he'd had enough, he was out of there. Not that he was learning a great deal in any case. Apart from where to score cannabis and who in the unit might join him in smoking it. Often, he was ejected from the centre for being 'under the influence' therefore 'unteachable.' (See letter above!)

It was debatable how much teaching went on anyway. He never brought any books or worksheets home. At least now I would find out if he had made any progress throughout his time there.

"He's gifted at art," said his 'key-worker,' Lynn, who spoke in a throaty voice and smelt of cigarettes, even though she sat at the other side of the table. "We think he's a potential candidate for art college."

"Well, that's something." I waited for the 'but.' If Tom had purpose; ambition...anything, maybe he could be diverted from his current path. It was wonderful to hear something positive, a chink of hope.

The class numbers in the centre were tiny compared to 'normal' classes; a maximum of eight teenagers were in each one.

"But he'd have to get off the cannabis," she continued, bringing me back down to earth. "He's stoned every day. There's no way he can concentrate or learn anything in that state."

"The only person who can get Tom to stop smoking cannabis is *Tom*. All kinds of drug interventions have already been attempted by his last school *and* by the Youth Offending Team. He's got to *want* to stop."

"How much money do you give him?" *Great they are blaming me, as usual.*

"The bare minimum." I looked straight into her face. "But I suspect even his lunch money goes on weed."

"Have you tried giving him sandwiches?"

"Of course I have." Leaning forward, I clasped my hands together. "He won't even put them in his bag. Anyway, if I don't give him any money at all, he's unbearable *and* more likely to steal stuff from home."

For a moment she sat, frowning as though she was rehearsing her reply. "We should discuss that 'unbearable' side you mention. Whenever he's *not* stoned, he's usually short tempered. In fact, we've had a few incidences of him swearing at other pupils or staff."

"I can imagine. I know exactly what he's like." I glanced down at the sheet of notes she had in front of her. "Anyway, other than artwork, how's he getting on with his other lessons?"

"Well, he's got interesting ideas but the attention span of a flea." She chuckled slightly but it was not a genuine laugh. "Even when we do manage to interest him, it's short lived. So he disrupts the others whose concentration skills are no better than his."

"But you're coping with him, aren't you?" Without waiting for an answer, I continued. "It's just that he's had dreadful problems in his schools before." *That was an understatement.*

"He's not one of our *better* pupils." She looked apologetic. "But we've encountered worse, don't worry! If he can kick the weed, he'd stand a fighting chance."

"I've begged, lectured, threatened and argued with him. It's out of my hands. He's aware of the dangers in smoking it; I've made sure of that. Base 10 have too, *and* his Youth Offending Team drugs worker."

"Well, if that's the case, there doesn't seem there's much more we can do." She looked thoughtful. "Not until the decision to sort the drugs problem comes from within him. Anyway, moving on from that... I'm afraid there've also been several complaints about him urinating outside. Obviously, at his age, it's unacceptable." As she screwed her lips together, the lines around them became more prominent. "The girls and female staff within the centre should not have to bear witness to it."

"He's been doing it since he was small." Leaning back on my chair, I clasped my hands behind my head. "It's happened at every school he's ever been to! I'm not sure if he's trying to shock people or can't be bothered finding a toilet." I glanced out of the window, noticing the metal fencing surrounding the building. "God only knows why he still does it now!"

"If you could have a word..."

"For what good it'll do." I raised my eyes to the ceiling, noticing the peeling paint. The classroom was barren. The furniture might have been cast out by a mainstream school and the walls were crying out for displays that might offer enthusiasm.

. . .

Later, as I headed to the exit, I noticed the walls of the disinfected corridors were just as devoid of any effort. Free rein had been granted for pupils at the centre to unleash their creativity at graffiti 'art' but there was no evidence of any learning or any link to the curriculum.

THE CHILD AND ADOLESCENT MENTAL HEALTH SERVICE (AGAIN)

AUGUST 2009, (15 YEARS, 8 MONTHS)

My first encounter with this service I remembered, back when Tom was eleven, had been constructive. Although there had been no magic wand or medication offered; Victoria, the child psychiatrist, had been thorough and non-judgmental.

At the time, the suggestions and advice she had offered had been a Godsend. The fact that she had diagnosed something, albeit Conduct Disorder instead of ADHD; had added weight to my claims that Tom's condition was beyond any mistakes I might have made as a mother.

Unfortunately, I was not as lucky with the 'experts' that now confronted us at each appointment. When I say 'us,' I mean 'me.' And when I say 'confronted,' I mean 'besieged.'

"Do you not think your negative attitude is making things worse?" One of them suggested. Tom would be saving up these comments to fire back at me later.

"*You'd* be negative if you had to live with him." Tom and I glared at each other, the echoes of his attitude on the journey here still lingering.

"But surely in front of him," the younger woman, the 'psychologist' was speaking, "a positive manner would be more helpful."

"It was *you* that suggested Tom should be present for all these meetings." My reply carried a note of rebellion. "There's no point in me lying. I need to tell it like it is."

"Yes, and we'll stand by that, for now anyway." She smiled. "He should be here to have his say. We're concerned that it won't do his self-esteem any good, hearing you being a little *pessimistic*."

The other woman nodded.

"It's not doing *my* self-esteem any favours being sworn at and insulted every day."

"We must remember who's the adult here." I shrank under her stare.

Tom seemed laid back as he drew SpongeBob SquarePants repeatedly. It was a nightmare persuading him to these appointments, requiring coercion to the point of bribery. I wished they had a camera in their waiting room. They would have been able to witness the full might of his nastiness. He had swiftly switched from hostility towards me as we waited, to be all sweetness and butter won't melt in front of these women.

"I try to say sorry, but *she* won't let me." I listened to a sample from his stock of 'one-liners' reserved for occasions such as this:

"She thinks more of my brother, Alex, than me."

"I'm going to get my head down and do well at school."

"I hardly smoke any cannabis now. People who do are stupid."

"I'm going into the army when I leave school."

"I'm going to work hard and prove my mum wrong."

The women intermittently smiled and nodded at the repertoire I had been subjected to already on numerous occasions. It was frequently 'trotted' out to people in *authority*.

In this case, I was mildly amused to notice that the younger woman and Tom almost *flirted* with each other throughout our appointments. There was no interest from them in respect of Tom's latest exploits; they wanted to talk about the past, and only the past.

Halfway through the appointment; Tom and I, and the 'experts,' were split for them to speak separately with either Tom or me.

"Anne and I have spoken, and we feel that history is repeating itself," the psychologist said after the 'split' at that meeting. "You suffered being rejected in your teens by your own mother, so you're now allowing the same thing with *your* son."

Shifting uncomfortably, I felt myself being scrutinised, like a specimen beneath a microscope.

"How do you feel about that?" She added.

"It's rubbish!" I was trembling as I leaned forward in my chair. "I only wish Tom had been given *my* mother, he would've been long gone. She couldn't have coped with a fraction of what I've had to."

"You must admit you're in danger of rejecting him." Her tone was calm. I wondered how she could take this view from only seeing us a handful of times.

"You're wrong." I sat back. "It's because of my own background that I've persevered for so long. My role as a mother is something I treat seriously. Why else would I keep trying to get help for him?"

"We don't see any underlying medical condition that he needs *help* with." Her eyes conveyed her unspoken words: *I'm the expert here!*

My heart plummeted. *What a waste of time!* "But you're basing your opinions on limited time spent with us in an environment that's not even natural."

"We're basing our *judgement* on the interaction we've

witnessed. As well as the previous reports we've seen." She flicked at the pages of her file resting on her knee. "Even an educational psychologist previously thought that your relationship with Tom indicated an attachment disorder. And he was only nine then."

I snorted. "He observed him at school for an hour. How can he seriously make an informed judgement in that time?"

"Nevertheless," she skirted around the question as she pursued her argument. "I feel that future appointments would be better spent addressing your own mother's treatment and rejection of you, and how you're going to prevent your relationship with Tom from further deterioration."

"If he stopped taking drugs, stopped being abusive and stopped getting arrested; that might be a start."

"But *you* must take responsibility for how he's turned out."

"I did not bring him up to take drugs and break the law! Listen, we're getting nowhere." Grabbing my handbag from the floor, I then dumped it onto my knee. "If you think I am going to rake up my childhood in front of you, you're mistaken."

"I understand it could be painful for you." Her voice was calmer.

"It's not relevant." I fished in my bag for my keys. "Addressing Tom's issues is what matters."

"We're going to offer a specialist counsellor for him to meet with fortnightly. He can get things off his chest and perhaps discuss his drugs issues. But in the case of yourself; we can't force you to engage with help if you don't feel able to."

"I don't *need* help!" I got to my feet. "Not personally anyway! I need help with *Tom!*"

Her face was flushed, though probably not as much as mine. I felt utterly failed. Blamed and judged.

"I hope one day you're not reading about something he's done in the papers." I strode to the door. "Because the way things are, anything's possible. Tell him I'm waiting in the car."

THE WEEKLY NEWS

SPATE OF LATE-NIGHT SHOP BREAK-INS. POLICE SUSPECT LOCAL YOUTHS

POLICE and local traders were today appealing for help in finding what they believe to be youths, who are responsible for at least four break-ins at four shops within the last week. The latest, which took place in the early hours of yesterday morning, was captured on CCTV both inside and outside the shop.

It is believed the thefts are linked; they have all been targeted within a mile radius of each other and have all suffered similar losses; cigarettes, large quantities of alcohol and confectionary.

If any member of the public has information which may lead police towards the culprits, they are asked to contact the local police station or ring Crimestoppers, on 0800 555111.

ARREST NUMBER 6

"COME ON TOM!" Jangling my keys, I shouted up the stairs for the third time. "We've got to be at the dentist in twenty minutes. Get your teeth cleaned *now!* I'll wait for you in the car." Eventually, he emerged, looking as though he had been dug up from somewhere!

"You should get yourself home at a decent hour," I ushered him out of the door so I could lock it. "You need your sleep you know, instead of rolling in after four in the morning. And I need mine. God knows what you're doing until that time." It was more of a question than a statement.

"Stop chatting shit Mum." He closed his eyes. "My head can't take it today." We passed the local shop which was being boarded up. Two of the windows had been smashed in. A police car was outside. Tom appeared to be grinning to himself.

"What's going on around here?" I said, suddenly recalling the newspaper article. "That's the fifth shop in a week to have been broken into. It must be the same…"

Stealing a glance at him, reality dawned. "I hope it's nothing to do with you, because if the police were to ask, I'd have to say

I didn't know where you were last night, well not until four in the morning anyway."

"Why d'you always have to think the worst of me?" His voice was feeble as he tried to load anger into it. "It's got fuck all to do with me!"

"Stop swearing." I slammed the palm of my hand against the steering wheel. "What gives you the right to swear at me? You'll get out of this car and walk in a minute."

"I didn't want to go to the bloody dentist anyway." He took a sip of water from the bottle he was carrying.

When we arrived, he shot to the toilet. The waiting room echoed with the sound of him vomiting. Everyone looked at me as I squirmed in my seat.

"You'll have to ask him to wait outside." The receptionist was unable to hide her revolt. "Obviously the dentist can't see him in that state."

"What's the matter with you?" I hissed as I led him out.

"Too much to drink, that's all." He resumed his retching in the car park. Swiftly, I abandoned him, anxious not to watch or hear him either.

For the rest of that day he slept. Until we received a loud banging at the door.

"Tom Clifford," barked a policeman. His female colleague stood at his side.

"He's asleep." I groaned inwardly at the thought of having to cancel that evening's plans, to be his appropriate adult *yet again*.

"We need to speak to him in connection with local shop thefts," stated the policewoman, stepping towards me. "You'll have to wake him."

"Tom! The police are here! They want to speak to you!"

"Tell em to fuck off." Twisting round to see whether they had heard him, I felt my face flush. From their expressions, they evidently had.

"Don't be stupid." I began up the steps. "Get up!"

"I can't," he whined.

"You'll have to. *Now!*" I bolted up the remainder of them until I was bawling at his huddled form from the landing.

Finally, he emerged, dragging himself downstairs and towards his would-be captors.

"Tom Clifford," announced the female officer. "We're arresting you on suspicion of burglary. You do not have to say anything. But it may harm your defence if you do not mention when questioned, something which you later rely on in court. Anything you do say may be given in evidence." I knew these words well. The policeman handcuffed him.

"Burglary!" I leaned against the wall. "I might have known *he'd* be involved!"

"It's the one at the Spar last night that we want to speak to him about. But there *are* several others. Come on Tom, get your shoes on."

"But I'm not feeling too clever." He looked dreadful.

"Well a nice lie down in the cell should bring you round." The officer turned to me. "Can I ask that you make your way down in about an hour?" He checked his watch as he spoke. "We'll hopefully be ready to interview him by then."

It was a balmy summers evening. Every eye in the neighbourhood was on Tom, as he was marched out in handcuffs. Watching from the window, I jumped as the van door slammed behind him. The engine roared out of the street and died away, like all my hope. I rang Martin.

"What did I tell you?" It irked me that he sounded almost triumphant. "I knew he was up to something. He's not been badgering us for money as much over the last few days!"

. . .

Half an hour later, Martin arrived home.

"I called into the shop on my way back. It was *Tom*. I've watched the CCTV with my own eyes. You should come back with me and see it for yourself." He rattled the car keys at me. "Just so you're not in any doubt."

"I couldn't." Continuing with my ironing, I slammed the iron down each time, trying to dispel my frustration. "What would the owner think of me?"

"He was OK with me. It's not *us* who burgled him!"

"I daren't!" Grabbing one of Tom's T-shirts from the pile, I could smell the Lynx that lingered on it.

"I *want* you to see it. There's him and another lad."

In the end I gave in. Within minutes, I gingerly opened the boarded-up door. Thankfully the shop had no customers.

"This is Tom's mum," Martin announced, with an air of importance.

"I-I'm sorry," I stammered, unable to look at the shop keeper. "I can't believe he's broken into your shop. I'm ashamed of him!"

"It wouldn't happen in our culture. We Sikhs, we make sure our children are not bored." The way he surveyed Alex as he spoke conveyed his expectance that he too, would turn out like Tom. "Plenty to do, you see."

Martin spoke again as he gestured up to the security screen. "Can you show her the tape?"

It was so grainy I imagined that the Crown Prosecution Service would declare it as not reliable enough evidence, as they had previously. There was no doubting it was him though. He had attempted to conceal his face in his hood, but I could tell it was him from his stature, his movements and his clothes. And I would be more than willing to say so in court too.

"I'll do everything within my power to make sure he's punished for this," I assured the shopkeeper before we left.

At the police station I had to hang around for ages before they interviewed him. It was like waiting to be hung, drawn and quartered.

This time, Tom had requested the services of a solicitor, which took me by surprise. Eventually he arrived, pin-striped and brisk. The desk sergeant told him that I was Tom's mother and perhaps I should be included in their pre-interview discussion.

"I don't think that's a good idea," I decided, remaining firmly in my seat. "You're paid to defend Tom. I'm not on his side whatsoever. I'm only here because I *have* to be."

"Right, OK." The solicitor seemed a bit taken aback.

As it was, he did not make any difference to the interview and hardly uttered a word.

"Where were you this morning at 1:07 am?" The officer referred to some notes.

"In bed," Tom nodded.

"Can you verify this? For the benefit of the tape, I'm directing this question to Tom's mother."

"No. It was after 4 o 'clock in the morning when he returned home."

Tom glared at me.

A duplicate tape showing Tom going into the shop and stuffing his jacket full of beers and spirits was played on the overhead portable.

"Is this you?" The officer asked him.

Tom nodded. "Yes," he said. His whole stature portraying his defeat.

I would now like to move onto your whereabouts on the evenings of the 5th July at around 2am, the 29th June at around midnight and the 27th June at around 1.30 am in the morning?" The stuffy room quietened apart from the continual whirring of the tape. I spent a few moments trying to calculate which days of the week they were referring to. I was able to provide an alibi for two of the dates.

"As far as I know he was in bed. But the thing is with Tom, that even after the house is locked up for the night, he will climb out of windows if he wants to get back out." Tom's expression was thunderous. "So, I can't provide a *cast iron* alibi."

"Fair enough." The policeman scribbled something down. "We'll see how the CPS respond to that."

In the end he was charged with one count of burglary. His court appearance was less than a week away, on the same day as he had been summoned for non-attendance at appointments with his youth offending worker, one in the morning and one in the afternoon. With a sinking heart, I realised that I would be in for a long day.

I went equipped with a bag full of reading matter, sandwiches and a flask of coffee. But I was frisked as we arrived at court.

"You can't take those in," stated the official, taking the flask and mug from my bag.

"Why not?" Several onlookers sniggered.

"Because they could be used as weapons." He locked them into a cupboard. *Of course, why didn't I think of that!*

"Do I look like the sort of person that would use a flask as a weapon? No, on second thoughts, don't bother answering that."

I was kindly permitted to retain my spoon.

"The case is adjourned for pre-sentence reports," declared the magistrate, looking somewhat bored. "You will return three weeks from today. Your mother will attend with you. All rise."

Sighing, I rose. I was sick of the sight of these places. Never in my life had I been on the wrong side of the law, yet I was being ordered about like a criminal.

THE SUBSEQUENT COURT APPEARANCE

Staring straight ahead, I tried to concentrate on the glimmers of sunshine permeating the gloom through the skylight. I wanted to be reminded of the day beyond the confines of these walls. I could not wait to get back out there.

I listened to Tom regurgitating his repertoire to the courtroom. "I don't know what I was thinking. I just followed the others." Tom heaped regret and sincerity into his voice. "I'll never do anything like it again."

"What *do* you want to do with your life Thomas?" From the expression on his face, the magistrate seemed genuinely interested.

"I want to make something of myself. I'm going to get my head down at school, get a good job and stay away from all the idiots I know."

"Do you not think that you, yourself, have been behaving like, how did you put it - *an idiot?*"

"Yeah, I mean yes, but I'm gonna change." He stood up straight. "You'll never see me in court again, I promise!"

"Good because if I do, you'll not be leaving through that door, you'll be leaving through that one." He gestured to a door behind the witness stand. "So remember," he wagged his finger. "If I see you again, you might as well bring your toothbrush with you!" *Gosh, two 'warnings' in one!*

This time he got twelve hours at an attendance centre, and another twelve months added to his supervision order. There was, of course, a fine imposed of £115, payable by me.

I COULD HAVE PAPERED THE WALLS WITH THESE TOO

Magistrates Court

Division:135
Case Number: 14099874638

Notice of fine and collection order

The Court has found Thomas Clifford guilty of the offences shown under Offences and Penalties below and ordered you, as his parent or guardian, to pay £115.00.

Date 15 July 2009
Offences and impositions Burglary other than dwelling – theft.
Amount £ Comp 30.00
Costs £ 85.00
Total £ 115.00
Time to pay £ 5.00 per week commencing 18 July 2009

The Court has made an Order to collect the sum due.

Application for time to pay can be made to the Court in person or by post stating the grounds on which the application is being made. Alternatively, you can contact the Fines Officer on the number above and speak to a member of the fines team.

Failure to pay will make you liable for further enforcement. This could include:

Deductions from your earnings or benefits

Increasing your fine by 50%

Clamping, removal and sale of your vehicle

Registering the account in the Register of Judgments, Orders and Fines
(affecting your ability to obtain credit)

A distress warrant being issued to the Court Bailiffs for the seizure of goods
(incurring additional costs)

Continued default – imprisonment

All enquiries regarding this notice should be made to the above address.

Acting Justices' Clerk

A WARNING TO ALL YOUTHS

Twelve hours in an attendance centre. A deterrent you might think. What is an attendance centre? I will explain.

It is held within a school building. Well this one was. Tom had to attend there on a Saturday morning between 10 am and 12 am.

On one occasion the supervising officer was unable to gain access to the school building so Tom was sent home and two hours of time were 'quashed.'

According to Tom, the two hours were passed in a variety of ways.

- Watching videos
- Having 'circle time' to talk about feelings
- Playing pool
- Playing table tennis
- Completing worksheets
- Playing darts
- Playing dominoes and other tabletop games

ALEX'S PARENTS EVENING

SEPTEMBER 2009 (15 YEARS, 9 MONTHS)

"ALEX OCCASIONALLY DISCUSSES things going on at home." His teacher stated quite matter of factly as I was sitting down.

I became flustered as Mrs Smith's statement sank in. *Oh no! What had he been saying!*

"I guess he's got to vent it somewhere." I tried to meet her eyes. "He puts up with an awful lot from his brother."

"So I gather," she smiled. "Has there been any improvement on that front, or are things still as hard?"

"I'm afraid not. We do our best to shield Alex but it's not always possible."

"He *does* appear to take it all in his stride." Her smile broadened. "He's remarkable!"

"I know. He's a little star." I gestured towards the seat where I knew he sat in class. "He knows about things and has heard words that no seven-year-old ever should."

"Well you'll be pleased to know that none of it is affecting him at school."

"It's not at home either. I think it has the opposite effect. Alex vows he'll never be *anything* like Tom."

"We're pleased with him. He's hardworking, contributes to discussions and is doing well."

"That's fantastic!" Her praise of him made me feel warm.

"You should be proud of him. He's helpful, polite; if I had a class full of Alex's, I would be a happy teacher."

"What about friends? Is everything OK there?"

"Oh yes. There's no one he doesn't get along with. There's one or two boys he spends more time with than others, but no, you've nothing to worry about!"

Tears sprang to my eyes. "You don't know how brilliant it is to hear you praising one of my children. It's such a different story to the parents' evenings I've had in the past."

"I can imagine!" She put her hand on my arm. "It's been a pleasure to give you such a positive report."

ARREST NUMBER 7

This is a message for Tom's Mum. It's his youth offending worker. Just returning your call. Apparently, you wanted to check Tom turned up for his appointment. I can confirm he has – he left the office about twenty minutes ago. If you can ensure he keeps attending and remains out of trouble, that should keep him out of court. Call me back if you need to talk further. Bye for now.

About thirty minutes later my phone rang.

"Is that Tom's mum?" It was a voice I did not recognise.

"It is." He could *not* have been arrested: he had only just left his appointment.

"This is PC Lawrence. I'm ringing to let you know we picked Tom up about quarter of an hour ago."

"Picked him up! Are you sure? He's been at a youth offending appointment."

"Well it doesn't seem to have done him much good. We got a call from Boots. He was nicking a pair of designer sunglasses."

"Oh, I don't believe it."

"We'll need you to come down to the station. Is that OK?"

"Erm yes," then I remembered. "I mean no, my car's in the garage having a new clutch done."

"Is there anyone who can bring you down?"

"No, not really." For a moment, I felt triumphant, believing I could get out of his interview whilst maintaining a clear conscience.

"What about another relative? Someone else who could act as his appropriate adult?"

"There's no one." I thought back to the first interview he had undergone, after the burglary. "Can't you get someone from the Youth Offending Team? They've done it before."

"It would be simpler if you attended. What time are you likely to get your car back?"

"Tomorrow."

"Oh. Right. Hang on a minute." There was a bit of scuffling and scratching for a moment as he conferred with someone. "OK, we can't let him out till we've interviewed* and charged him. For that we need *you* here. We'll send a car out to collect you."

Gulping, I glanced out of my window. "A police car? But my neighbours-"

"I'm sorry." He did not sound it. "It might make the difference between us letting him go today or keeping him overnight in the cells. The car will be with you in about half an hour."

Martin thought it was hilarious. As the *marked* car pulled up outside my house, I pelted outside, hoping to avoid the neighbourhood glare. Of course, most of them were tending to their lawns, cars or whatever and my mode of transport was witnessed by all. I resisted the urge to give a queen-style wave as I left the street.

The policeman barely uttered a word as he drove. His driving was appalling. Too fast and too close to the left. On arrival, he rammed the car up the kerb outside the police station, narrowly avoiding a lamppost.

"Er thanks," I offered, climbing out quickly. "Do you know you're on double yellows?"

"It doesn't matter." He waved his hand. "We're allowed."

*Bog standard interview, bog standard questions: *Were the sunglasses yours to take Tom? Were you intending to pay the shop back Tom? Did anyone give you permission to take them?* We spent all evening there until he was eventually charged and bailed.

~

A week later, he pleaded guilty in court and received a 'severe' reprimand, a lifetime ban from Boots stores countrywide, and I, of course, got court costs.

OUT OF CONTROL

Tom shot towards the stairs. There was something frantic in his eyes as he held onto something up his sleeve.

"What've you got there?" I put the washing basket on the hallway table.

"Nowt." Unusually for him, guilt was etched all over his face.

"Show me."

He tried to bolt off in the direction of the landing, so I raced after him.

"Do one will you," he shouted as I grabbed his sleeve.

"I want to know what you've got."

"Fuck off. Gerroff me!" He tried to shake his arm from my grasp.

Letting go, I re-captured him on another part of his arm. There was a soft bulge and a rustle of polythene.

"Get the fuck off me!" He tried to shove me away with his foot. He had lowered himself to the landing floor and was literally snarling at me. Both our hands were fastened around the bag. Neither of us were letting go. Whatever he had; it was a sizeable amount.

"Fuck off, fucking whore, fucking get off me."

Fuelled with anger, I won the battle. I held the large bag of cannabis aloft. Using my limited drugs knowledge from the internet, I guessed he had about a hundred quid's worth.

"Not in my house!" Muttering the words through clenched teeth, in a robot-like fashion, I lurched towards the toilet.

"Mum, no, please!"

In hindsight, I should have phoned the police and let them deal with it, but I gave myself no chance for logical thinking. In one fell swoop I had flushed the bag away.

"You stupid slag. Fucking slut!"

His venom echoed in my ears as I walked down the stairs.

I had been so determined to get the drugs off Tom that I had been oblivious to Alex observing our 'altercation' from the bottom of the stairs. He looked petrified. Before I had reached the bottom to console him, Tom threw a glass after me. It skimmed the top of my head and narrowly missed Alex.

Seconds after the smash, Martin burst through the door.

"What the hell's going on?" He looked from me to Tom to the floor. "I could hear this shit from the bloody street!"

"He had drugs," I gasped. "I flushed them down the loo. So he chucked a glass at me." I pointed at the floor. "It nearly hit Alex." Barely able to breathe, I fought to get the words out.

"You've two minutes to clear up this glass!" Martin barged past us into the living room. "Before I launch you out of this house; once and for all!"

Amazingly, Tom obeyed this instruction before retreating to his bedroom.

Through the night, I have a glass of water next to the bed. Mercifully, on this night I started to take a sip *before* switching the lamp off.

"Have you put ice in my water Martin?" There was a 'rattle' within my drink.

A closer look showed my glass to be swimming with shards of glass.

"Do you know what damage you'd have done if you'd taken a big swig in the night? Not to mention if you'd swallowed any."

"Why did he put it here?" I said. "Why didn't he throw it in the bin?"

"Why do you think?" Snatching the glass from me, he peered into it. "He wants to get his own back for flushing his precious drugs away."

"Don't be daft." I scrunched my face in protest. "I know he's angry, but he wouldn't hurt me."

"Wake up Sarah. He's just tried to."

A DIFFERENT GP

On the brink of tears, I slumped before the new GP. "I can't cope anymore. I'm not sleeping and feel exhausted. Can you prescribe me something?"

"Pills are all very well Sarah, but they only mask things. They don't address the problem. Tell me about what's going on."

"I feel so low and out of control." I stared down at my hands. "It's crossed my mind to swallow some tablets, fall asleep and never have to face it all again."

I saw concern in her face. "Problems at home? Or work?"

"It's mainly my teenage son." I lifted my eyes to meet hers. "The whole thing's making me ill. I can't even face working. I'm a newly qualified teacher and I've already been signed off." Tears leaked down my cheeks.

"Ah yes, I see that. You've been signed off for two months now. Tell me more." She tugged a tissue from the box beside her and passed it to me.

"I've had a million problems with him, right through his childhood," I tried to steady my voice through my tears. "But for the last three years, it's been abuse on a daily basis. He's into cannabis and even smokes it in the house sometimes." I dabbed at my eyes. "And he threatens me if I don't give him money."

"How does he threaten you?"

"Following me wherever I go until I give in." Pausing, I blew my nose. "Sometimes it's worse, like threats to slap me, usually when my husband isn't around, or he'll threaten to smash up the house or my car. He steals from us too. Nothing can be left lying around. And I'm in and out of court and police stations. I lost count of how many times he's been in trouble over the last couple of years."

"You have another child too," she glanced down at her notes. "How's all this affecting him?"

"To be honest, Alex copes pretty well and tries to stay out of Tom's way as he gets bullied otherwise."

"Is it physical bullying?"

"Not usually. I keep a close eye on things. It's more name calling, a bit of shoving perhaps if I don't get there in time."

"What if I were to make a referral to Social Serv..."

"That's all been tried -," I interrupted. "They apparently only deal with abused children, not kids that are out of control."

"To be fair," she whisked a pen from her desk. "They've a duty to protect your youngest son from your eldest. From what you've told me, he must be witnessing far more than he should."

"I feel guilty enough already. What could Social Services do?"

"They could offer respite with Tom." She tapped the pen thoughtfully against her chin. "That would be a start."

"And what about giving me tablets?"

"I'd prefer you to talk to a counsellor first." Rummaging around on her desk, she found a card which she slid across to me. "Offload it all. I promise that will be more beneficial than any medication I could offer you."

PROFESSIONAL NUMBER 16 - THE COUNSELLOR

OCTOBER 2009, (15 YEARS, 10 MONTHS)

SPILLING MY PROBLEMS FELT SELF-INDULGENT.

The first appointment was spent going over background stuff. "Tom's even taking our home," I said. "None of the neighbours speak to us and we were evicted from our last home because he burgled the next-door neighbour." I rested my elbows on the arms of the chair. "I'm too ashamed to even hang out my washing. I've coped and coped but it's all making me ill now."

"Which is why you're here." Reaching over, she patted my hand. "We're going to get you through this."

"I can't relax anymore." I rubbed at my forehead. "There's no way of knowing what's coming next. I think he's sensing how stressed out I am and is bullying me even more. I've no fight left."

Unlike previous conversations with other professionals, I was able to consider the effect Tom's behaviour was having upon *me*. The counsellor did not seem to be blaming me and the more I said, the more I sensed I could trust her.

"As a child, I was neglected and abused before being rejected completely." My voice wobbled. "But history is *not* being repeated which is what the child psychiatrists are implying. But the negativity I'm feeling towards Tom is awful. I can hardly bear being in the same room as him at the moment."

By my third and fourth appointments, the counselling was helping.

"The care and concern you have for your son is obvious," she said. "I think," she paused, "that rather than history *repeating itself,* it's actually a cruel irony that you've had both a mother *and* a son who have treated you as they have."

My eyes burned with tears. "History *has* repeated itself. But not in the way the so-called *specialists* are saying."

"What do you mean?" She leaned forwards in her chair.

For several moments, I searched for the right words. "I was *forced* to be apart from my family as a kid. I *had* to stay in my room and eat on my own. Tom excludes *himself.*"

"Go on."

"My mum would only let me in the house when my dad was in. No matter what the weather, I was locked out. So now, when I'm worrying about where Tom might be at night, and I'm listening to the wind or rain, it's harder because I was *made* to go out in weather like that."

She nodded. "I can see how that would be difficult for you."

"I do want the best for him. I'm terrified that one day I'm going to get a visit to say he's dead or something. Sometimes I wish the courts would lock him up. At least then I'd know he was safe."

"Does he ever open up to you? Or say anything about what's going on for him - perhaps where he is at night?"

"He hardly acknowledges me these days. But he's having sessions with a male specialist at the Child and Adolescent

Mental Health Service; when I can get him there. Usually, he kicks up a stink about going."

"Are you part of that?" She wrote something down.

"No, I was to begin with, but it wasn't working out. I was being blamed for the lot. Now, he's supposed to go on his own. I drive him and wait in the car, but every bribery tactic is needed to get him in the car in the first place!" Despite the angst, I smiled.

"Why do you think they were blaming you?" She tilted her head to the side.

"Because it's easier. Finding answers within Tom is too difficult. It's easier to point the finger at the mum who's had a rough childhood *herself* and had a baby when still young. To be honest, I can't believe how they've talked down to me. They've made their minds up without talking to any of Tom's family, like his dad or stepparents."

"How's things with his stepdad? Martin, isn't it?"

It might help me to let things out. After all I was in a confidential counselling session.

"Martin acts like he's doing me a favour by staying. He's said no other bloke would put up with Tom."

"How do he and Tom get on?"

"They don't. It's hell. But whilst Martin's around, Tom has a bit of a deterrent."

"Is that the only reason you stay with him?"

I pause. I'd not considered this before. "I do love him, I think. I mean, we've been together a long time and we've been through a lot."

"But?"

"I'm not in love with him. I don't respect him, and he drinks too much. With him and Tom, home is somewhere to be avoided. Luckily, I've got friends and family I can escape to when I need to. Now that I'm signed off work, I tend to stay out of the way through the day, but I've got to be home in the evening to keep Alex in his routine."

"It all sounds hard. You talk about spending time with Alex – do you ever get chance to spend time with Tom?"

"I've tried. I really have. He's not interested." I thought back to the time when we had tried to spend time together on a regular basis. It only happened twice.

"If Tom *was* to open up, and you had the chance to make him really listen, what do you think you'd say to him?"

"I guess the main thing is *please don't throw your life away."* I looked at her. "He could have a really good life if he wanted it. He's bright, intelligent, not to mention a lovely looking lad and really, I'd support him to the end of time if he'd give me the chance."

"And what would you hope to say to him in the future?" Her hand gestures supported her as she spoke. "Let's say in about ten years from now."

"I want to be proud of him; I never have been proud. That's terrible isn't it? I'd love to be able to say. *I'm proud of the way you've turned your life around.*"

"You've shown with what you've said, that it's not all doom and gloom." She smiled.

I shook my head. "But it's all one-way. He doesn't care about *me* or even his little brother." My voice trailed off. "He wants whatever he can get. I honestly can't see him *ever* turning his life round or there being an end to any of it." A tear plops onto my skirt. I'm surprised by it as I didn't realise I was crying. "He's going to drag me, well all of us, down with him."

"You've mentioned feeling *dragged down* or being frightened of being *dragged down* several times." She passed me another tissue. I wondered about *her* then. It's one way, is counselling. I wanted to ask her if *she* had kids but realised that wasn't how it all worked. "What do you mean by being *dragged down*? What is it that you're scared of?"

"Depression, I guess. It's bad enough already - I can't let it get any worse." My voice shook. What I needed was a good cry really.

"You're stronger than you think," she said. "Surely you can see that?"

I shook my head. "I'm worried I'm not being a good mum to Alex. I worry about us being kicked out of our house or not being able to get back to work. I've no confidence anymore – I can't even walk down the street." The appointment was coming to an end. "All the neighbours are talking about me."

"But you're not just Tom's mum. You've got to keep hold of that. You're Sarah too."

THE GP (AGAIN)

"I WANTED TO SEE YOU STRAIGHTAWAY," the GP said, pointing to a chair. "Have a seat."

I waited for her to continue as I sank down and rested my bag in my lap. "Is it about the referral?"

"Yes." She took a long breath. "I've had a bit of a shock, to be honest."

"Why?" I was momentarily hopeful. "Are they offering some help?"

"No." Her face bore a strange expression. "Quite the opposite. As I promised, I rang them and went over the situation with a 'duty' social worker. She told me that they wouldn't be pursuing the referral."

"Why not?" I fiddled with the strap on my bag.

"Mainly because Tom is nearly sixteen." She paused. "I explained about your family being at breaking point and needing respite." She lowered her eyes. "The woman I spoke to was unhelpful. Eventually, realising I was getting nowhere, I asked to speak to someone more senior."

"And?"

"I got the answer you warned me about. They don't do

anything to alleviate situations borne out of behaviour issues; they exist solely to prevent child abuse and neglect."

"I've been told that every time."

"But I wasn't happy, and I made it clear that Alex should be considered with regards to being bullied *and* his older brother's influence. After a while the woman seemed annoyed and told me if I wanted to push things, they, and I'll use her words exactly, *would come and remove the youngest one.*"

"What! She said that! She'd take Alex away!" My heart was thumping, and I felt dizzy. "They won't! They can't! What are they on about?"

"I was shocked too." She fiddled with paper clips on her desk. "When I asked her to clarify what she meant, she repeated that if I wanted to force them down the child protection route, they would remove Alex, not Tom."

"Did you give them any details?"

She shook her head. "Just my name and practice details initially but no, nothing about you, Tom or Alex."

"Can this be left alone?" I heaved a sigh of relief. "I'm scared to death they'll pursue it."

"Don't worry. If they were to come back to me, I'd say the situation has been resolved and we don't require their *help*!" She drew 'air quotes' as she said the word *help.*

"Can you promise me that nothing more will come of this? You've got me really worried."

I had been having enough difficulty with sleeplessness and was to manage on even less now. I had a constant dread lurking within me. *What if they tried to take Alex?* I would rather have died than allow it.

ON HIS OWN DOORSTEP 2

I HAD NOT BEEN in bed long. But after two glasses of wine, I was dozing off but awoke again with a start as the doorbell went.

I tugged a cardigan on whilst glancing at the glow of the digital clock. 11:37pm. *Blimey, he was home before midnight!* That's if it was him, not the police, or a 'hoodie.'

Tom hurtled through the door and past me without a word. He darted into the living room. As I went to close the door behind him, I heard a peculiar popping noise, coupled with an inaudibly angry voice. Tom was peering around the living room curtain.

"What're you doing?"

"Nowt."

Hearing footsteps on the stairs, I realised Martin was on his way down. "Can't you hear what's going on out there?" he said. "It's his bloody mates."

"They're no mates of mine. Not anymore."

There was another similar but louder popping noise, then another. Accompanying them was the sound of shattering glass. Flinging the door open, I was shocked to see two of Tom's friends beating the hell out of the windows of the house opposite us, with what looked like broom handles.

"Stop it, you idiots!" I belted towards them in my pyjamas. Somebody had bought this house. Even the 'sold' sign had been uprooted. They had battered three out of the four front facing double-glazed units. One of them held his broom handle towards me whilst the other commenced work on the fourth window.

I stared into his glassy eyes. Something other than rage was clearly powering him. "You don't scare me, you know. You're just a little lad. Won't your mum be wondering where you are."

"Get Tom out here!" He demanded.

"Why?"

"Just get him out here!" He was frothing at the mouth. The ghostly faces of our next-door neighbours were visible, observing the 'action' from their upstairs window.

There was only me who'd had the nerve (some might say stupidity!) to try and stop these lads before they wrecked more houses or cars.

"Put the stick down!" Martin strode towards the one still trying to demolish the fourth window. "You're both off your heads. You're going to be in some right shit if you don't stop it!"

He paused for a moment, "I want Tom. Get him out here now!" Another swipe of his broom handle popped the final unit.

"He's a pussy!" Stated the other, swaying as he spoke.

"What do you mean by that?" I was curious as to what role Tom had played in causing this.

"Keep em talking," Martin hissed into my ear. "I've rung the police."

The one who finished the final window off sloped down to the ground. For a few moments, we all stared at one another, as if wary of each others next move.

Then I remembered. '*The security guard!*' Without uttering a word to anyone, I tore off; slightly impeded in slippers, towards the apartment in which he was usually 'holed up.' Again and again I rang the doorbell. A dim light flickered above. No answer. I began hammering on the door.

"Call yourself a security guard!" I bellowed up at the window. "What a joke!"

At that moment it was flung open. "What you on about? I'm only on duty till midnight. It's past that now."

"So you sit back whilst idiots smash in one of the houses? You're a disgrace. You should be sacked!"

"I didn't hear owt!"

"Course you didn't! Well you'd better shift your lazy arse out here and help us keep hold of them till the police get here?"

"I'll be down in a minute." His head disappeared and the window slammed.

It was more like five minutes before he turned out to help. There was still no sign of the police that Martin had dialled 999 for. Both teenagers seemed subdued. One remained slumped on the ground and the other was propped against the garden fence. They were simply idiotic boys who were out of their depth *and* their heads.

There was no sign of Tom. Although he had taken no part in the smashing of the windows, I suspected he must be somehow responsible for the aggravation of these boys. The way they had pursued him up our street suggested so anyway.

"What have you taken?" The 'slumped lad's' face had turned visibly paler in the light of the streetlamp.

"A bit of this." He struggled to focus on me. "A bit of that. Dunno. Can't remember."

"Why've you done this?" Martin gestured towards the smashed windows. The *security guard* stood over him, in case he made a bolt for it. But to be honest, I doubt he would have had the energy.

"My head went." His head was lolling to one side. "Can't take the pressure anymore."

Twenty minutes after Martin had made the call, the police finally appeared in a riot van.

"Fucking bitch. You never said you'd rung the filth!" Martin battled to keep a grasp on him as the van screeched up. The security guard caught hold of the other one as he tried to get to his feet. Three policemen leapt out of the van and sprinted towards us.

"About bloody time too," I clapped my hands. "It's lucky we've done your job for you and managed to keep hold of them."

Two officers had one of the lads pinned to the floor. His limbs were flailing in all directions. Clearly, he had got a burst of energy from somewhere. As they leant on him, one of them plucked an aerosol from his pocket. I realised it was CS gas.

"No!" I said, "Don't spray him."

His finger poised over the trigger of the can. "Surely three of you can get handcuffs on two drugged up lads, without having to resort to that."

The aerosol was replaced in his pocket. As the handcuffs were clicked on, all fight seemed to drain from the lad, like a washed-up fish.

In contrast, his mate was going quietly.

"Can I have a drink of water?" he seemed to be directing the request at me. "I feel like crap."

"Can you hell." The security guard yanked him towards the van by the hood. "You're off with them."

"Just a minute. I'll get him one." Crossing the road to our house, I found Tom still cowering behind the curtain.

"You've got some explaining to do." I walked past him towards the kitchen.

The two lads were taken off and an officer came inside to take a statement.

Tom feigned complete ignorance to the situation and claimed not to even know the lads, even though I knew that they had called for him on several occasions.

"Can I ask," the officer turned to me as I showed him out, "Why did you prevent us from gassing that thug...and give the other one a drink?"

"They didn't seem in control of their actions, not from what I saw. I've got two lads myself. And that's what *they* are." I glanced across the road at the damage they had caused. "Under all that crap, they're still someone's boys."

FACTS ABOUT ME

<u>ALEX, aged 8</u>

1. My favourite place to swim is Waterworld.
2. I like to spend time on my PlayStation.
3. I am a member of Club Penguin.
4. I enjoy going to cubs.
5. I have got a cute dog.
6. I have got the worst brother in the world.

<u>Why My Brother is the Worst Brother in the World</u>

1. He has stolen many things from me.
2. Yesterday, he slammed the door on my head.
3. I don't like him anywhere near my dog.
4. Because of him, we only have half a happy family.
5. Even my teachers know about him.
6. He hurts me and squashes me.
7. He says things that are unkind and swears.
8. He watches weird TV shows and won't let me watch anything.

9. He takes my PlayStation so he can have a go.
10. He is awful to my mum.

GRAPPLING FOR SURVIVAL

"WHAT'S WRONG WITH YOUR NOSE?" Martin screwed his up. "I can't believe you can't smell it!"

I wrenched laundry from the machine. "I can."

"So what're we going to do?" Standing with his hands on his hips, he studied me as though I should have a solution.

Exasperated, I abandoned the washing basket, stormed upstairs and began thumping at the bathroom door.

"Get rid of that now! Or I'm ringing the police!"

"Course you are!"

I am not sure what was worse; the stink of cannabis, or the smell drifting from his bedroom. The door was wide open, emitting potent deodorant, stale socks, sour milk, old food and who knows what else. It looked like a cesspit.

Only the day before, Tom had moaned there were no glasses in the kitchen. I counted nine in his bedroom now. All partially filled with rotten milk or spat in. Cigarette ends floated in three of them. The floor was strewn with rubbish and laundry. His bin overflowed with half-eaten food. Even his sheets were covered in spilt food and cigarette burns. It had been two weeks since I had attempted to restore any order in there.

"Are you mad?" Martin had asked, watching me gag as I scrubbed an undistinguishable substance off his windowsill. "He's going on for sixteen. If he wants to live like a pig, then let him." I wondered sometimes whether Martin would ever say anything kind or supportive to me, about anything.

For two weeks I had resisted the urge to go in there, even to remove pots, rubbish and clothes. Deep down I knew Martin was right. I clicked the door shut and returned to the kitchen, furious.

"Sarah, calm down!" Martin poured me some wine.

"How can I? Have you seen the state of his room?" I threw my hands in the air. "Or smelt the stink up there? I've got an asthmatic son asleep in the next room! It's not as if Tom can even be reasoned with. He does what he wants. I want him out of here! I do! I've had enough!"

"What are you playing at Tom?" Martin asked when he appeared in the kitchen a short time later.

"Smoking a bit a weed in the bath." He flung the microwave door open to inspect his evening meal.

"*My* bath, *my* house!" I rammed a pan into the dishwasher. Martin shot me a look.

"If I smell it in my house again, it won't be *me* banging on the door." I banged the dishwasher shut. "It'll be the police."

"It's a bit of fucking weed!" He swung the microwave door till it slammed closed.

"It's a class B drug!" I wrestled with the urge to throttle him. For slamming the door, smoking drugs and being a general shit.

"You chat shit Mum." The microwave binged. "You don't know what you're on about. They'd have to find it on me first."

"Just get your tea and quit while you're ahead Tom."

As his tea reheated, Tom started opening and closing doors to the cupboards and the fridge.

"What're you looking for now?"

"Summat to eat."

"You've got a pork chop meal warming in there." I pointed at the microwave. "You don't know how lucky you are, having a meal waiting for you every night. It was cooked over four hours ago. I must be a right mug!"

Smirking, he stuffed two bags of crisps into one pocket of his 'trackies' and a handful of biscuits into the other. He added three yoghurts, an ice lolly, two bananas and a breakfast bar to his tray. I then observed as he filled a pint glass till it was brimming with milk, then greedily necked it and refilled it again.

I jumped slightly as the microwave pinged. The pork chop aroma had overcome the chemical cannabis smell. Adding the steaming plate to his laden tray, he headed towards the stairs.

"Are you sure you've got enough to eat Tom?" I stared at his tray in disbelief. "I wouldn't want you to be hungry or anything."

"Leave it Sarah," Martin shook his newspaper open. "It's the cannabis making him think he needs all that. You should be used to it by now."

Another plate and glass to add to his collection. I fumed, whilst also worrying that the consumption of so much food and milk at one sitting might make him sick in the night.

My heart sank the next morning because it was only 7.20 am when I heard Tom banging around. I preferred for him to sleep in. I got dressed, knowing he would be downstairs, bullying Alex if I left them unattended. However, I wasn't fast enough! Hearing him bawling and swearing, I hurtled towards the stairs. The dog bolted past me on the landing before cowering behind my bed, Alex tore after her, eager to explain.

"Tom was playing with her," he panted. "She was giddy, and she jumped up. I think she hurt his ear with her paw. But it was an accident!"

"So he screamed at her like that! Tom!" I leant over the banister, "please stay away from the dog in future!"

"She's a little bitch!" He appeared at the foot of the stairs. "She's lucky I didn't boot her."

"You hurt my dog and I'll..." gasped Alex.

"You'll what, you little div?" Tom took a couple of steps up the stairs but then paused. "Shut your ugly little trap!"

"How can you talk to him like that?" I closed my eyes as if hoping to shut his words out. "He's your little brother!"

"I wish I wasn't." Alex folded his arms. "When I'm older and tougher than him, I'll sort him out then."

At this point, I should probably have offered words of correction, but I could see where he was coming from.

The door banged a short time later, indicating Tom's departure from the house. I heaved a sigh of relief then felt guilty for it. This was my way of life. Relief when he went out, a plummeting heart when he reappeared. It was not right, and these feelings provoked continual guilt within me. Sagging down next to the patio doors I basked in the peace. This was to be shattered by the barking of the dog. My cup clattered to the floor as I startled when noticing a youth, about Tom's age, scaling along the high wall which bordered my back garden.

"What do you think you're doing?" I flung the door open.

"Looking for me bike."*

"Did you not think to ring the doorbell and ask rather than trespassing?"

*We had warned Tom that no bikes were to be brought back to our house. There had been three in as many weeks, probably stolen.

FEAR OF REPRISALS

NOVEMBER 2009, (15 YEARS, 11 MONTHS)

I WAS LIVING on a knife edge. Each time collective voices gathered outside, it seemed to yield a gang of hooded youths. Sometimes Tom was among them, at others it would be his 'friends' calling for him. Although they didn't actually *call,* instead they would manically rev their car engines in the street.

I leapt at the sound of the ringing doorbell, answering the door to yet another policeman. I scanned the street for onlookers as I asked him in.

"What's he done now?" I switched off the TV.

"We've had a complaint from the owner of the off-licence." The policeman loomed large in my living room doorway. "Apparently Tom has been captured on CCTV concealing two large bottles of cider under his jacket."

"Oh, for God's sake!"

"The shopkeeper was too afraid to challenge him. Apparently, there was a large gang of them outside the shop. So he rang us instead."

"Well I don't know where he is right now. I can let you know when he gets back."

"That won't be necessary. The shop keeper doesn't want to press charges." "Why not?"

"He's scared of what might happen." He shrugged his shoulders. "Having his windows put through, that sort of thing." "That's dreadful. God, I'm so ashamed of him." "Well that's why I'm here." He ventured further into the room. "To give you the opportunity to put things right. If you cover the cost of the cider, no more will be said."

"Are you joking? So he thieves and I reimburse it." I pointed at myself. "But he'd do it again. It could even become an informal arrangement between me, him and the shopkeeper!" I laughed, hollowly. "No! I'll tell him to go back and pay back the cost of the cider himself, but I certainly won't be covering it!"

"Do you think he'll agree to that?"

"Of course not! Which is why the shop keeper should press charges. And you should make sure he and his shop are protected. Let the courts bloody deal with him!" "Well, we can't force him to press charges. But I'll have another word."

In the end Martin went around to speak to the shop keeper. Tom, of course, had laughed in our faces when we had told him to pay for what he had taken.

"Don't ask for a penny for the rest of the week," I said. "I'll be giving the money to the shop instead."

He didn't seem to care. As soon as my back was turned, he took my bottle of wine and several cans of beer from the fridge, as well as two of Martin's new Blu-ray DVD's.

Martin was red-faced when he returned from the shop.

"Do you know how embarrassing that was?" He slammed the door. "You can go next time."

"I'm sorry." I dropped my hands into my lap.

"*You're* his mother."

"I couldn't have gone in. I'm too ashamed."

"Well the little shit has been back in the shop today. I don't know how he has the nerve. When they refused to serve him, he spat at the window!" His voice was ascending with every word. "I'm off to the pub."

I was glad. I hoped he'd never come back. I often dreamt of a quiet home for me and Alex. Home should be a place of sanctuary. Mine was hell.

A LOSING BATTLE

Tom yanked a glass from the cupboard. "Why're you so tight?" And banged it onto the worktop. "It's only a pair of fucking trainers."

"You don't deserve them. Get off your backside and find a Saturday job. You want trainers." I slammed the bottle of squash in front of him. "You buy them."

That evening he returned home wearing muddied socks.

"Where're your trainers?" I glanced up from my magazine.

"I lost em."

I laughed. "How do you lose a pair of trainers?"

"I got em stuck in mud." He peeled his socks from his feet.

"Well, you'll have to wear your old ones." Trying to feign an air of indifference, I returned to my magazine.

"I sold em to my mate ages ago."

"Tough." I was bubbling with fury, though I wasn't showing it. "You think you can chuck a perfectly good pair of trainers away and I'll buy you new ones." My blood pressure must have been going through the roof!

"Sarah, you thick cow." Martin slammed the remote control

down. "He's not *lost* his trainers. They'll be in the garden somewhere."

"They're not," Tom asserted, with a smirk.

"Don't speak to me like that," I hissed at Martin then I turned to Tom. "Well, you're gonna be walking around in your socks, aren't you?" I nodded towards the pair he was clutching.

"Well I won't be going anywhere." His face reddened as he raised his voice. "Not to school, or to my appointments. I'll be here," his finger pointed towards the floor. "And I'll follow you around the house all day, making your life hell until you sort them for me."

"Get out of here now!" I yelled. "Either up to your room or out of this house. I've had enough!"

"I'm not going nowhere." Tom threw himself into the chair. "Not till you get me my trainers."

I stood my ground for two days. Tom's old trainers never reappeared. Some pristine new ones did though. Tearing the box open, Tom grinned. I couldn't believe Martin had gone against me; it was a further two days before I spoke to either of them.

AT RISK OF LOSING ANOTHER HOME

Dear Mr and Mrs Pearson,

We refer to the anti-social behaviour contract that was signed by yourselves when your son, Thomas, first offended last year. Despite the cautions that police officers have issued, Thomas continues to behave in a way that contravenes the terms of the behaviour contract.

We would draw your attention to the following behaviours, many of which are affecting the local community and have invited complaint:

- Using foul and offensive language whilst in public
- Climbing on the property of other people.
- Entering private gardens.
- Graffiti.
- Acting in a drunk and disorderly fashion.

- Urinating against people's fences.

He has recently been the subject of a complaint where a local resident, upon finding Tom in his garden, was verbally abused. He was then subjected to Tom urinating against his front door after he had returned inside.

You will agree that this form of behaviour in the local community is unacceptable and as such, we have a duty to inform your landlord. As you will no doubt be aware, you are responsible not only for your own conduct, but for that of anybody who resides with you or visits you.

The next step in our proceedings will be to refer your family with a view to obtaining an anti-social behaviour order. This may result in the loss of your tenancy as you will be in breach of your tenancy agreement.

You may, at this point, wish to take advice from a solicitor or the Citizens Advice Bureau.

Yours sincerely

Anti-Social Behaviour Unit.

DON'T CALL ME MUM!

NOVEMBER 2009 (15 YEARS, 11 MONTHS)

The following morning, I dropped Alex at school before setting off on the ten-minute drive towards Tom's pupil referral unit.

"Stay there," I ordered as he unclipped the seatbelt to get into the front seat after Alex had got out. "I don't want you sat at the side of me. Not after the letter I've had!"

"I don't even know why you're taking me to fucking school." He rammed his fist against the back of the passenger seat. "I'm not going in." He was always at his absolute worst on a morning and had, today, surfaced from his room in the darkest of moods.

"You *are* going in!" I pulled up at a junction and glared at him. "Do you think I can cope with *you* at home all day?"

"Well you'd better be giving me some money then." Sliding back in his seat, he folded his arms.

"You must be joking." My voice rose. "After the letter we've had?"

"*What* letter?"

"Weren't you listening last night? The letter threatening to throw us all out."

"Oh that letter. Nah, I wasn't listening." He looked out of the window.

"I thought you were ranting again."

"Ranting!" I slammed at the button for the car radio to turn it off. "I have every right to. I'll give you ranting."

"So do I get some money or what?" He leaned forward again.

"Tom, do you realise what you're doing to us?" I was struggling to concentrate. "We might all be getting kicked out because of you."

"You're chatting shit again Mum." He looked impatient. "Course we won't get kicked out."

"After the way you've been carrying on." Wrenching the letter from my pocket, I hurled it into his lap. "What'll we do if we lose our house? I can't believe you don't care about it!"

"I want some money." He didn't look at the letter. "I'm not getting out of this car until you give me some!"

"You bloody are!"

"Make me."

"Tom you're getting no more money out of me. You can forget it."

"Fucking tight bitch!" He booted the back of my seat.

Screeching the car up at the side of the road, I lashed out behind me but missed him. "I'm sick of you *abusing* me." I began to cry, mainly with suppressed rage. "I can't take any more of you."

"Stupid cow. Sort yourself out."

"How can you talk to me like that?" I rested my arms, then my head against the steering wheel. "I don't know how you live with yourself."

"Quite easily."

"You'll know about it when you're older and you don't have anyone." I wrenched my head back up. "You're a nasty piece of work! Don't think I'll put up with this forever." I drove the final stretch in silence. Pulling up outside the pupil referral unit, I waited. "What are you doing?"

He did not move. "I'm not getting out. Are you deaf or summat?"

"Get out of this car before I launch you out!" I thumped the steering wheel.

"Give me some fucking money Mum, now!"

"***Don't call me mum!*** Don't you *bloody* call me mum! You've no right. Not with the way you treat me."

In the end I hurled four-pound coins through the window of the passenger seat. He darted from the car to gather them up, allowing me the opportunity to speed away without having to hear what he shouted after me. Hatred bubbled up and escaped through my eyes as tears. I hated him but hated myself more for hating him. *What sort of a mother was I?*

In a trance, I drove on. There was no way I could go on living with him. Bit by bit, I was being destroyed. At that moment, I decided to *force* the authorities to help. Yes. I would inform them that he could not return home that evening. That I had reached breaking point. It would be better for us all this way. Especially him.

If you flick back to the beginning of this book, part of the phone call I made is included there.

LETTER TO THE MP

18 November 2009

DEAR MR GREGORY,

Your secretary has advised me to provide information about my circumstances prior to our meeting.

I live on the edge of your ward and I rent my house through a housing association. My problem is anti-social behaviour perpetrated by youths in the area, of which my 15-year-old son is one of the ringleaders.

Eighteen months ago, at our previous address, my son began to offend. Firstly, he burgled our next-door neighbours and was arrested. He was about to be released due to lack of forensic evidence and the police were struggling to charge him, so they asked me to speak to him.

I persuaded him to 'do the right thing' and own up. Because of this admission, he was brought to court. However, the court ordered me to pay compensation of £600 to our neighbours and Tom was barely punished.

He then went on to cause over £500 of criminal damage. This was in addition to all the other anti-social behaviours he was displaying in and around the home. This swiftly resulted in a written contract having to be drawn up with the anti-social behaviour team.

Our landlord also asked us to leave the property.

We moved to our new home over a year ago, a move that we were delighted with. However, Tom has quickly acquainted himself with the local delinquents, and we have been issued with a written warning regarding his anti-social behaviour which has included being drunk, causing trouble around people's homes, burglary of a shop, shoplifting and urinating against people's doors. We have been told that further behaviour of this kind will result in us losing our tenancy.

We will be deemed to have made ourselves intentionally homeless as we have failed to control our son, therefore will be unable to secure future social housing.

Since this written warning, Tom has continued to shoplift, drink excessively and has been brought back on several occasions by the police. At the weekend, we discovered that a further complaint will now be made to the anti-social behaviour team. The police state that Tom is not a follower within this gang; he is one of the instigators.

In the last eighteen months, I as his mother, have attended the police station with him to act as his appropriate adult about nine times and have been to court on fifteen occasions. The court have given him supervision and tagging orders, both of which he has breached time and time again, landing him back in court and in turn, forcing me to have to pay the costs. The court have not punished him at all for his crimes.

The rest of us, as a family are law abiding people and have struggled with Tom since infanthood. Even back then, he was hyperactive and destructive. School have also battled with him and by high school he was causing vandalism, truanting, bullying, fire setting and smoking cannabis in school. He has no respect for authority and will be verbally abusive when challenged. He now attends a pupil referral unit, having been excluded from school.

This is also the case at home. He bullies his younger brother and is severely abusive to me. This has several times resulted in him issuing threats or causing damage. He towers over me and intimidates me.

We have tried to ensure he complies with his court orders and have attempted every imaginable way of keeping him in the house at night so he cannot go out causing trouble. If we try to ground him, he laughs in our faces so I gave him a financial incentive for him to come in on time, in the hope that it may engage him more: 10pm weekdays and 11pm weekends.

After the house is locked up for the night, Tom frequently uses knives to unscrew the window locks and escape.

In addition, he steals from us. We keep valuables with us and lock things away such as the laptop and camera. Tom has sold most of his own possessions and many of ours. A couple of these thefts were reported to the police, but we were made to feel like time wasters.

Over the years we have seen various child psychologists and specialists; sought help from the 0-19 team three times, the Child and Adolescent Mental Health Team twice, we've been let down by the courts, although the Youth Offending Team is supportive.

Social Service's help has been repeatedly sought, especially since Tom's conduct, particularly at home, has a negative effect on my younger son. My GP tried to obtain help for us with Tom from Social Services recently but was informed that if she wanted to pursue the case for my younger son, social workers would simply come and remove him.

I feel desperately 'failed by the system' and am worried about the threat of us losing our home. I have employed many approaches, both recently and in the past but our family is now at breaking point. Tom loiters around outside our house with large gangs of hooded friends and we are obviously finding ourselves ostracised from our neighbours. Attempts to move his friends on are met with threats and taunts.

As the local MP; you will be aware of the problem with anti-social behaviour and will be keen to deal with it. If we were a family condoning his behaviour, I would expect eviction from the community. But we are as powerless as the local shopkeeper who dares not press charges against those who shoplift from him in case his shop windows are smashed.

Many people have suggested I contact you for assistance. I do not know what to do next and hope you may be able to advise me further.

Many thanks in anticipation of your help and your time, I look forward to meeting with you.

Yours sincerely, Sarah Pearson

I am not sure what I was hoping to achieve with this letter. But I'd fruitlessly sought help from my GP, Social Services, The 0-19 Team and The Child and Adolescent Mental Health Service. I felt utterly failed by the judicial system and had eventually been advised by various quarters to try our local member of parliament.

Anti-social behaviour was riding high in the media and was rife within our local community. I was sure the MP would be interested in being instrumental in 'stamping it out' within his ward. After all, there was an election looming.

And what better person to have on board for him, than a parent of one of the troublemakers?

"I hope you don't mind me bringing my little boy along?" We sank into the thick carpet. Wax polish and expensive aftershave hung in the air. The MP sat behind his desk, sparkling under a grand chandelier.

"It's always a pleasure to meet my younger constituents." He offered Alex a handshake. "So, how can I be of assistance?"

"I left a letter with your secretary last week," I explained as Alex and I sat. "Our situation would take so long to explain, that the allocated ten minutes wouldn't be enough time. I thought it would help if you already had background information so were aware of our situation before meeting us."

"Ah yes, the antisocial behaviour problem." Glancing at the timer before him, his brow furrowed. "I'm afraid I haven't had the opportunity to read your letter in depth. How old is your son again?"

"Nearly sixteen. I've already dragged him to a multitude of specialists and got nowhere." Raising my eyes from the lacquered table, I allowed my eyes to meet his. "You're my last hope."

"Well, I'll do what I can, of course." He clasped his fingers together on the table. "But I'm not sure what I can ..."

"It's not as if we've brought him up like this," I persisted.

"We've tried everything with him. Now he's a teenager, he's becoming unstoppable. And it's worse now he's hanging about with similar lads. They all want stopping." I was gabbling. It was partly nerves, and partly because of the time constraint. "I'm suffering as much as everyone else in the neighbourhood, if not more!"

"Does he have any sort of criminal record yet?"

"You could say that!" Despite the desperation I felt, I laughed. "It's all in the letter I wrote you. But the police and the courts have done nothing apart from punish *me*!"

"I'm not sure whether-"

"We're going to lose our home!" I was hardly pausing for breath. "They all hang about outside! The police have informed us he's on their 'hit list' for eviction from the area. I don't know what we'll do if we're evicted."

"It doesn't seem fair that an entire family should lose their home because of one individual. When is he sixteen?"

"In two months." Glancing at Alex, who was perched quietly beside me, I felt guilty at him being there and having to listen to this conversation, however, there had been no one to look after him.

"Ah, well then," the MP slapped his hand upon the table. "The answer's staring at us. He can secure independent accommodation when he reaches sixteen."

"It's not as simple as that. Who on earth would give a tenancy to a sixteen-year-old?"

"Is there any family who'd take him in?"

"No."

At least the man was attempting to *sound* helpful! But he was floundering. The outcome I had been seeking was that he would want to throw his weight behind us; and perhaps have influence with the police and housing office.

"Leave it with me." He rose to shake my hand again. "I'll have a thorough look at your letter, make some enquiries and get back to you, hopefully with answers or at least a bit of advice."

I heard nothing further. I sent an email via his secretary but did not get a reply either. Obviously, the MP was not unduly concerned about antisocial behaviour in his ward.

ARREST NUMBER 9

It had been an exasperating morning; supply teaching with an impossible class. I escaped with my lunch and my book to the tranquillity of the car, rather than encounter a staff room bustling with strangers.

My need for solitude was probably associated with my poor confidence; a street-full of condemning neighbours and a lifetime of being ostracised. These combined elements had ensured that my self-esteem was now at an all-time low.

Chewing on my sandwich in the silence, I decided to ring Martin to check on things at home.

"You must be telepathic." He answered on the first ring. "I was about to call you. Are you on your own?"

"I'm in the car." I fiddled with the half-eaten sandwich in my lap. "Just having my lunch. Why, what's up?"

"He's been arrested again. His school have been on the phone."

"Oh, bloody hell!" I leaned my head backwards against the seat. "What's he done now?"

"School found a top-of-the-range sat nav and BlackBerry phone on him; they wanted to know what Tom was doing with these things so I told them he must have nicked them. Apparently, they were going to confiscate them and let the police know. He's then tried to do a runner, but they've managed to hang onto him till the police got there."

"Here we bloody go again! Another evening of fun and games." Catching sight of my reflection in the rear-view mirror, I noticed the shadows beneath my eyes.

"Apparently the stuff has been pinched from a car around the corner from our house. It'd been left in the car. He was probably planning to flog it after school."

"But they've got it back now?" I picked at my sandwich.

"Yeah but they're gonna be asking him about other car thefts that have gone on around here. They say there's been a few."

POLICE SEARCH 2

DECEMBER 2009, (15 YEARS, 11 MONTHS)

"WE NEED to search your house, I'm afraid. It shouldn't take too long." Extracting two pairs of rubber gloves from her bag, the policewoman passed a pair to her male colleague without looking at me. "Have you had your house searched before?"

I nodded. "Where do you need to look?" I swiftly mentally assessment the state my upstairs rooms had been left in. "Everywhere?"

"Mainly in Tom's bedroom." As she spoke, she scanned her eyes around my living room. "To be honest, I'm satisfied we won't find any stolen goods concealed elsewhere, aren't you?" She turned to her colleague.

"Well, yes," he agreed as he wiggled his fingers into a glove, "but we still need to have a quick look around."

I led them up to Tom's room.

"Gosh, it's tidy," she remarked as she entered his tiny bedroom.

"You wouldn't have thought that a week ago." I lingered in the doorway, observing as she tugged a box from beneath his bed. "It was an absolute hovel! But we'd run out of glasses and cutlery and I'd got to a point where I couldn't bear *not* to clean it in here. It wasn't a pleasant job."

"Do these belong to him?" She held up the electronic wires and mobile phone chargers that nestled amongst Tom's bits and pieces.

"No. This one says *Tom-Tom* on it." I pointed towards the logo. "So does that one. They would only work with a sat nav. This one looks like a mobile phone charger though." I looked at it. "Nokia. He's never had a Nokia phone."

"Do you know where he got these from?" She reached out and took them from me.

"Of course not!"

"It looks like he's been busy." She turned to her colleague as he ransacked Tom's sock drawer. "Anything?"

"No." He nodded towards the bundle of chargers she clutched. "It looks like that's the lot."

"So, what happens now?" I signed the form consenting for the removal of the wires.

"Well we've got the sat-nav and the phone back. But he'll still be charged with theft. We'll be asking him about these wires as well." She slid them into a polythene bag. "We'll give you a call to let you know when we're ready to interview him. Have you been an appropriate adult before?"

"Just a few times," I groaned.

Flinging the door open, I was curious to see an immaculately dressed, unsmiling woman before me. I had expected the police or someone in a hood.

"I'm here about your son." She looked beyond me. "Is he here?"

"No. He's-," I stopped. "Who are you anyway?"

"I want a word with him." She stepped towards me. "He's robbed our stuff."

"Do you want to come in?" I held the door open. No way was I conducting this conversation in the street. Her perfume drifted up my nostrils as she breezed in and followed me to our lounge. My gaze swept over the dusty TV, discarded magazines and used mugs. *I should've tidied up!*

"Have a seat," I beckoned to a chair.

"No, you're alright thanks." She turned to face me. "I'll stay where I am."

I could feel myself disintegrating.

"You're lucky *I'm* here, instead of my husband, to be honest." Her tone was icy.

"Look, I can't tell you how sorry I am about what he's done." I stared at her patent shoes which burrowed into the carpet pile."School caught him with both items and..."

"The sat-nav *and* the Blackberry?"

"Yes. Luckily. They phoned my husband, Tom's stepfather. They've confiscated the things and told the police."

"Well thank God for that," she sighed. "My husband was facing the sack. There was confidential stuff on that phone. It's not even his, it's the company's. He shouldn't have left it in the car."

"He wasn't expecting my son to come along though, was he?"

"He forgot to lock the car," she continued. "Apparently your son, as well as a few other lads, are prowling around the estate, trying all the car doors."

"Look," I took a deep breath. "The stuff's safe and he's going to be held accountable for it. I'm off up to the station whilst they interview him."

"Do you think I'll get our things back if I go up for them?" Her attitude towards me had softened somewhat.

"I've no idea, but I don't see why not."

"My husband will be relieved. It was hard stopping him

from coming here. He'd have torn your son limb-from-limb. He's fuming, so he still might, you know."

"Listen," I spoke slowly as I sought for the words. "You've got every right to be angry but please talk your husband down?" I looked at her. "We have been to hell and back in the last couple of years with him. We have no idea where it's going to end?"

"I've got a lad myself and he'd never dream of pinching." She looked suddenly haughty.

"He's into cannabis," I said as though that justified things. "We're fighting a battle we can't win. It's not like we aren't trying with him. If he'd been punished by the courts in the first place, we might not be where we are now."

"I feel sorry for you. You seem like a good mother." I could see she was scanning the picture frames scattered around my lounge; smiling images of my sons at varying stages of childhood.

"I'll speak to my husband," she promised, starting towards the door. "We'll get our things back and as long as your son never comes anywhere near us again, that should be an end to it."

"Thanks." I went to show her out. "For being so reasonable."

"I hope things improve for you." She turned back before leaving. "It must be difficult."

"It is." I said, mostly to myself, as I closed the door behind her.

IN COURT YET AGAIN

SCANNING the face of the magistrate, "It's your poor mother I feel sorry for." I tried to work out whether he was being genuine or sarcastic. "Do you suppose she enjoys trudging back and forth to this court, shamed by you, because you have no control over your behaviour?"

"No, and I'm sorry for what I've put her through." Tom was giving an Oscar-winning performance as usual. He stood, like a soldier 'at ease.' "I'm never going to pinch again. I'm glad I was caught, and that they've got their stuff back."

"A commendable speech Thomas. But do you mean it? I've met your sort before. Many a time, unfortunately."

"Your honour," announced a man, rising from the 'prosecution' bench. After being acknowledged, he continued. "The prosecution request that this matter be referred for a pre-sentence report." He cleared his throat. "We think it appropriate that all options be considered now. There are too many previous convictions for this case to be concluded with a simple reprimand and court costs."

The magistrate looked thoughtful as he paused for a

moment. "Am I right in thinking that the stolen property was recovered and returned to its owner?"

"Yes. But we are concerned Tom will offend *again* if this incident is treated more leniently just because the property was recovered."

He nodded. "I will adjourn for two weeks. In this time a pre-sentence report that considers 'all options' will be prepared by the Youth Offending Service. I will take their recommendations."

"All rise." The usher rose to his own instruction.

"You could get sent down Tom," I warned. "You'd better prepare yourself." Leaving the gloomy court room, we emerged in the public waiting area. My eyes strained to catch his expression in the sunlight. It was belting through the glass roof, before bouncing back and forth in the white marble interior where we now faced each other.

"That'd make you happy, wouldn't it Mum?" His face was etched in a scowl.

"Don't be daft. You straightening yourself out would make me happy."

"Don't lie. I'm not bothered if I get sent down anyway. I've got mates in the young offenders' place. It's a piece of piss in there anyway." He grinned. "Just play pool and that."

"Tom." It was a woman from the Youth Offending Team. One who usually saw Tom through rose-tinted glasses.

"Alright love," he grinned, swaggering back towards her.

"I need a quick word. It's about the pre-sentence report." She smiled. "Follow me please."

Obediently, we trailed after her, as though drawn by lengths of string, into the room where Tom had received a 'roasting' after his first ever offence. That seemed long ago now.

"Have a seat." Across the table, she leaned towards Tom.

"Am I gonna get sent down?"

"We've been told to *consider all options* so yes; it is a

possibility, *if* the magistrate decides to go *against* the recommendations of our report. We will be arguing for you *not* to be given a custodial sentence. I don't think it would have a positive effect on your situation at all." She smiled at me then, evidently expecting gratitude.

"Why?" If I was to be honest, part of me wanted him to receive a custodial sentence. Mainly to shock him into sorting himself out, but also to afford us, as a family, some respite. "Every other punishment has been tried with him. Nothing works."

"Have you fucking heard *her?*" Tom would not even look at me. "She actually *wants* me to get sent down. Some fucking mother."

"I don't Tom." I sighed. "I want *you* to get punished for a change. Instead of me."

"We'll be arguing for further reparation and the opportunity for Tom to consider how his behaviour affects others," the woman continued, obviously trying to maintain a balance between us.

"An opportunity for him to *talk the talk*, you mean." Leaning back in my chair, I gave a hollow laugh. "While I get a fine and costs again."

"I know this must all be difficult for you but..."

"You've no idea. I'm sick to death of being dragged to this place and police stations. And getting punished on *his* behalf." I laughed again. "Do you know, I've never committed a crime in my life!"

The court *did* go along with the recommendations of the Youth Offending Team. As predicted, I got costs and a fine. Tom got further reparation, an order to attend a victim awareness course and weekly sessions with a drugs worker. I was heartened about this final sanction but doubted as to whether Tom would engage with help around his drug use.

"You should be thanking your lucky stars you didn't get sent down," I said to Tom as we left court. "For a moment, I thought those magistrates were considering it. Especially when they 'retired' for ten minutes."

"So did I. Thank fuck I'm outta there!" He had more of a jauntiness about his step than when we had first arrived.

"Tom," I cringed as we passed two women. Their disgust at his language was written all over their faces. "Will you stop swearing in front of me?"

"Look at my new trainers," he moaned, ignoring me as he raised a foot from the pavement. "One of em's scuffed! Can you take em back and change em?"

"Don't be daft." Shaking my head, I laughed. "You can't take trainers back because they're scuffed."

He stamped his foot back down. "I've not had em long."

"Look, I didn't want you having them in the first place. And I certainly don't want to discuss them."

For a few moments, we walked side-by-side in silence.

"So, are you gonna give me any money?"

"I can't believe your cheek." I stared at him. "I've just been told to pay over a hundred quid and you're hounding me for money. No chance. Not a good time to ask!"

"Come on Mum." He nudged my arm. "Don't be tight."

"I'm not paying those costs anyway. You are." I pointed at him. "You can have a couple of quid a day until I've got them paid off. Then if you stay out of trouble, I'll up it a bit."

"A couple a quid! What the fuck am I supposed to do with that?"

"I wouldn't knock it Tom. I should be saying that you get

nothing at all." I reached into my purse and plucked out two pound coins. "Here, that's all you're getting."

"You can shove them up your arse!" He slapped at the hand offering the money.

"Fine." Dropping them back into my purse, I snapped it shut.

"I need some fucking money Mum and if you don't give me any I'll-" He stopped dead.

"You'll what?" Slipping my purse back into my handbag, I winched it higher up my shoulder.

"I'll smash your fucking car up!" He flailed his arm in the direction of where I had parked it. "Why are you being a dickhead?"

I swung around and faced him. "I've spent all morning in court, been fined yet again and now you're abusing me." I tried to get around him on the path. "Get out of my way. Get the bus home. You've got a bus pass." I nudged him. "I can't take any more of you!"

"Like the fuck I will, you stupid bitch!" He grabbed my arm.

I swung my bag at him, "Get away from me!" One or two people were watching us. By now I was too angry and upset to care.

"Money or I'm going nowhere!" He still had hold of my arm.

"If you think you're getting in my car you've got another think coming."

"You won't even have a car. I've told you what I'll do." Marching behind me, he was crimson with anger.

"So you're threatening me, are you?" I was so upset, I felt winded. "I've a good mind to report you."

"To the police?" He laughed. "Weirdo! What'll they do."

"Leave me alone Tom." By now I was openly weeping in the street, but I wasn't bothered. "I'm warning you."

"Or what?" He tugged at the strap of my bag. "You'll hit me with your handbag again?"

We reached the car. I tried to get in and lock it, but he jumped into the passenger seat.

"Get out." I pushed at his shoulder. "What did I ever do to deserve a son like you?"

"Get a load of yourself! What a fucking state!"

"You made me like this!"

"Money Mum, then I'll go." He stretched his hand out towards me.

Rummaging in my bag, I fished out a five pound note and thrust it at him.

"Is that it?" He snatched it.

"Get out of the car," I couldn't look at him. I needed him away from me.

I cried the entire journey home; I was surprised I didn't turn the car over. Tears of guilty hate leaked from me. I sobbed so hard that by the time I got home I felt ill.

It was several hours before I dragged myself from the sofa. And only to answer the door. I wondered what bad news it yielded this time.

"Is Tom in?" I looked from one boy to the other. They were younger than Tom. They didn't have a hood between them, and I noticed that they were both wearing 'proper' trousers and smart shoes. Not the usual appearance of someone calling for Tom!

"Er...no. He's not here. Who shall I say called?"

They glanced at each other, looking uncomfortable. Then one spoke. "He's stolen some money."

"Has he?" I leaned against the doorframe. "Do you want to tell me a bit more?"

The other boy looked down. "We don't want any trouble."

"If Tom *has* stolen from you," I folded my arms, "*he'll* be the one in trouble. How much has he stolen?"

"Twenty pounds." He fiddled with the zip on his bag. "My mum's going to kill me."

"How did he steal it? Did you leave your bag somewhere?"

"Kind of." He glanced at his friend.

"When was it taken?" I hoped they would say it was earlier that day, when Tom could not possibly have been anywhere near them.

"About two hours ago."

"Are you sure it was Tom?" I looked at them again. They were at least two years younger than him. "How well do you know him?"

"It was definitely him." The other boy puffed his chest out. "We don't want any hassle; just our money back. Can't *you* give it to us?"

"Me? Why should I?" I stepped back inside my hallway. "If you're telling the truth and Tom *has* stolen your money, then you need to tell the police. You've nothing to worry about. The police will deal with him."

"But *you* won't give us it?" He looked at me.

"No. But, listen, I'm on your side. If Tom's stolen from you, it should be sorted. Let your parents know what's happened. Let them decide. I'm sorry," I flung my arms in the air. "I can't say any more than that."

As they left, I replayed the conversation. *Menacing young boys for money!* I waited for his return so I could confront him.

"It was for cannabis." Tom tugged a bag of crisps from the cupboard. "They wanted me to get em some."

"But that makes you a... a *dealer!*" My hand flew to my mouth.

"How does it? I didn't get em any?"

"So you took their money and kept it?" I slammed the door he had left ajar.

"No, I spent it," he spoke through a mouthful of crisps.

"Well if they've told their parents, you'll be having a visit from the police soon." I glanced up at the clock.

"As if they'll have told anyone." He took a carton of juice from the fridge. "That they wanted to buy weed."

My eyes moved to his feet. "What have you done with your trainers?"

He took a large gulp of juice. "I swapped the scuffed one in the shoe shop." He wiped his mouth. "The one on display was my size, lucky eh?"

I shook my head. He had left court, after making his declarations of 'change,' been vile towards me, fleeced two boys out of twenty pounds and stolen a trainer.

ARREST NUMBER 10

THE NEXT ARREST was at a police station I was not familiar with; in the centre of town, fifteen or so miles from our house.

"We've got him in custody," a male voice said. "We need you here as soon as possible please."

"What's he done this time?"

There was a rustling of pages. "He's stolen a bottle of beer from Sainsbury's to the value of £1.46."

"Pardon?" I wondered if I had misheard. *"£1.46."*

"Yes."

"But it'll cost me ten times that in petrol and parking." I shook my head. "You've got him locked up for £1.46?"

He exhaled. "I agree it does seem ridiculous." His voice held a hint of regret. "If it was his first offence, we would ask you to cover the cost. But because of his already, extensive criminal record, we've *got* to prosecute him."

"I understand."

The city centre police station, like a bustling cattle market, was bleaker than the one he was usually held at. Shouts from cells rattled around the walls. Uniforms swarmed everywhere. A stench of stale alcohol hung in the air, made worse by two drunks I watched being dragged in. They were so drunk, they had to be supported whilst their rights were read.

I studied the list of occupied cells. The spaces next to cells 24 and 41 advised *do not use, to be steam cleaned.* Nice.

I wondered how long I'd be here for this time. Martin had agreed to collect Alex and I passed the time by firing texts off to friends and family I hadn't seen for a while. For some time I'd been considering how many relationships I'd allowed to slide; partly because of time constraints but mostly down to my self-esteem. I hated people coming to the house as it was all too unpredictable. I lived with two angry, bullying males where *anything* could kick off at any time. The friends I had left barely tolerated Tom and Martin, having seen and heard about how I was being treated.

After a while I was joined by a man whose son had been 'wrongly incarcerated after a neighbourly row.' I was treated to a rendition of his entire life story as well as an account of his evening. Nodding politely, I longed to say *get lost* and *leave me alone.* Eventually, a policewoman must have taken pity on me.

"We'll put you in the interview room until we bring Tom through." She led me into one of the all-too-familiar airless green rooms. "I thought you needed rescuing."

"You're not kidding!" I smiled at her. "Thanks!"

An alarm wailed through the station like a wounded animal. The officer, along with an array of identical uniforms ran towards one of the cells. It was like a TV scene. Eventually, she reappeared, with a male officer and Tom, clad in paper trousers. He bowed his head as he followed her into the interview room.

"I'm sorry Mum." He slumped beside me, his paper trousers rustling. "I can't believe I've been caught for something so stupid!"

"It's not about being caught!" I blustered, twisting myself to face him. "It's about stealing in the first bloody place!"

"I know."

"Well this shouldn't take long," the policewoman unwrapped the tape and slotted it into the machine. "Right I'm going to start the tape, then read your rights. Do you need them explaining?"

"No."

"Off we go then." The recording machine emitted a lengthy beep, signalling the interview had commenced.

I listened peripherally as Tom responded to a series of ludicrous questions.

"Did the beer belong to you?"

"Who did the beer belong to?"

"Did anyone say you could take the beer?"

"What did you do with the beer?"

"Were you intending to go back into the shop and pay for the beer?"

"Whilst you are here," the policewoman glanced down at her notes, "we've also been asked to investigate a complaint about the theft of a firework."

"A firework?" Tom's expression hovered between innocence and puzzlement.

"Yes. A *dud* firework." She looked to be stifling a smile. "It was removed from the display of a shop that's opened in your main street. We've got you on CCTV trying to light it sometime afterwards."

"Oh for God's sake!" I wasn't supposed to speak during the interview, but the words came tumbling out.

"Have you anything to say Tom?"

"OK. It was me. But it was my mates too. And it didn't work anyway."

"That's not the point Tom. Stealing is stealing."

Tom was placed back in his cell, pending the CPS's

decision. I resumed my wait on the metal bench. The man from before smiled as I retook my position. His son's predicament had developed in the time that had elapsed. *Come on, hurry up!* I prayed silently as his whisky-laced words washed over me.

"We've highlighted the court date on the sheet," said the desk sergeant, sliding the sheet towards Tom, now wearing his tracksuit bottoms again.

"He's to go to court?" I raised my eyes to the yellow ceiling. "For £1.46 and a dud firework?"

The sergeant then slid another piece of paper towards me, side on.

"For a lad of not even sixteen, his record is astounding." His hand rested on it as he waited for my reaction.

"I know." I scanned the list. "And before you start assuming I'm to blame, this is not how he was brought up. No one else in our family has *ever* stolen a thing."

"It's not just thefts though, is it Tom?" He arched his eyebrows. "Criminal damage, burglary, graffiti, breaches." He whistled. "You've got a hell of a lot of convictions for someone so young."

"I'm gonna sort it out," Tom stated faintly.

"Course you are!" he snatched the sheet back. "I meet your type all the time. You'll be inside by the time you're eighteen. Your sort never learns."

Tom reddened to the roots of his blond hair. He seemed rattled. For a moment I panicked that he might answer back but he didn't. That would have been a sure way to have earned extra time in the cells. Grabbing the summons, I muttered thanks to the man, and shepherded Tom towards the door.

ANOTHER COURT APPEARANCE (LOST COUNT AGES AGO)

THE MAGISTRATE STARED AT US, "Theft of a bottle of beer to the value of £1.46. Stealing a dud firework," and then at the people on the prosecution bench. "Is that it?"

"Your honour," a woman from the bench sprang up like a jack-in-a-box. "He's got a substantial history of different types of thefts. It seemed appropriate to prosecute for these, albeit more trivial acts of theft, too."

The magistrate shook his head as he replied. "What is it you want me to do with him?"

The duty solicitor rose to his feet. "Tom deeply regrets his actions. He recognises that to steal these items was foolish, and indeed occasioned in what he has referred to as *moments of madness.*"

"Indeed," echoed the magistrate twisting towards where we stood. "Have you anything to say for yourself Thomas?"

"I wanna say how sorry I am." Clasping his hands behind his back, he shuffled from one foot to the other. "It was stupid, and I regret it."

"Regret you got caught you mean," the magistrate's voice

had a note of intolerance. "Not only are you a thief, it would seem that you're not actually a *good* one!"

Laughter bubbled within me as an image of Tom permeated my mind; the frustration that would have been upon his face as he attempted to ignite a fake firework!

"And you're his mother?" His voice swiftly quelled my emerging mirth. "How do *you* feel about him stealing?"

I started to get up.

"You may remain seated." I compliantly dropped back into my seat with a thud.

"I am, of course, ashamed of him." I clasped my hands in my lap. "And I can't believe we're here again."

"Quite." He whispered something to the people sat at the bench in front of him.

"All rise." There was a rustle of clothing and a creaking of chairs in response to this order.

"Right Thomas," began the magistrate. "I've decided that in view of the value involved in this theft, I shan't impose any punishment on this occasion. It is, however, imperative," he slapped the heel of his hand onto the desk, "that you continue to comply with the terms of your supervision order."

"I will, I promise," Tom nodded earnestly. "Definitely."

"If you are returned to this court for any more acts of theft, you must be aware that you *will* be leaving here in a prison van."

Tom nodded.

The judge then muttered something else to a clerk. "Court costs in this matter," he continued, averting his eyes towards me, "are payable by the defendant's mother. Please collect the details on your way out."

HAPPY NEW YEAR

(16 YEARS)

Tom

CHRISTMAS WAS SHIT. All I got was clothes and a crap phone. My Mum had gone on one, big time, because I'd taken the mobile she'd bought me, out of her room two days before Christmas. It's not as though I stole it or owt. I just had it a bit early. It was mine wasn't it? She went berserk as usual. I looked in Argos and it only cost fifty notes anyway.

Most of my mates got decent phones and gold chains and that, but not me. Their mums weren't tight like mine. It didn't even have a memory card so I could save some tunes. *What good's that?* So I took her memory card. She doesn't use it anyway. It was a week before she even noticed I'd pinched it.

"What right did you have to take *mine*?" She was always fucking screaming.

"It's not as if you need it, is it?" *Well she didn't.*

"It's got all my photos on," she bawled, frothing at the mouth. "I want it back."

"It's not got 'em on anymore." I turned to walk out of the room. *Oh shit, I'm gonna get it now!*

"You mean you've wiped it?" She looked as though she was in pain.

"Yeah, there weren't many pictures on it anyway."

"How dare you?" *That bloody voice!* "All those pictures of the dog as a puppy, and Alex, and..." *Yeah right. Precious dog. Precious Alex. That's all she bleeding cares about!*

Still, she picked me up after I'd been out on New Years' Eve. I'd been to an all-nighter. It was the bizz. Was still buzzing when her car pulled up. Could nearly block her out going on at me.

"What do you think you're doing reversing bloody charges again?" As usual, she was driving like an idiot. "You've put about twenty quid on our bill in the last few weeks. Where've you been anyway? It's half six in the morning. Don't you think I deserve a lie in on New Year's Day?"

And on, and on. In my head, I tried to replay one of the tunes from the club. Anything to drown the drone of her voice. I should've charged my phone, so I could've plugged myself in to some tunes, and not have had to endure *her.*

"You've bust the fridge-freezer, as well. Leaving the bloody door open all the time. I'd only just been shopping too. We've had to put it all in the shed. You don't give a toss, do you?" And on she went.

I'd had enough of the lot of em if the truth be known. Which is probably why I got wrecked on Christmas day. I drank so much that mum left me with her brother. Said she'd had enough of me. It was him who got me drunk anyway.

He fell out with me the morning after though. Caught me wearing one of his coats under mine. Well he's got loads a stuff, hasn't he? It's not fair. Then he found the pouch of baccy I'd sneaked into the pocket as well.

They all had a right blast at me. Mum's said she won't take me to their house again. Am I bothered?

. . .

On Boxing day, I was dragged to a naff 'family' party. Some old dear that my grandad knows, who's eighty or summat. I wasn't complaining though. Posh house, nice grub and as much drink as you could hold.

Mum went barmy cos I filled my pockets up with a few bottles. Well what am I supposed to do when it's all free? I must have topped up from the night before cos I was soon wrecked again.

Spoiled a family photo! Sweet. Can't help it if I felt sick, can I? Didn't get out of the shot in time. Mum looked like she was gonna die of embarrassment. Serves her right. She couldn't get me into the car quick enough.

"You're a disgrace!" Her anger made her even uglier than usual.

"All right Sarah, calm down." At least Martin was being reasonable for a change. Normally he was a knob head.

"And your language in that house was disgusting!" She whacked her hand against the steering wheel. "You sound as though you come from the gutter!"

"Shut the fuck up you weirdo!" I was starting to feel sick again. No wonder, having a mother like her. "Your voice goes right through me!"

"I can't wait to drop you off at your dad's." She turned to eyeball me, then twisted back to the road. "It's time *he* dealt with you. It's been ten months since you last slept there."

"It's not my fault if he doesn't want me!"

"It is. And I can't say I blame him either."

"That's just it, innit Mum? None of you want me." A wave of self-pity washed away the wave of sickness. "I'd be better off dead." I looked at Alex, the little shit. Mum *never* shouts at him.

"Oh shut up!" But the expression on her face showed I'd made her feel guilty. Sweet.

. . .

Luckily, I made it to the bog when we got to his house. Only just though.

"Thanks a bunch!" I could hear my dad's voice in between my retching. "How the hell's he got into that state? What have you brought him *here* for?"

"He's all yours. I need a break. If only for one night."

She left straightaway. Normally she'd have stayed for a drink so she could slag me off to Elizabeth. Seemed like she couldn't get out fast enough.

I slumped next to my dad, still feeling dodgy.

"You stink!" Was about the only conversation he was offering.

"Chill Dad." I slapped his arm. "I'll be gone tomorrow."

I thought I'd got rid of the silly cow but ten minutes later, I could hear her voice screeching down the phone to my dad.

"Right OK. I'll ask him. Yep. We'll check. Right, we'll have a look. I'll ring you back in a bit." A man of many words, my dad.

"Right mate." He turned to me. "Your mum's pretty upset."

"She always is." I raised my eyes to the ceiling.

"Apparently an expensive phone's disappeared from that birthday thing you were at." His face was fixed on mine.

"And she thinks it's me?" I leapt from the sofa. "Well that's fucking great innit? I get blamed for fucking everything!"

"Stop swearing Tom. That's gonna get you nowhere. Did you nick it or not?"

"No. Course I didn't. I've got a phone! Anyway, there's no point me even saying owt." I stormed towards the door. "Everyone'll blame me anyway! You needn't think I'm off home tomorrow. No way am I facing her, going on at me about it. It wasn't me!" I slammed up the stairs, away from the lot of em.

. . .

So that was it. Christmas and New Year. Another shitty year to look forward to. Me mates mostly had sound families. Not me though. I couldn't stand mine. I couldn't wait to get away from em. Especially my mother. Now that I'd turned sixteen, maybe I could.

LETTER FROM THE CHILD AND ADOLESCENT MENTAL HEALTH TEAM

7 January 2010

Dear Sarah,

We are writing to confirm that we are discharging Tom from our service as he has stopped attending the meetings with his counsellor. We hope this will not stop him accessing therapy in the future if he needs to talk to someone. He would have to do this either via his GP or by accessing other young people's services.

We refer to our previous conversation when we confirmed that the conclusion of our assessment was that Tom did not have any underlying mental health diagnosis. It is our view that the emotional and behavioural difficulties Tom has presented with from an early age, reflects his experiences within your family system. *

We acknowledge this is difficult for you to hear without some sense of blame, which we discussed with you previously, and our hope was that we could support you with thinking about this, in terms of how relationships develop within the family, how this impacts upon the children, and how you might respond to current difficulties within this context.

We know, Sarah, that you experienced a difficult early life history and childhood, and we feel that this has inevitably impacted on your relationship with Tom. We acknowledge it was too difficult for you to engage with any work on this, which resulted in us focusing on individual work for Tom, and we offered him appointments accordingly.

Unfortunately, we are unable to offer any further appointments as he has not attended on a consistent and regular basis. We hope things have improved and we wish you well for the future.

Yours sincerely

Child and Adolescent Mental Health Practitioner

*Blamed again.

IMPOSSIBLE

It was on days like this that I questioned how much longer I could go on.

5.41 am Woken by doorbell. Tom collapses in door, looking like the living dead. Lie awake listening to him clattering around in the kitchen as he reheats his dinner; cooked for him the previous evening.

9.05 am Telephone call from Youth Offending Team to inform me that he missed the appointment that he should have attended the day before. The court summons is on its way.

10.00 am Post arrives. Huge phone bill caused by Tom ringing mobiles and making reverse charge calls. Warning letter due to non-attendance at last reparation session.

10.35 am Tom starts moving around upstairs. Downstairs, I await his arrival on tenterhooks; preparing ourselves for the inevitable bad morning mood.

10.50 am Tom throws Alex out of the chair, snatches the remote control and sits down. Told to *fuck off* when I reprimand him.

11.10 am Whilst I make a drink, he grabs my laptop. When I remind him of the fact that it is only six weeks since I gave him my old laptop, he admits he has sold it.

12.30 pm I feel instantly less on edge as the door bangs behind him. The entire house stinks of Lynx deodorant and the remains of his sullen anger.

12.42 pm Martin discovers that Tom has stolen £10 from his wallet. An argument develops between us.

3.35 pm Tom appears in the kitchen. I interrupt him stuffing his pockets with as much 'convenience' food as possible. He is once again 'off his head.' I avoid confrontation.

7.45 pm He storms past me as I stand in the doorway between our kitchen and lounge. He opens the microwave door before slamming it shut. "Is that it?" He says of his dinner.

7.55 pm I watch sadly as he takes his tray upstairs, preferring to eat alone in his room.

9.10 pm I put my head around his door to offer him a drink. He is asleep.

11.40 pm Engine revs outside our house. Driver repeatedly sounding horn. I open my window and angrily ask the driver of the car what he wants. "Tom," he replies.

Tom bangs around in his room for several minutes before heading downstairs to use a knife for operating the kitchen window lock.

WARRANT FOR ARREST (MINE!)

Magistrates Court

Division: 135 Case Number: 14099875463

A WARRANT HAS BEEN ISSUED in respect of the unpaid sum of £95.03, payable on behalf of Thomas Clifford by his parent Sarah Pearson. The sum of *£95.03, as ordered by the court, is unpaid, therefore this warrant is granted in order that enforcement can commence.

In order to prevent this arrest, you can make full payment quoting the reference above to the Fines Officer. All enquiries regarding this warrant should be made directly to the court. ** Failure to pay immediately will result in your arrest and/or imprisonment if default continues.

Acting Justices' Clerk

. . .

*I *had* stopped paying - a letter had been sent to Tom to say the debt had been cleared. A cheque had even been issued to *him* for £5, in respect of an overpayment *I* had made!

TWO-FACED

FEBRUARY 2010 (16 YEARS, 2 MONTHS)

As it was Martin's fortieth birthday, we had persuaded Elizabeth and Peter to have Tom for four nights, enabling us to go with Alex and the dog to a log cabin in the Lake District. Tom would have been bored rigid and in any case, our previous holiday experiences with him had put me off taking him with us forever.

Even though I was some ninety miles away from him, my handbag remained on my shoulder (this had become ingrained,) and I fretted constantly about what he might be up to and with who. I was paranoid he might break into our house whilst we weren't there or cause mayhem in our street with his mates. Sometimes, I wondered if I would ever relax again.

Elizabeth updated me regularly. As it approached midnight on our second night of freedom, she informed me that he had not yet returned to their house. Knowing the buses would soon stop running, I began to panic. I had visions of him being in trouble or stranded somewhere. Yet obviously I was powerless to do anything.

She texted me soon after to say he had arrived but with a massive gash on his cheek. He seemed drunk or stoned, she said and had told her that he had been in a fight and threatened with a broken glass. I didn't sleep that night.

The next morning, I received another text message. Tom needed stitches but was adamantly refusing to go to hospital. His story had now changed to that he had fallen in the street onto some glass.

OPINION OF MY MOTHER-IN-LAW

Divulged by Martin after a telephone conversation with his mother.

"Well something must have made him like this! Didn't Sarah show Tom enough love when he was younger?"

ANOTHER BREACH CHARGE, ANOTHER COURT APPEARANCE

The Youth Offending Team had begun listing Tom's court appearances on Fridays. His key worker had learned that this was *my* day off so I could not be excused from attending with him. I thought at sixteen-years-old, he should be accountable for his own behaviour. I would have to wait until he reached seventeen for that though.

On this occasion, he was being 'breached' *yet* again for non-compliance with his supervision and reparation orders. I had arranged to meet him outside the courts.

I smelt Tom before seeing him as I walked towards the revolving court doorway. The security officer screwed his face as he began frisking him.

"You'll have to excuse him," I explained. "He must have been spraying testers in Boots. One day he'll learn that less is more!"

The two men did not smile, or even reply. Obviously, someone of my standing did not have the right to be conversing with them. Instead I choked on my own laughter but more probably on the overkill of aftershave. It made my eyes sting as we took the lift to the youth court.

Once outside the courtroom, my mood darkened. Tom was stoned; very stoned indeed.

"Are you stupid or something?" I hissed, my face burning as several people looked at us.

A lady wearing a Youth Offending Team badge came over to us. I'd not seen her before, but she obviously knew who Tom was.

"Don't worry Tom," she sat beside him. "You're going to be fine in there. We'll be arguing for the court to keep an eye on your attendance for a month. They *should* leave it at that. So hopefully they won't be doing anything with you today."

"So, he gets *no* form of punishment for defying his court orders." I leaned forward in my seat so she could see me from beyond where Tom was slumped between us.

"At least he's honest." She patted his shoulder. "When he forgets, at least he admits he's forgotten. He doesn't try to invent an excuse."

"He doesn't forget." I shook my head as I spoke. "He *chooses* not to attend, even though I remind him."

She ignored me. "We've got a soft spot for Tom you know. There's a lovely lad lurking beneath all that bravado."

"Tom Clifford," called a girl who can't have been much older than he was. "Can we have five minutes before you go in? Jennifer Phillips." She offered her hand. "Henry Hague Solicitors."

I shook the manicured hand. "Have I to sit in with him?"

"Of course," she beckoned for us to follow her into the interview room. I was swamped by the waft of sweat which must have lingered from the previous interviewee.

"Right." Her voice was highly pitched. "We're here today on charges of breach."

Tom shifted in his seat, looking as though he was struggling to keep his eyes open.

"Do you accept the charges Tom?" She shifted papers around in front of her.

"Yeah, I forgot about my appointments, that's all." He was barely audible.

"That's rubbish," I tried to nudge him into alertness. "I make sure he's fully aware of his appointments."

"OK." She gave me a strange look. "I think we'll keep that quiet in there! I understand, Tom," she went on, "that you've got a bit of a drug problem. Is that affecting your ability to attend your appointments?"

"I smoke a bit of weed sometimes, that's all." He seemed to be slipping further down beside me. "But I haven't touched it in ages."

"He's talking rubbish." I lifted my eyes towards the ceiling. "He smokes the stuff seven days a week. He's stoned now, as you can see."

"Why are you doing this to yourself Tom?" Her voice was gentle.

"It's my mates and that, innit."

She peered at me through her glasses. "Is he getting any support with his drug problem?"

"We've tried." I sat up straight. "Support can only be given to someone who wants it. He seems to prefer to carry on. He knows there's an alternative."

"Don't chat shit Mum. I haven't touched weed in ages."

"How can you sit there and say that? You're off your head now! How could you be so stupid?" I grabbed his arm. "Turning up here...stoned!" I just wanted to walk out, be like a normal woman of my age, go to the gym, meet a friend for lunch. My life was a relentless round of utter shit.

"I'd like to speak to Tom on his own," said the solicitor. It was a demand rather than a request. She probably knew as well as I did that I was not the best person to be accompanying Tom to court. *How could I be on his side anymore? After all he had and was continuing to put us all through?*

Minutes later they emerged from the room. She indicated for me to follow them into court.

I pottered behind as she lurched in on high heels. The magistrate signalled for everyone to sit, apart from me and Tom.

"State your name," commanded someone from the bench.

"And your address."

"And you are accompanied by-?" He glared at me over gold-rimmed spectacles.

"Sarah Pearson."

"You may sit," he beckoned to me. I dropped to my seat like a stone. "You stay standing," he ordered Tom.

The charges were read then the lady from the Youth Offending Team was invited to speak. I listened attentively as she portrayed Tom as being amenable to work with; honest and committed to sorting himself out; just in with a 'bad' crowd.

The solicitor took over, citing Tom's main issue with attendance as being that his reparation order had to be executed on a Saturday morning. This, she stated, was bound to pose problems given the fact that like most teenagers, he socialised on a Friday night.

Surely, they're not going to find sympathy with that, I thought.

"Remind me what this order was originally imposed for," demanded the magistrate, flicking through papers.

"Your honour." A lady on the prosecution bench rose from her seat. "It was for an act of burglary and a further act of shoplifting in September of last year."

"I see." He rhythmically rubbed at his chin whilst appearing submerged in thought. I watched as he spoke in a low voice with his colleagues. He then cleared his throat and looked towards me.

"It would seem, Mrs Pearson, that an electronic tagging device might be the way forward here. Clearly Tom is struggling to comply with his orders, particularly the one that must be attended on a Saturday morning." He stretched his arms out, then clasped his fingers together in front of him. "If we can ensure he is at home each evening; that would surely sort our problem."

"Am I allowed to disagree?" I stammered, feeling insignificant as my voice echoed around the courtroom.

"Well, yes, you are. It is, after all, *your* home where the equipment would be installed."

"Electronic tagging has been tried twice already." My voice wobbled into the air. "It has resulted in me having to endure a driveway full of hooded youths smoking cannabis and making loads of noise while Tom leans out of his window or the front door to spend time with them.

"I see."

"It makes family relations even worse than they already are. They are already stretched to breaking point."

"Could you elaborate on that please Mrs Pearson?

"Shut the fuck up Mum!" Hissed Tom. From the look on his face, I knew the magistrate had heard.

"You can gather from that sentence, how much respect he has for me." I was feeling a bit braver. "You should hear him at home. The abuse I get is incredible." I took a sharp intake of breath before continuing. "I have a younger son, who's eight. The example Tom sets is terrible; not to mention the bullying he has to endure."

"Stop fucking lying Mum," Tom elbowed me in the arm.

The court was silent. They seemed interested in what I was saying.

"To have Tom at home each evening from 7pm again would be unbearable. He steals and verbally abuses us. His mates are as nasty when they're outside. Our neighbours don't even speak to us anymore."

"Why do you think he's behaving like this?" One of the other magistrates spoke.

"Drugs." The shame radiated from me. I imagined them struggling to make sense of this scenario in their probable sheltered existence. But then, they'd have probably heard it all before. "He steals to fund his cannabis addiction. I've tried to get him help but he doesn't seem to want to stop."

"*Do* you want to stop Tom?" The first magistrate addressed him now.

"Yeah of course I do, but *she* gets on my case all the time." He jabbed an accusing finger in my direction. "She never lets up."

"You wouldn't be the first teenager to say that about their mother," said the same magistrate. "How about school? Do you enjoy school?"

"Yeah, I wanna knuckle down and get good exam results," Tom said. "I wanna go in the army."

"Well, that's a commendable job." All three magistrates seemed impressed. "Do you think you could help him with looking into that, Mrs Pearson?"

"Of course, but if he refuses to even go to school then I don't see how he'll get into the Army." I shook my hair from my eyes. "He failed in mainstream school and has ended up at a pupil referral unit as it is. Look, I'm sorry to sound negative, but you don't know what I've been through. This must be the twentieth time I've been in this court. I've been his appropriate adult at the police station around the same number of times. I've had enough of it all. We're going around and around in circles."

"Have you *always* had problems with him?" The third magistrate spoke again.

"Where do I start? Put it this way, since he was two years old, I've taken him to every specialist known to man. I've never had much help though, which is why we're here today."

I could sense the eyes of the youth offending woman on me. I addressed her directly.

"Look, I can imagine what you're thinking. You might think the sun shines out of his backside. That's because he can talk the talk. What he can't do though is follow it through. You'll all realise it sooner or later. You ought to try living with him. Try having to fit locks on all your doors and take your handbag everywhere, even to the loo." My manic voice reverberated around the room. "I can't even leave Tom unattended with my younger son because he hits him. Then there's the abuse each day because I won't give into his demands for money.

"We're not judging you." The youth worker's voice was gentle. "We can all see you're in an intolerable position."

"We'll retire for several minutes. We need to consider this between us." The three magistrates rose from their chairs and filed out after one another.

"You stupid cow." Tom looked thunderously at me. "I'm gonna get sent down cos of you. Why couldn't you let em tag me?"

"Because I couldn't stand it again! No way! If they do send you down, it's *your* fault, not mine. It's *you* who breaks the law. *You* who commits the crimes." I pointed towards him as I spoke. "You think you don't have to do the punishment though. You've had every bloody chance to sort yourself out!"

The rest of the room was silent. They were probably all judging me. Blaming *me* for his behaviour. Feeling sorry for *him*.

Five minutes was like an hour. Deep down, I *was* worried that what I'd said might be responsible for a custodial sentence.

After all, this was about the eighth time he was before them on breach charges. Surely there was only so many times he could be let off for it.

My stomach lurched as they re-entered the courtroom. Everyone stood. One of the magistrates smiled towards me. *Why is he smiling?* Perhaps I was about to be granted respite? Or maybe he thought I would be relieved that Tom was about to be given another chance?

It turned out to be the latter. He was given further hours of reparation to do and another 'stern' warning.

"We'll be keeping a close eye on you. A note will be kept on your file. You *really* are on your final chance. *Any* more charges, *any* more breaches, you'll be dragged back in front of us, personally. Do you understand?"

"Yes," Tom nodded furiously.

"So, if there *is* a next time, bring an overnight bag with you, as you'll be needing it."

DOES ANYONE EVER LISTEN?

I PICKED UP THE PHONE, "Is that Tom's mum?" I was puzzled as I didn't recognise the voice this time. The call would most likely not be bringing good news.

"Yes." I replied. "Can I help?"

"It's Mr Johnson, head of the learning centre speaking. I'm ringing to let you know Tom's not feeling too well."

It was Monday morning. Tom had hardly been at home all weekend apart from Sunday. He had come in at noon and slept for most of the remainder of the day. Clearly, he had overdone whatever he had been inflicting upon himself. I tried to convey this to the 'head of centre.'

"I believe he's genuinely ill, Mrs Pearson. He doesn't look too good at all."

"Well hopefully he'll learn for next weekend then."

"We need you to come and collect him."

"I'm not collecting him." My voice rose up. "If you can't have him in school then he'll have to make his own way back on the bus."

"He doesn't look well enough for that."

"Look, I'm not being rude, but his *illness* is self-inflicted. I'm afraid I haven't got an ounce of sympathy." I had my day planned out. I needed to go shopping before going to the gym. I was then meeting a friend for a coffee. *Some normality*. I wasn't about to let Tom hijack my day.

"But we have your permission to let him go."

"Yes. I'm surprised he's bothered about permission," I snorted. "Normally he'd find a way out when he wants to leave."

"Like I said, Mrs Pearson, I don't think he's well enough for that."

It was several hours before Tom made an appearance at home. He stumbled in, stoned, turned out the kitchen cupboards then spent the rest of the evening, in his room.

The next morning after he had left, I decided to ring his school.

"I'm calling to let you know that Tom's on his way."

"Oh, is he better now?"

"There was nothing wrong with him, as I'd suspected. After he'd been *allowed* to leave yesterday, he spent the rest of the day getting wasted with his mates."

"Right...I'll let Mr Johnson know."

"If you could. Tom is usually below par on a Monday, but it's only because of what he does to himself over the weekend."

"We'll bear that in mind in future, thanks."

"I did try to tell this to Mr Johnson yesterday. It seems Tom put on a good performance."

"*This message is for Tom's Mum.*" It was the following Monday. *"This is Mr Johnson speaking, head of the learning centre. Just a message to let you know that Tom's on his way home. He's got earache."*

. . .

My laugh echoed around the silence of the kitchen, bouncing like missiles off the walls. *Was this man an idiot or what?*

Here is a message I *could* have left in response later that day (I resisted though!)

This message is for Mr Johnson. This is Tom's Mum speaking. Just a message to let you know that Tom came straight home; after being let go from school with 'earache.' As I have recently highlighted, Tom is addicted to cannabis. He suffers the after-effects at their worst on a Monday after the excesses of the weekend. However, he seems perfectly OK today and is certainly well enough to bully me for money. Thanks to him not being in school, I have spent the afternoon enduring the company of his friends outside my house. No doubt their language, general conduct, engine revving and drug smoking has been noted by my neighbours.

I wonder if you could explain why you haven't paid any attention to the comments I made a week ago – do you think you know Tom better than I do?

QUOTE FROM ALEX

MARCH 2010 (16 YEARS, 3 MONTHS)

"He stays out all night and sleeps all day...
He's like a bat Mum."

MORE THAN CANNABIS

I FLUNG the door open to two policewomen. "Oh no.

"It's OK, it's positive news for a change."

"Oh?" This I *was* interested in hearing!

"There was some trouble in the town centre last night, brawling, that sort of thing. Tom stayed out of it, even though we lifted several of his mates. We were impressed with him. As we were passing by your house anyway, we decided to give you better news for once."

"Thanks for that." Tension drained from me. It certainly made a change to hear something positive. I was happy but at the same time, irked by the net curtains I noticed twitching across the road.

"He *is* mixing with a dire crowd though," said the other officer, her smile fading. "They'll drag him down if he's not careful."

"I *do* know about his friends." Folding my arms, I propped myself against the frame of the doorway. "Which is why we don't allow *any* of them in the house. We've tried to talk to Tom, but at the end of the day-"

"I know- it's hard- but perhaps him staying out of last

night's trouble is a sign he's turning a corner."

Tom didn't return home that night. If he had I would have praised him to the skies for staying out of the trouble that had occurred. It was 8.30am the next morning when he surfaced, looking as though he had not slept for weeks.

"Thanks for ringing to let me know where you were." I looked at his scrawny form. The weight was tumbling from him. "Do you think you should get ready for reparation?"

"I came to ask for some money. For bus fare and something to eat."

I thrust a note at him, then watched as he walked down the garden path to his friend who was waiting on the wall, hiding behind a hood.

"I bet he's not going," Martin said.

"Don't be daft, he wouldn't be that stupid."

Later that afternoon, as I relaxed with my book, my heart plunged as I noticed a police van pulling up. Martin and I went for the door handle in unison.

"I'm afraid it's not such good news today," the police officer said. "Is he in?"

"No, I've not seen him since this morning. What's happened now?"

"We've been called out to investigate a noise complaint. When the door was answered, we smelt drugs. We went in and managed to seize a substantial quantity."

"From Tom?"

"No. As we entered, he leapt from a window. Which makes him look pretty suspicious." Her gloved hands held a bag of white powder aloft. "If his prints are on this, he's in trouble."*

Tom seemed done in when he returned that evening. It was the worst state I had ever seen him in. His eyes were raw, his skin blotchy and his lips swollen. But it was his nose that worried me most. It was misshapen; as though he had been hit. His clothes draped from him as though he were a clothes hanger. He looked ill, very ill.

"Look at the state of you," I shrieked, grabbing hold of his shoulders to take a closer look at him. "What on earth have you taken?"

He mumbled incoherently, exuding the air of a down-and-out instead of a healthy sixteen-year-old with his entire life before him. After he had staggered up to bed, I slunk onto the sofa and rested my head in my hands.

"That isn't drink," Martin said. For once he didn't have his usual condescending tone. "I couldn't even smell it on him, could you? Did you see the state of his eyes? And his nose? God knows what he's been on."

"I know." Fighting my tears, I lifted my head. "He looks terrible."

All through the night I was kept awake by Tom snorting as he tried to clear his nose. It was late afternoon when he surfaced. By then he had slept for nearly twenty-four hours.

The more I considered it, the more I knew it wasn't cannabis usage. Whilst searching around drugs websites, I found the following article:

Arrests after teenage M-CAT users die

Police are investigating the deaths of two teenagers who are thought to have taken the legal drug mephedrone.

Police said the boys had taken the drug known locally as M-CAT, which appeared to have contributed to their deaths.

Two men aged 26 and 20, and a 17-year-old boy have been arrested in connection with the incident.

Det Ch Insp Michael Paxton said both teenagers had been out drinking until the early hours on Monday.

Police said the first teenager was pronounced dead at his home at 1200 GMT. We would encourage anyone who may have taken the drug or knows somebody who has taken the drug to attend a local hospital as a matter of urgency.

Statement by Det Ch Insp Paxton

Just after 1620 GMT, officers received a call about the death of the other teenager. Post-mortem examinations are being carried out.

The Police are currently carrying out investigations into their deaths. From our investigations we have information to suggest these deaths are linked to M-CAT. We would encourage anyone who may have taken the drug or knows somebody who has taken the drug to attend a local hospital as a matter of urgency."

Six people, including two of those arrested, who are thought to have taken the drug have attended hospital. Three of those have been discharged with no symptoms.

The substance, which has become popular on the UK club scene in recent months, is legal in the UK but is subject to a Government safety probe. Its side-effects are thought to include psychosis, palpitations, burning throat, nose bleeds and insomnia.

*We didn't hear anything further in relation to the confiscated white powder. Tom explained how he had jumped from the window in a panic, assuming he would be blamed.

TRYING TO GET THROUGH

APRIL 2010 (16 YEARS, 4 MONTHS)

I WAS worried sick about him. "Is this *really* how you want to be spending your life?" Obviously unable to face it, he had pushed his Sunday roast away. It was one of his favourite meals usually.

"Tom, you're a young lad." I put my fork down. "You're either in some sort of trance, or you're asleep, or ill. What're you doing to yourself?"

Suddenly he looked upset. "I don't know. I want to sort it out Mum. Honest, I do."

"Then why don't you?" From across the table, I rested my hand on his. "You're not on your own for God's sake. You've got me. I'll do anything to help you, you know."

"He's feeling sorry for himself." Martin said. "Are you sure it's just drugs Tom? Or perhaps you've done something else you regret this weekend?" He continued shovelling dinner into his mouth without looking at Tom. I looked at him, hoping he'd choke on it.

"Why do you always have to think the worst of me?" Tom sipped his water, head bowed.

"Experience."

"Next weekend," I began, trying to steer them from

confrontation, for Alex's sake. "Why don't you do something with *us*? Remove yourself from the temptation of your mates." Jumping up, I then began stacking plates as I tried to persuade him. "I know we can be a bit boring, but you could choose what we do. The cinema, bowling, something to eat, anything."

"I will," he agreed, twisting himself around in his seat to face me as I started filling the sink. "I want to get away from that crowd anyway. Make some decent mates."

"Talking the talk again Tom?"

I glared at Martin as he spoke between mouthfuls. It was time to change the subject.

"Have you spoken to anyone from 'careers' at school yet? I could get you some forms organised for college?"

"I'll ask tomorrow." Absently, he drove the salt and pepper pots around the table.

"You could have the world at your feet, if only you'd sort yourself out." Pausing my bashing around of pans. I looked at him. "I'm worried about you."

"There's no need. Chill Mum"

"Oh, come on, you don't bother to come home half the time. You don't even ring me to let me know where you are."

"I've not got a phone anymore," he avoided my eyes.

"But you've only had it five minutes. Where is it?"

"I flogged it."

"How much this time?" Martin slammed his cutlery onto his plate.

"Don't start Martin." I glared at him. "I paid for it. But I should have known he'd sell it." I marched from the sink and sank onto the dining chair. "Go on then Tom, how much?"

"Thirty quid."

"*Thirty quid*. But it cost bloody eighty!"

MORE SLEEPLESS NIGHTS

MUM." I sat up, responding to Alex's tapping on my bedroom door.

"Hang on." Rubbing the sleep from my eyes, I found my way around the bed in the darkness.

"I can't sleep again. I've been laid awake for ages. Can I get up for a bit?"

I glanced at the clock which glowed across the room. 3:26 am. "Alex, it's the middle of the night." I took his hand. "You must try and get back to sleep."

"But I can't." He padded at the side of me back to his room. "I keep hearing things."

"Like what?"

"Someone outside." As he got back into bed, he pointed towards his window.

"There's no one outside." Peeking through his curtains, I then shook my head at him.

"Has Tom come home?"

"Not yet."

"So even if I *do* get to sleep, he'll only wake me up with the doorbell." Tears filled his eyes as he remained sat upright in his bed. "I want to go to sleep Mum, but I can't."

I stayed with him whilst he had a drink, before tucking him back up and leaving him. Within an hour he was rapping at my door again.

"Bloody hell!" Martin tugged a pillow over his head. "It's the third night in a row he's been like this."

"It's not his fault!" I sprang back up again. "It's no wonder he's unsettled with everything he has to put up with!"

"Well go and see to him then!"

Alex's bottom lip trembled as I opened the door to him. "Come on, it's OK, I'll take you back to bed." I reached for his hand. "Don't listen to Daddy."

The next day I stocked up with lavender spray, hot chocolate and a CD of *calming classical music for children.* None of it worked though. Meanwhile, in the days that followed, Alex was working himself up into more and more of a state.

"I'm scared of it being night-time." His eyes were dark against pale skin. "I'm worried I won't be able to sleep again."

"You will, I promise."

"I can't stop worrying about it. It's making my head hurt."

"Well," I said. "Every time you get a worry in your mind, you must chase it away by thinking something happy."

"Like what?" He frowned. "We're not even going on holiday this year, are we? We can never do anything because of *Tom.*"

"We'll still do nice things, you'll see. We can go for trips out for the day or you can have a friend round, or..."

"I can't have a friend round." His voice trembled. "Tom will be mean to them like he is to me."

. . .

Alex's sleeplessness continued for well over a fortnight. He worked himself into an incredible turmoil about it. Usually, other than his asthma, he never caused me any worry. But I was on the verge of taking him to a doctor as he looked exhausted.

But miraculously, he slept for the entire night without waking. Then he slept the next night. I felt so guilty about it all.

KNOTTED UP INSIDE

It was the middle of the day, but I had come home early with a migraine. Tom and Alex were at school, Martin was out, and the dog was sleeping in her basket downstairs. As I lay on my bed in the quiet house, the pain in my head began to ease.

BANG! BANG! I was jolted into life. The dog was barking hysterically at whoever pounded at the door. BANG! BANG! BANG! She began to growl. Then thumping began on the back door as well. Too in pain to move, I listened. BANG! BANG! It went on for at least five minutes. Whatever it was, I couldn't face it now.

The hum of deep voices was drowned in an engine being fired up. Vehicle doors slammed and an engine revved. *I had to know who it was!* In order that they didn't see me, I peered around the curtain, recoiling at the police van. *What on earth had he done now?*

Later that afternoon, I got the chance to ask him.

"How should I know?" He slung his coat across the sofa. "Maybe it's that drugs thing from the weekend." He tugged ham and butter from the fridge. "Or it could be about graffiti. Me and me mate nicked some spray cans. But we cleaned it off like."

"I can't see the police sending the big riot van for that Tom." I passed him the bread from the cupboard.

"A few of my mates nicked a couple of boats from the side of the lake. Maybe it's that. It was the other day when I was at school. They took em out for a laugh and that. It was nowt to do with me." His eyes met mine as though he was searching for belief.

"Well if that's the case, I'll ring school and they'll confirm when you were there and tell the police." I headed for the door. "If you've done nothing wrong, there's no need to worry."

"I haven't. And if anyone says I have, they're lying."

ARREST NUMBER 11

I COULD NOT SLEEP YET AGAIN that night. *What had Tom done?* The police would not tell me anything when I rang to ask. They would only say that they were intending to return the following day to arrest him. If I failed to ensure he was 'available,' they had threatened to return in the middle of the night.

It was after three the next afternoon when the riot van reappeared. How I kept him in the house all day, I will never know.

"I am arresting you on suspicion of car theft and street robbery," asserted a plain-clothed man who had introduced himself as CID something or other. "You have the right to remain silent, etc."

"Street robbery!" I sat on the stairs.

"Whoever's saying I was there is making it up!" Tom, however, allowed the men to handcuff him.

"Come on lad, we'll discuss it down at the station." Two of the uniformed officers led him down the drive towards their van. I resisted the urge to wave at our neighbouring observers.

The plain-clothed 'CID' hung back to search our house.

"Will this take long?" I sighed. "I've to collect my eight-year-old from school shortly."

Later that evening I had to attend the police station in my capacity as 'appropriate adult.' Tom had opted for a solicitor. We had a brief discussion before the start of the interview.

"I'm not naming any names," Tom rested his elbows on the graffiti-covered table.

"That's fine," nodded the solicitor, scribbling onto a notepad. "Just tell them you're fearful of repercussions. You can also, as I'm sure you're aware, say *no comment* at any time."

Moments later, two CID officers entered the airless interview room. One of them was the man who had searched our house earlier. The other man I recognised but could not place.

"Don't I know you," he looked at me as he sat down, his chair scraping against the floor.

God, where do I know you from? Please don't let it be an embarrassing acquaintance!

"Ah yes, I remember; this isn't the first time we've met Tom, is it?" A flicker of recognition crossed his face. "I seem to recall arresting you for burgling your next-door-neighbour some years ago."

"Two years."

"Right, let's get started." The other officer unwrapped the tapes.

There was a pause and then the long tone was emitted from the machine, signalling the interview was commencing. We all had to state our names; Tom was again read his rights then asked if he understood what he had been arrested for.

"It wasn't me," he protested, leaning back in his chair. "I know who it was, and it wasn't me. I shouldn't even be here."

"Let's deal with this one thing at a time." One of the CIDs

asked the questions while the second transcribed the conversation onto an A4 pad. His handwriting looked like spiders venting their anger all over the page. "Firstly, the street robbery. Describe to me, in your own words, exactly what happened on the evening of last Friday, 25th April."

Tom drew a deep breath in. "I was at a party yeah, and a few of the lads decided to go out for a bit and they came back with this bag yeah, but I wasn't with em."

"Let's go back a bit." The officer formed a backwards gesture with his hands. "Who was at the party?"

Tom looked reminiscent. "There were a few lasses, me and three other lads."

"Names?" The second CID spoke now with his pen poised.

"I don't know any of the lasses second names. And I only know two of the lads."

As Tom reeled off the names of the 'partygoers,' the second CID scribbled them down. *So much for him not being willing to name names.*

"What about the other lad?"

"I don't know his name."

"Can you describe him for us?" The first officer leaned forward in his chair.

"Well he looks a bit like me really. Blonde hair, nearly 6 foot."

"What sort of build is he?"

"I dunno."

The officer read out a description. "White male with blonde hair. Aged between 15 and 17. Wearing dark blue jeans, a light blue shirt and black trainers. Athletic build."

"Yeah that's right," Tom affirmed, nodded and raised his eyes to make contact with theirs. "That's what he looks like."

"Don't you think he sounds like you?" This line of questioning was pursued for a while, but Tom was not budging. No way was he admitting to anything, just that the 'character,' as he dubbed him, had been a 'mentalist,' hurling verbal abuse at people in the street, kicking bins over and making strange suggestions about what they might do to obtain some money.

"How are you aware of all this, if you stayed at the house when it was all going on?" The CID sat back in his seat and clasped his hands behind his head.

"Cos one of me mates told me." Tom cocked his head, defiantly.

"Did you handle any of the stolen property?"

"No." He shifted in his seat.

"Could your fingerprints be on any of the stolen property?"

"No."

"Was it *you* who punched the victim in the face?"

Tom glanced at his solicitor. "No comment."

Tom was then asked a series of further questions, all requiring a 'yes' or 'no' response. To which he replied, "*no comment*." To all of them.

The other CID officer then shifted the focus onto the car theft. He stated the approximate time that it had occurred.

"Where were you on Monday morning between one and five am?" His voice sounded robotic.

It was like being part of a TV drama.

"In bed."

"Can you confirm this?" All eyes flickered to me.

"*As far as I know* he was in bed. But I can't be sure. He climbs in and out of windows through the night."

"Shut up Mum," Tom glared at me.

"Don't talk to your mother like that."

After thirty-nine minutes, the interview was concluded. Tom was informed that he would be expected to participate in an ID parade. If the victim picked him out, it would be necessary to re-interview him.

. . .

It was a filmed ID parade. Like in all sombre situations, I suppressed an inappropriate urge to laugh.

"Right Tom, I want you to choose a t-shirt to wear," trilled the man conducting the filming. He was a cheery, bumbling man, with a humongous red nose and a beer belly. "I'd advise choosing a light coloured one." Half a dozen t-shirts in assorted colours were spread on the table.

"Why?" Tom rummaged through them.

"Because," the man fiddled with his computer, "the description that's been given of the suspect, describes a lad wearing a *dark* t-shirt."

Tom took off his own t-shirt and tugged a pale green one over his head. It was a colour he would never dream of wearing but it suited him anyway.

"Good." The man, manoeuvred Tom onto a 'spot' in the centre of the room. "Now, I want you to look that way towards the camera and then back the other way. Keep your face straight and your hands by your sides."

Tom, with his scar centrally upon his cheek, looked every inch the yob as he was captured on film.

"OK." He gestured for us to join him. "We'll slide your picture in with some others. I want you to pick another eight lads from these photos." He pointed at the screen. "Choose images with a similarity to yourself."

After they had all been decided upon, we reviewed the 'parade.' I have to say, he looked right at home amongst the other 'suspects.'

By this time, he had been in custody for six hours. I expected them to release him.

"Do you think he's telling the truth?" One of the officers looked at me. I hardly dared to say it out loud. Although I felt guilty about it, I could not lie. I shook my head.

"We don't believe a word either," agreed one of the CID officers. "But if he isn't picked out from the line up tomorrow,

I'm afraid we have no evidence to place him at the scene. We'll keep him here tonight anyway."

"All night?" His words stung like a slap. Although I knew Tom was probably in it up to his eyeballs, it didn't stop me fretting about his state of mind. It was dreadful leaving him. Especially after the occasion when he had thrown his head against the cell wall. Maybe I should have relaxed though. At least I knew where he was for a change.

The following day, I could not face work. My insides were churned up. The thought of my son, along with two of his 'friends,' cornering, attacking and mugging a defenceless boy gnawed away at me. *How desperate must he be for money?*

To distract myself, I drove to the supermarket, but trudged around, unable to focus, probably doubling the time the shopping would have normally taken. At the checkout, I queued behind a woman and a teenage lad, who must have been about Tom's age. Blinking away tears, I watched the boy help his mother load shopping onto the conveyor belt like it was the most normal thing in the world for a son to help his mother with the shopping.

An image of Tom, sitting alone in a cell, where he had been since this time yesterday, refused to leave my mind.

That afternoon at four, he was released without charge, having spent nearly twenty-four hours locked up. He had not been chosen from the line up, so returned home, jubilant.

"He's guilty as sin," Martin observed. "If I'd been locked up all this time for something I hadn't done, I'd be fuming! In fact, I'd be suing the police for wrongful arrest! Tom seems relieved that he's got away with it! Again."

LEAVING SCHOOL

Tom was approaching his final days at school. I went to a parent consultation evening. No progress had been made in terms of what he might do beyond school. He was in danger of falling deeper in with his inappropriate friends and their collective criminality.

His English teacher and a 'key worker,' were enthusiastic about his drawing talent.

"If only he would develop it," one of them said. "But he has no concentration skills whatsoever." Her voice echoed around the classroom. I was sad to see it still devoid of any artwork or displays. "And he continually disrupts the others."

"No change there then."

"What do you mean?" She folded her arms.

"I've been having this conversation with his teachers for years. He's *always* been disruptive and unable to concentrate."

"Was he ever diagnosed with anything?"

"The closest I got to a diagnosis is when he was eleven and was identified as having a 'conduct disorder.' I think it's ADHD but when I was trying to get him recognised with that, it was still a new *thing*."

"*We* haven't been made aware of any problems before high school." She glanced sideward at her colleague.

I laughed. "I can't believe the lack of communication between services. I've had serious problems with him since babyhood. I've begged for help. I never got it. That's why we're still in this situation now."

"Well, there's nothing on his file." She flicked through it as though something would suddenly leap out at her.

I shook my head. What could I say? It was clear they wanted insight, but I did not have the energy to rake over our history yet again. The future was all I was interested in discussing now.

Eventually, we concluded that with my help, Tom would receive as much support as he would accept ahead of his forthcoming G.C.S.E.s. They would also get hold of some careers advice and information about art college.

This, like many promises, never happened. It was left to me to investigate everything and apply to college. With four exams looming, he officially left the referral unit. I bought revision materials and tried to get him on board. But I didn't manage to persuade him to do a stroke of work.

MORNING CALLS

THE SITUATION at home was becoming more out of control. Whenever Tom walked in, he seemed to be 'off his head.' It is the only way I can describe it.

At times he would wake us an hour after we had gone to bed; sometimes in the middle of the night; or it would be at about four or five in the morning. I am not sure he had any concept of time. I had come to suspect that he had gone beyond cannabis in his drug use. He was snorting mephedrone, or M-Cat, as it had been dubbed. It was terrifying.

Early one morning, when he hadn't been home all night, we were awoken by Tom and his 'friends' at the side of our house. It was 5.21 am. Martin headed to the landing window.

"They're measuring something out." He said as he watched. "We should get the police here."

"They'd have moved before they got here. Look how long they've been in the past."

"Maybe I should get photos then," Martin suggested.

"And what if they see you?" I leaned back against my

pillows. "Don't bother. I don't want my windows putting through."

When confronted later, Tom shrugged and promised it would not happen again. He then loaded his pockets with food before disappearing. Later that evening he came home in a right state.

"Oh my God!" I grasped at his shoulders. "Your mouth looks as though it's been stung by a wasp." His nose was swollen too.

"Leave me alone!" He stamped up the stairs.

It was 5.32 am the following morning when we were awoken again.

"Tom you dirty bastard!" Leering and whistles ensued, then several bangs as stones, or whatever, were thrown at his window, bouncing off the glass.

I lay, frozen to the spot with my hand resting on the dog's back to try to stop her from growling. There was no point confronting them – it wasn't worth the abuse. But my next-door neighbour risked it.

"Go away and wake someone else up," she shouted from her window. It was a fair request.

"Fuck off silly bastard."

Oh God, please don't let this get out of hand!

"Go away little boy."

"I'll put your fucking windows through." It was a different voice now. It sounded like there was at least four of them.

There were laughs, shouts and a few more whistles before it went quiet. Martin was dressing. There was no point going back to sleep. I was too wound up.

Later the man from next door came to the door. "I want names. Then I'll know who to report when my windows go through."

"I'm sorry. If there was anything I could do, I'd be doing it.

I've confronted them myself and got the same abuse as your wife."

"She's terrified," he continued. "We've three kids to consider."

"I know. If they turn up again, I'll call the police. I'll have a word with Tom too, for all the good it'll do."

These were obviously not satisfactory enough responses. But I was sure he would sense my lack of control in who decided to cause trouble in our street.

"We're on the same side as you." I persisted. "Obviously, I want them all stopping as well."

"The thing is, we've got one of the *idiots* living *here* with us." Martin gestured upwards to Tom's window. "If I had *my* way, he'd be out."

"I'm trying to sort it out," I added. "*I* want Tom in his own place too. Then maybe things will ease off. The rest of them would have no excuse to hang around. I'm sorry it's impacted on you. It isn't fair and I'll do whatever I can."

I spent all that day with a blistering headache, probably due to lack of sleep.

Tom looked horrendous when he came home. He staggered into the living room.

"What's up with you?" Martin glanced from his newspaper.

"Feel like shit." He was clutching his stomach.

"Been on that stuff again, have you?"

"It's the last time." He sank into a chair.

"We've heard that before."

"I mean it this time. I'm never feeling like this again." He was bent double.

"Is it that Mephedrone?" My brother Chris, over for dinner, spoke from behind the computer.

I nodded. It was good to have him over. Have someone on

my side. Tom's behaviour and Martin's hostility had alienated the friends who might have called once upon a time. But being isolated had become my norm.

"M-cat's serious shit, that, you know. It's wiping people out. Haven't you heard?"

Tom sat back up again. "My nose is caving in."

Chris continued. "It's as addictive as heroin. You don't know what it's mixed with either."

"How *are* you feeling, *exactly?*" I felt sick. All sorts of scenarios were whirring around my head; sudden heart attack, fit, internal bleeding...

"I'm aching." His hand flew to his head. "And my head and nose are killing. I'm gonna have no nose left and it'll cost a few grand for a new one."

Chris and Martin laughed. I didn't.

"Feel like I'm gonna have a heart attack or something. My heart's beating really fast."

"I think it's best if we get you looked at, don't you think Tom?"

"No! No way."

"Right. Well we'll think about that again soon if you're no better. When was the last time you ate something?" I'd thrown his meals away for the last two nights.

He shrugged.

"I've saved you some dinner." I started towards the kitchen. "You should try and eat a bit then have a lie down."

Picking at the food a few minutes later, he seemed agitated.

"Would you say you've taken much of it Tom?" I flopped onto the chair beside him.

"They're all at it. Round at a house. And now I can't stop."

"How do you afford it? I thought drugs were expensive."

"Not M-Cat." He pushed food around his plate. "You can get it for the same price as a pack of fags."

"Are you addicted to it?"

"I think so. I can't stop anyway. Not now."

"I'd better make an appointment at the doctors. Maybe we can get you into a clinic or?" I would have robbed a bank to cover the cost.

"It's not that bad. Look, Mum, I'm gonna sort it out, I'm gonna change, I promise you."

I put my hand on his arm as he struggled on with his meal.

"I'll help you. We'll discuss this when you're a bit better. For now, though, I'm off to bed. And you should do the same when you've finished that." I pushed my chair pack and stood up. "I've been up since half five. Get some rest Tom. Put your TV on and try to relax. You'll be OK, I promise. You need to get this poison out of your system. Give me a shout if you need me." I went to bed. But exhausted as I was, I couldn't settle. I kept abruptly waking every so often with feelings of dread.

The next morning, I did a bit more research about Mephedrone. All the symptoms he had been suffering from the previous evening were listed. I was worried to read that users become psychologically dependent on it. Furthermore, its use had been implicated in several heart attacks. It was classed as a 'narcotic' substance, a progression 'up' from cannabis, heading towards the 'biggies' like heroin and crack.

By eleven o'clock, I was starting to panic. There had not been a sound from Tom's room. The fact that he was not yet out of bed was usual. But normally his bedsprings would creak as he moved. Or we would hear him going to the loo. Because I had not even heard him cough, I asked Martin to check on him.

"Why me? You go." He switched the lawnmower off.

"I can't. I'm scared." I kicked the grass he had mown into a pile.

"Of what?"

"He said last night that he felt like he was dying. What if he has?" Tears leapt to my eyes.

"Don't be stupid. I'll give him a shout."

Relief washed over me when I heard Tom moaning at being woken up. It was at that moment that I came to a decision. Until I was certain that he was not going to be tempted by any sort of drugs, he was getting no more money. Not from me, anyway.

THREAT OF EVICTION

4 June 2010

Dear Tenants,

Re: Nuisance to Neighbours

I have received a complaint regarding your conduct towards one of our tenants.

The complaint is:

Youths congregating outside your house in the early hours of the morning shouting up to your son's bedroom window.

. . .

I would inform you that this department takes incidents of nuisance to neighbours and anti-social behaviour seriously and is determined to take steps to prevent them from being repeated. This may include taking legal action.

I would like to give you the opportunity to discuss the complaint and I would ask you to contact me as soon as possible. We can then agree how the matter can be rectified to ensure that no further complaints are made against you.

Yours sincerely,

Housing Officer

We were going to get thrown out! Where would we go? What the hell would we do?

COMING TO A HEAD

JUNE 2010, (16 YEARS, 6 MONTHS)

THE NEXT EVENING Tom returned downstairs after we had all gone to bed. I stared into the darkness, knowing I would get no peace until I discovered what he was up to. As I tiptoed down the stairs to investigate, I was greeted by the familiar herbal stink.

I realised he had sneaked out of the kitchen window, which had been left ajar, leaving the house vulnerable. I dashed to the front door, hoping he would still be nearby, but he had vanished into the night.

When he reappeared the next morning, I was already up. His vile mood exuded as he barged past me. Mercifully I did not have to remain in the house for long, as Alex was in a football tournament. I packaged him into the car, trying to ignore the insults that Tom was directing from his bedroom window. His venom flooded the street.

"Slag! Fucking tight bitch!" He bellowed into the Sunday morning calm. Obviously, he was displeased at the fact that I hadn't left him any money.

As he launched something from his window at my car, I sped away. The meek and mild mood he had displayed the previous day had not lasted long.

A reasonably sympathetic 'senior housing officer' rang us back that morning, agreeing that we were unable to control the behaviour of *other* youths. But he warned Martin that if we did not begin to control *our* youth, we would be facing eviction.

The man said our neighbours were all maintaining a 'log' of any adverse behaviour from Tom and his accomplices. *No wonder I was unable to hold my head up in the street.* All information was being reported back to the police, the housing office and the neighbourhood watch meetings. (Which *we* hadn't been invited to.)

As I had vowed, I did not give Tom any money over the next few days. I bought a stash of cigarettes, cans of pop and pre-paid bus tickets. There was no way I was going to attempt another bus pass; he had lost them countless times.

I drove him to several exams at the pupil referral unit, so that he definitely sat them. As we sat side-by-side in the car, I encouraged him to put together a portfolio for his forthcoming art college interview and discussed with him about how he was managing without mephedrone. The conversations were one-sided, and he seemed subdued.

I was sitting at the kitchen table working one morning when Tom announced himself, not with, *good morning mum* but with, "I need some money." His exams were over, and he was clearly bored. It had been five days since I had given him anything.

"Tom you know what I said." My stress levels were immediately elevated. *I had to stick to my resolution.*

"I only want bus fare."

"I'll give you a ticket." I fished around in my bag.

"What if I want cigs?" "You can take some with you." I thrust a packet of cigarettes and a bus ticket towards him. He did not seem happy with the fact I had an answer for everything.

"Wouldn't it be worth a fiver to get me out of your hair?"

"No."

"If you don't give me it, I'm going to annoy you until you do." He began whistling and tapping his feet. Ignoring him, I continued shuffling through paperwork.

"I mean it. I'm going to really get on your nerves."

"I'll stay out of your way."

"Then I'll follow you around. C'mon Mum." He jumped up from his seat. "I need some money."

Gathering my computer and bits of paper, I decided to shut myself in my room. I had loads of work to do and was not going to let him bully me.

"I'm off upstairs." I started towards the door. "We've discussed this. You know why I'm not giving you money."

"I'll sit outside your room all day banging on your door."

"Tom. You're not going to win this." I swung around to face him. "Back off."

His face darkened. "I fucking hate you, you stupid bitch." He stepped towards me. "Do you *know* how much I hate you?"

"I think you'd better go out." I backed away, noticing the hairs on the back of my neck rising. I'm not sure whether it was fear or anger. Probably both.

"Fucking whore. Tight fucking whore."

My temper was starting to go. I dumped the computer and papers back onto the table.

"Get out of my house." I tugged at his expensive hooded top. "Get out! I can't take it anymore."

"Fuck off." He tried to wriggle free of my grasp on his hood. "Get the fuck off my jacket you slag."

"I mean it Tom," I shrieked. "I want you out of this house until you've calmed down. I don't have to put up with this." I retreated into the kitchen.

"You either give me money or I'm going to sell summat," he shouted.

"Try it." I tried to sound not bothered. "I'll ring the police."

"You'd better say goodbye to the TV." He yanked the plug from the wall.

"Tom, stop this or I'm ringing Martin." I stormed back into the living room.

"I'll fucking smash the house up!" He began kicking the wall in the living room, quickly resulting in two holes in the plaster."

Grabbing my phone, I dialled 999.

"You fucking bitch!" He lunged at my phone. "You're not getting me locked up."

"Watch me."

He grabbed his coat and trainers as I was connected.

"Police please." This was unreal. *I was ringing the police because I feared my own son!* I fought to regain my breath and my heart was thudding in my ears. Tom was still in the house as my call was connected. I chose to carry on.

"My son's being verbally abusive. He's booting my walls in." I garbled at the operator.

"What you fucking lying for!"

He left before the police arrived. Thankfully, they didn't treat me like a timewaster as I had feared.

"What is it you want us to do to help you?" The policewoman asked gently, after I had relayed what had happened.

"I think the fact that I've rung you has shown him I mean business. But I guess I'd like you to give him a warning."

"Would you be willing to go to court and testify against him?"

I laughed sarcastically through my tears. "Court. They won't do a thing. They never do."

"I know," she agreed. "It frustrates us too. Anyway, it's your call. We can put a warrant out for him, but you'd have to be willing to follow it through."

I hesitated. "I think I'll leave it but if there's a next time I'll follow it up, all the way."

"You won't get a choice again. I must make you aware of that. I know he's your son but we're classing this as a domestic abuse incident." Her words stunned me as she made several jottings in her 'pocketbook.'

"Next time, we can do what's known as a *'victimless prosecution.'* If he'd still been in the house when we got here, we'd have arrested him. It would have been taken out of your hands."

I understood perfectly. They left soon after, promising me the whole incident was 'on record' and I could use it against Tom should anything else occur.

I rang Martin.

"He's out," was all he said. I ended the 'conversation' before telephoning Tom's youth offending key worker.

"I can't cope anymore," I said. "Martin wants to chuck him out *now*. I do too, if I'm honest, but obviously I won't."

"Why not? He *is* old enough now. He'd have to move into a hostel. But he'd only be there for a month or so before something more secure was sorted."

"There must be an alternative."

"Sarah, I doubt he'll get offered a council flat. Not for years." She fell silent for a moment. "I can arrange for our housing officer to do a home visit. She knows of one or two supported housing schemes, so might have a few suggestions. If you're willing to *officially* threaten him with homelessness, I think he'd fulfil their criteria."

Hope flooded me. "I think it's the *only* way. Can you sort me an appointment? If I know there's movement, I can hang in here a bit longer."

"He ticks all the boxes. Young person. Family breakdown. Threatened with homelessness. Substance misuse. Offending behaviour."

It was a miserable list but at that moment it was debris in a turbulent ocean. Something to cling onto.

"I want him out." Martin ran his hands over the holes in the wall then turned to me. "You hold the key. I can't throw him out. You're his mother. It's your call."

"I'm onto it." I told him about the housing schemes, thinking he would be pleased.

"That could drag on for bloody months." He slapped the palm of his hand against his leg. "How much longer can we go on like this? We can't have a holiday. We can't trust him with a key to the house. Everything has to be locked away from him." His tone heightened as he reeled off the situation. "He won't change, you know. Things are getting worse as far as I'm concerned."

"I know. But I'm going to do everything I can."

"But why should *I* have to live like it?" He threw his arms into the air. "Why should Alex? Even Peter doesn't want to know. And he's his *father*. So why the hell should I?"

"Cos you've been here since he was this big." I flattened the palm of my hand beside my knee. "I don't believe you can chuck him out with nowhere to go, any more than I can."

"Watch me." He folded his arms and looked at me with an air of defiance.

"He might leave for a couple of days but then what?" I held my hands out. "He'd be back, pleading. Could you lie in bed at night, listening to him hammering at the door, shouting that he's nowhere to sleep or hungry?"

"No," he said.

"We've *got* to do this properly. He needs a flat where he'll be properly supported. And helped with his drug problem."

It was only me preventing him moving. Martin did not want him there. The neighbours didn't. Alex certainly didn't. Neither did I, but I had to do what was right.

Within days, we had another visit. Martin dealt with it. I was grateful I was out. He rang me after they had gone.

"The police have been."

"Hang on. I'm driving. Let me put you on speakerphone. "I clipped the phone on the dashboard.

"There was two of them." As I drove the car around a bend, I strained to hear what he was saying.

"He hasn't done anything," Martin explained. "They wanted a word about him and this anti-social contract thing."

"They've already written to me about it." My relief was palpable at the realisation that he had not actually *done* anything.

"I know. But they're saying things haven't improved. And they're right, aren't they? Anyway, they had a sheet with about ten photos on. There was a picture of Tom among them and I recognised about six of the others."

"So?"

"They're the lads they're going to force out of the area apparently. They don't care how they do it but have said enough is enough. The visit was to warn us of what's going to happen."

"I can't handle any more of this." I pulled over so Alex could only hear one side of the conversation.

"They asked if we could contact the housing association about being re-housed," Martin went on. "Or if we've any family we could stay with. I told them we're not going anywhere; we've done nothing wrong and shouldn't have to lose our home because of Tom. One of them said we won't have a choice soon."

"What are we going to do?"

"Look I don't know how. But we're going to *have* to get Tom out. If we don't, he's going to take us *all* down." I knew Martin was right. "We'll be in a hostel or something before we know it, if we don't get it sorted. Can't you have another word with his dad? See if he'll take him."

"No point. I know what the answer will be. Look he's sixteen. Hopefully one of these supported housing schemes will come to something."

"What's up Mum?" Alex asked.

"Nothing. Don't you worry about anything." I rested my hand on his arm. "I've just got to sort a few things out."

"One of them noticed the holes in the wall," Martin continued. "What did you say?"

"The truth. I think she's going to tell the housing though. She mentioned criminal damage."

"Look we'll fight this." From nowhere, a sense of fight emerged. "All the way. There's *no way* we're getting thrown out. I'll get a solicitor involved. We've got rights. We've done nothing wrong."

"We're responsible for everyone in our house. That's what they're saying. If Tom's out of control, we're liable."

"That's just it. When hasn't he been out of control?"

HOLDING ON

TOM *DIDN'T* GET a place at art college. He had become so used to a one-to-one forum where he could discuss his issues, that he had not made this distinction in his college interview and had disclosed his drugs problems. Their reaction was understandably to doubt whether he would possess the concentration or commitment needed on the course. His future incessantly worried me and as the days wore on after his exams, Tom seemed increasingly lost.

Before leaving for work each morning, I had to hide my computer and Alex's games console. Often, we would return home to find his friends hanging out, usually fed and watered from my kitchen. I could have run away, leaving them all to it. I never knew what state things were going to be in when I returned. My home was beyond my control. These fears were worsened knowing that the neighbours were documenting it all. My hopes were now pinned on the forthcoming assessment with the housing officer.

. . .

Despite his promises, Tom did not return home when he was supposed to.

"We can't start without him." The woman sipped her tea. "There are forms he has to sign."

"Can't I do it?"

She shook her head. "We can discuss his support needs and accommodation availability, but I can't commit him to anything without meeting him."

"Of course." I cast another glance out of the window and along the street.

"So, are we looking at emergency accommodation?" She tugged some leaflets from her bag. "Do you require him out immediately?"

I recoiled. *What an awful situation!* "I want to make sure he's alright. He's so young, particularly emotionally." The woman scribbled away. "He needs support with his drugs and offending issues. As well as budgeting, living, all that kind of thing. And I'll help once he's in his own place. Keep an eye on him."

"Well that's a real positive." She looked at me.

"Really?"

"You'd be surprised how many kids I deal with are booted out and left to fend for themselves."

"I'm not kicking him out. But we're going lose our home."

"I've been briefed by Tom's youth offending worker. It sounds like things have been rough. She says you've done as much as you can."

I was grateful for this acknowledgement. "Really the only thing standing in the way of him needing emergency accommodation right now, is me. If it was up to my husband, Tom's stepdad, he'd be out straightaway."

Just then Tom walked, or should I say, stumbled, in. I realised he was out of his mind on something and hoped the housing woman wouldn't notice. However, there was no masking his state when he attempted to string a sentence together. Thankfully, he wasn't too stoned to sign his name several times on the paperwork.

The situation was looking promising. He was to be referred for a flat where he would have an allocated support worker. Help would be given with benefits, leisure time usage, budgeting and cooking. Due to his history of drug taking and offending, he was eligible. Although he seemed to think there was a benefit in lying about it all.

"I don't touch cannabis anymore," he said when she asked him about his history of drug use.

"Tom you're stoned now."

"Shut the fuck up." He accepted one of the forms.

"Tom don't talk to your mum like that." She passed him her pen. "Not in front of me please. It's awful."

"Well she doesn't know shit." His words were slurred. "She just thinks she does."

"How long are we talking before things start moving?" This was the question. *How long would I have to wait until I could have some sort of normal home?* Not having to lock everything away and lug my handbag around with me. Not to be abused and sworn at every single day. To be able to go to bed, knowing I would not be disturbed through the night, either by Tom returning at all hours, or his friends outside.

"Probably a couple of months." She swept her paperwork into a pile.

"Really? That quick?" The relief was immediately replaced by guilt.

"Can you hang in there?" She nodded towards the holes in the walls.

"I've hung in this long," I stood up. "A couple more months won't kill me, I hope!"

"I'll get the referrals in straightaway." She slid the forms into her bag.

"I'm sorry about the state of him," I showed her out.

"Don't worry, I've seen worse!"

After she had gone, I sank onto the bottom step of the staircase. Tom was not even seventeen, yet I was forcing him to leave home. It shouldn't have been this way. I would worry about him endlessly and would have to stop myself from checking up on him morning, noon and night.

For all our sakes though, I was going to *have* to let him go. It was time to allow him to sink or swim. Whatever was coming was out of my hands.

HANGING IN THERE

THE SUMMER HOLIDAYS could not arrive soon enough; I would be off work for six weeks and able to reclaim control over my house.

One night I was woken by a motorbike. It thundered up and down the street for about ten minutes. *The whole street must have been woken!*

It was 2:03am. Then a horn began sounding. Exhausted from the hectic day I'd had, I was paralysed.

Tom's voice cut into the night. "Gimme a minute."

After clattering around his room, he went downstairs then climbed out of the living room window. Wide awake now, I listened as the deafening engine roared again, before leaving the street. Gradually it faded into the distance. *What if Tom wasn't wearing a helmet?* My eyes flickered back open in the darkness, maternal urges overshadowing my exhaustion.

I prayed they would be stopped by police. I lay for ages, gazing into the void of the night, still hearing the motorbike's engine inside my head until after 4 am. I was going to struggle getting up for work at six, yet the more I worried about this, the more sleepless I became.

Finally, I must have dropped off. Martin nudged me at 4.35 am. Tom was re-entering through the living room window. Relieved as I was, I was also angry as I heard him crashing about in the kitchen downstairs.

Less than two hours later, I dragged myself out of bed. Tom had pulled the curtain rail out of the plaster during either his exit or entrance through the window. Rage coursed through me and I battled with a migraine all day.

I never looked forward to finishing work for the day; home did not feel like *home*. I never knew what I was walking into.

"What was I supposed to do all day without any bloody money?" Tom scowled.

I could have wept as I glanced around. I could not go on much longer. The kitchen was splattered with fat. All the milk had gone. Wrappers and half eaten food were strewn everywhere and he was, as usual, wearing Martin's socks.

What may sound trivial to others irked me. Even though Tom had a drawer full of his own socks, he would help himself to *anything*, even when it belonged to someone else.

I handed him a five pound note.

"Is that it?" He inspected it as though it was a dead mouse.

"We have this conversation nearly every day Tom," I started towards the kitchen with the shopping I had brought in. "I shouldn't give you *anything.* You cause me nothing but heartache, you don't lift a finger in the house and to be honest, you're old enough to get a job now."

"Yeah, right." Stuffing the note into his pocket, he set about getting ready. This consisted of him cramming his pockets with food, coating gel on his hair and spraying Lynx on himself with such voracity that he would be smelt streets away.

Eventually a banged door indicated his departure. He was not blessed with social niceties, such as *bye mum, see you later!*

As was often the case, I locked the house up that night not knowing whether Tom would be back, *or not*. Sleep found Martin easily; this was never the case with me. It was a luxury I had learned to forsake many years before.

It was a warm night. In the distance I could hear shouting. It sounded like a fight. The voices grew closer. There seemed to be a few of them.

"Gerroff!" The fight had found its way to the end of the street. I could see it from my window. Furious voices had descended into violence. With someone at the bottom of a pile of about ten lads; it looked like a rugby scrum. Only this was ten onto one. And that *one*, I realised in horror, was Tom. I fired down the stairs and out into the street.

"Get off him!" I ran towards them. "Leave him alone!" Several of them jumped up. The neighbours must have got sick of seeing me running wildly into the street, in my pyjamas, trying to avert some crisis or other. I stood, watching until one by one they released their grip upon him.

"Woman beater!" Said one, letting Tom go but shoving him as he did. "You'll keep." Tom stumbled towards me, his lip bloodied and eye blackened. The gang of boys diffused.

"Are you OK?" I caught him by the arm. "Why've they done this to you?"

"Just leave it mum." He tugged his arm away.

"I will *not* leave it. I should call the police."

"Then I'll be in even worse shit!" He checked back over his shoulder.

"Why?" I studied his face. "What have you done?"

"I haven't done owt, not that *you'll* believe me." He scowled, then winced.

"Sit there." I said as we arrived back home. "I'll get something to bathe your face."

"It's fine. I'm OK." But he sat anyway.

I returned to the room with water and cotton wool. "Why were they after you?"

"Some girl's saying I smacked her. She was my girlfriend but not anymore. I didn't though, honest mum." He stared at me as I wrung water out of the cotton wool. "I dumped her, and she's upset so she's making up lies."

"Are you telling me the truth?"

"See, I knew you wouldn't believe me. You never do."

"Alright, calm down!" I dabbed at his eye.

"Ouch."

"Tom if you *did* hit her, tell me."

"I didn't. Not that they'll take any notice. It was her brother who organised that lot." He gestured towards the window. "They'll be waiting for me every night from now on."

He looked defeated and I prayed that we would soon have an alternative. Mostly for his own sake as much as anybody else's, he needed to get out of the area. A new start was essential.

THE SUPPORTED HOUSING PROJECT

AUGUST 2010 (16 YEARS, 8 MONTHS)

"How long's it likely to take?"

The woman handed Tom the form to sign. "It could be a month. Or it could be a year. It depends on the turnover of residents. I have to say though..." She glanced down at one of the newly completed forms. "He'll be getting the highest priority awarded."

"Will he?"

"Yes. He's threatened with homelessness and because of his age, it shouldn't be that long. We always prioritise referrals we get from the youth offending housing worker."

The word *homelessness* pierced my conscience.

"I reckon I'd be alright here." Tom leaned back in his chair, clasping his hands behind his head as he looked over the grounds of the housing complex.

I had been surprised by it. The gardens were landscaped, and full of places to sit. Ironically, the accommodation had echoes of the chalets we had previously stayed in on holiday.

"Would you like to have a look at one of the flats?" The lady followed Tom's gaze.

"Please!" Tom and I chorused, rising to our feet.

The flat was newly painted in magnolia. The wood-effect lino on the floor looked new as well. It had everything he would need; cooker, fridge, bed, sofa; even curtains.

"You'd have a support worker," she watched as we looked around. "They'd have a meeting with you as soon as you moved in to see what you'd need help with."

"Everything!" I turned to her. "Cooking, cleaning, budgeting *and* shopping."

"Well he *is* very young." As Tom opened and closed kitchen cupboards, she seemed to be studying him. I could only imagine what must be going through her head about us.

During the interview, Tom admitted to having a *slight* cannabis problem and to *occasionally* going off the rails when he was *younger;* also having previously been in trouble with the police. *But that was all behind him now.* I had resisted the urge to complicate matters and had not contradicted the information he had given. *What would be the point?* It might make the difference between him being accepted onto the waiting list, or not.

Throughout the interview, he was pleasant and well-spoken. The woman must have been wondering what on earth had gone sour within our family for me to want him re-housed at such a young age.

I no longer wanted to elaborate on the details though. Things had to move forward. I was sick of having to justify myself, exhausted of going over and over the same background details and reasons for things. There was no point anymore in dealing with things in any other way.

His dad and Elizabeth were no longer able to provide any 'respite,' our reputation lay in shreds where we were living, and we were all facing losing our home. Unfortunately, the situation had come to this; it was either a case of *him* needing accommodation, or *all* of us.

. . .

Tom was incredibly upbeat as we left the supported housing complex and returned to the car. "I liked it there Mum. I hope they give me a flat." I nodded, guilt-infested. This was not *really* what I wanted. It was eating me up. But I was clueless as to what else to do.

"Will you drop me off at my mates?" His tone was far more amenable than usual.

When he got out of the car, he did not even harass me for money. His nearly six-foot form strode away before waving back at me! If I hadn't already been sitting, I think I would have keeled over in shock. I closed my eyes, trying to make sense of the turmoil swirling within me. Slipping the car into gear, I set off again. But once around the corner, I parked up and dissolved into tears.

The ringing of my mobile sliced into my depleted mood. It was his youth offending worker, the lady who had initially referred him for the housing assessment.

"How's it all going?"

"OK." I dabbed my eyes as I tried to steady my voice. "We've been to look at *Maple Court*."

"Oh, the supported housing unit. Yes, it's not too bad there. He should be OK."

"I know. It's just he's so young." A fresh tide of sorrow engulfed me. "I'm sure the woman who interviewed him was judging me, thinking, *why are you kicking your son out?*" I choked a sob down.

"She won't have been, don't worry. They're aware that young people referred there have a variety of issues. In fact, she was probably shocked that he was accompanied by his mother for the interview. Most young people in there are alone in life."

Tears were cascading from my eyes again. Holding the phone away from my face, I sniffed.

"Sarah, are you OK?"

"Not really. I feel so guilty." My voice wobbled. She would know I was crying.

"You've nothing to be guilty about. You've been through a hell of a time. You've got to let him go. I'm not saying it'll be easy, but maybe you're doing him the biggest favour you ever could."

"I don't see how."

"What chance does he have if he stays where he is? Amongst the others, amongst the drugs? What chance do any of you have? You've told me yourself you'll all be kicked out. Sarah, I think you've done as much as you can."

"It's not as if I'm going to turn my back on him." The lump in my throat was like a melon. "I'll still be helping him out and keeping watch over him." I shielded my face from a woman who walked past my car, peering in at me.

"I know that. You won't stop being his mum because he's not living with you."

"I wish I didn't feel so awful." I fished around in my bag for a tissue.

"You're bound to. It's a massive step. But with a bit of luck, it'll all turn out OK. It's up to Tom. He's not a little boy anymore."

"I know," I sniffed, wiping my eyes. "I suppose I was out on my own at his age and managed. And I didn't have *anyone* to lean on."

THE PHONE CALL

IT WAS A BEAUTIFUL SUNDAY MORNING. I sat, sprawled amongst the chaos I had caused in Alex's bedroom. Clothes, books, outgrown toys, bits of things; we were having a clear out.

Alex had initially helped but had then gone out to play football. In the distance I could hear him yelling with his friends.

From the next room, our room, I listened to the rhythm of the paint roller as Martin painted the wall. I had chosen lilac as it is supposed to be relaxing. *Odour free*, it had claimed. But the house reeked of paint. It was not an unpleasant smell though. Things smelt clean.

Tom had not graced us with his presence until after three in the morning and was still asleep. I looked out of Alex's window at the cloudless blue sky. It was nearly midday and *Tom was still sleeping.* Alex had been right when he had once likened him to a bat. My thoughts were interrupted by my phone.

"Can I speak to Tom?" The voice sounded official. Strange on a Sunday morning.

"He's asleep. Can I help at all?"

"Are you his mum?"

"Yes." *Please don't say he's in trouble again!*

"It's Linda, calling from Maple Court; he attended an interview here last week."

"Yes, that's right." *I hoped there wasn't a problem with his application.*

"I'm sorry to bother you on a Sunday but we've a vacant flat that we'd like to offer him."

I couldn't speak. I needed a moment to process her words.

"Are you there?"

"Yes. Sorry." I leaned against the boxes that surrounded me. "You've got an empty flat?"

"That's right. But we need to know *now* whether he wants to accept it. And for Housing Benefit purposes, he'd need to have it signed up by tomorrow."

"*Tomorrow?*"

"Yes, would that be a problem?"

"N-no, I shouldn't think so." The 'melon' abruptly returned to my throat. "When would he move in?"

"Well, we can complete the signing up process at five o'clock tomorrow, which gives us chance to do our checks on the flat during the day. So he could move in tomorrow night."

"That soon?" I felt dizzy.

"I thought that's what he wanted?"

"It is." Tears warmed my eyes. "It's a bit of a shock. Sorry."

"Should I go ahead and make the appointment for him," she said.

"Yes, I think so."

"Do you need to check with him first?"

"No, I know it's what he wants. He's told me."

"Right. Good. We'll see you tomorrow at five then. He'll need to bring evidence of identity and his national insurance number."

After the conversation had ended, I sat amidst the mess. I

am not sure how long I sat there. The room swam around me as I tried to steady my thinking.

Finally, I went to tell Martin. Perching on the edge of the bed, I watched him roller the paint onto the wall for a moment.

"Nice colour," I remarked, trying to keep the heaviness out of my voice. "You're doing a good job."

"Who was on the phone before?"

"Maple Court. Where I took Tom."

"The housing place?" Without looking at me, he continued to roller.

"That's the one." Tears spilt from my eyes.

"What did they want?"

"To offer Tom a flat." The words left me slowly. I could hardly believe it.

"WHAT?" Martin swung around. "You're joking. This soon? When?"

"Tomorrow."

"Tomorrow!" He dropped the paint roller in its tray. "You mean he's actually going to be moving out *tomorrow*?" He made no effort to disguise his excitement.

"That's what I said." I stared at the floor.

"Why are you crying?" He shook his head. "You should be pleased!"

"*Pleased?* Don't be ridiculous. He's my son." I left the room and went downstairs to distract myself in the kitchen. Martin soon followed.

"Sarah get a grip, for God's sake." He reached for my arm. "This is what we've all needed for a long time, Tom included."

I continued to stack the dishwasher, so I didn't have to look at him. The level of my shock had taken me by surprise. Had I allowed the stray tears to become sobs; they may never have stopped. Suddenly, Tom was my baby again and I was no longer certain that I could let him go. I had visions of my little blonde boy, and flashes of pulling him back from the road or stopping him from climbing too high.

Martin caught my elbow and forced me to face him. His voice became gentler when he realised how affected I was. I was grateful he wasn't being awful or sarcastic about this.

"Can you imagine what'll happen if we don't take this chance?" He caught my chin in his hand. "We'll all be booted out of this house within a few months. Think of it, Sarah. Think of what we've been through. But most of all, think of Alex."

I knew this was it. There was no way we could go back on things.

"I'm going out for a bit." I grabbed my car keys from the sideboard. "I need to clear my head."

I made the short journey to the next village, tears rolling down my face as I listened to the ebb and flow of the engine. I stopped at the supermarket to buy something for Sunday dinner. *What if this was the last time he wanted to eat his Sunday dinner with us?*

It was one of those scorching days when most people are glad to be alive. I approached the checkout, noticing that people were buying boxes of lager, chicken drumsticks and other barbecue things. There was happy energy around as children queued with their parents.

"Is that all you've got love?" A voice distracted me. "You might as well go before us."

"Thanks." I placed my silverside joint onto the conveyer belt. As I waited for it to be scanned, I caught sight of a little boy in the trolley at the next checkout. The breath caught in my throat as I saw his white-blonde hair reflecting the light that filtered through the supermarket roof. For a moment it was though a younger Tom had returned, to remind me of the enormity of the situation which was now presenting itself.

I couldn't face Martin who had gone back upstairs when I returned home so I dumped the meat, grabbed the dog and headed for the park with her.

We trudged in circles for what seemed like an eternity. The idea had been to try and collect my thoughts a little and give myself a bit of a talking to, but I was enveloped by a numb, foggy feeling. Though one foot went in front of the other, I felt incomplete. Nothing would ever be the same again. With every family I saw, every mother with her son, my depression deepened. I hated myself. *How could I be doing this to my sixteen-year-old?*

Tom was stirring when I arrived home. His mood seemed as dark as ever as he crashed around the kitchen. I took a deep breath.

"Maple Court have rung." I pulled a pan from the cupboard. "You know, the place where you saw a flat last week?"

"Oh yeah?"

"They've got a flat for you." I unwrapped the beef. "They want you to move in tomorrow." I waited for his reaction.

A grin that appeared to be a combination of relief and gratitude stretched across his face.

"You're kidding! Honest?"

"Yep." I dropped the beef in the pan with a thud. "How do you feel about it?"

"It's the bizz, I can't believe it." Leaning against the fridge door, he was seemingly overcome. "But what'll I do for money?"

"We'll get all that sorted out." I threw the pan into the oven. "Do you definitely want to go? Cos you don't have to, you know."

"Sarah." Martin jumped up from his chair. "We all know it's for the best."

"I know." I lowered my eyes so neither of them would notice the fresh batch of tears that were bubbling up. I busied myself in folding tea towels that were already folded. "I suppose we'd better get you sorted then."

"Shall I start packing? Have you got any boxes or owt?"

Without waiting for an answer, he sped upstairs. Sliding floorward against the kitchen cupboard, I sobbed into my hands.

"It's the end of an era," announced Martin, rubbing his hands together. "This is it. He's leaving home."

"He's too young!" I wailed, staring at the checked pattern on the lino.

"Pull yourself together, for God's sake." He searched in his pockets for his wallet. "I'm going for a pint to celebrate."

"You're all heart, aren't you?"

For much of the day, I continued in the same vein. I was unable to stop crying but somehow managed to conceal it from Tom. I could never have predicted the extent to which this would upset me.

"Just because you're moving out, it doesn't mean you're on your own." I had pulled myself together adequately enough to give Tom a 'pep-talk' as I ironed. I'll still be helping you." The steam curled up towards my face, its warmth providing momentary comfort.

"Yeah, I know."

"This is your chance." Filling the iron with water, I tried to stop my hand from trembling. "It's up to you what you do with your life."

"Yeah, whatever." He turned the volume up on the TV.

"For goodness sake, don't be having all your mates around. They won't give a toss about your home. They won't think twice about messing everything up."

"Alright Mum. Stop going on. You're doing my head in." His gaze remained fixed to the TV. I slammed the iron onto every garment, wishing misery could evaporate like steam.

He stayed at home that night. I listened to every creak and cough from his room, knowing I was hearing him in the next room for the last time. It was like a bereavement. I lay, staring into the darkness, waiting for tears or sleep to come. Tears kept winning the battle. By three o'clock I'd had enough of lying there and went downstairs. The early summer sun rose, marking the dawn of the final day I would have my son at home. Still crying, I drifted off to sleep on the sofa.

MOVING ON

AUGUST 2010 (16 YEARS, 8 MONTHS)

"I've packed me stuff Mum." Tom arrived at the bottom of the stairs, laden with bags. "It's all there." His mood had lifted enormously since the flat had been offered.

"Right." My heart was like rock. "I'll get you plates, towels and stuff like that packed. I'm not sure what's in the flat already but you'll want stuff of your own." I began tugging things from the kitchen cupboards.

"What time do I need to be back here?" He leant down to fasten his trainers.

"Where are you off?"

"Just round and about."

"Tom, don't be telling people where the flat is." I stacked plates into a box. "It's going to be your place, *yours* and no one else's."

"I know."

"It's where you can come and go, lock your door behind you and do whatever you want." I watched him as he swapped feet to tie his other lace. "Your space. Your sanctuary."

"All right Mum, you're going on again." He rose to his feet and dragged his hoodie from the coat hooks.

"Well, it's a new start, a chance for you to rid yourself of the idiots around here. You'll have me around to help. And support workers."

"I'm off anyway. Can I have some money?"

For the first time since I'd woke up on the sofa, I cried again as I watched him walk away from the house. As I looked at the pile of bags and boxes, I wondered if I'd ever stop.

Part of me wanted to get the move over with, but this conflicted with the other part of me that wanted to return his things to his room and call Maple Court to say he had changed his mind. But really, I knew this was not an option.

The day ticked by like any other. Trying to keep myself busy was hard as I was struggling to focus. Tom was back on time, so Martin helped him load up my car with his stuff. I couldn't bear to do it.

We travelled in silence, apart for the occasional chatter from Alex.

Maple Court was bathed in sunshine when we arrived; one or two of the residents were sat around on the benches. Tom jumped out of the car and headed towards the reception area as though he owned the place. I crept in behind him, not daring to meet anyone's gaze with my downcast, red-rimmed eyes.

"If you'd like to have a seat in there." The woman who had previously interviewed Tom beckoned us into a side room. Moments later she joined us, accompanied by a man, Carl, who was to be Tom's housing support worker.

"Right Tom. This is a copy of your tenancy agreement." The paper crackled as she passed it to him. "If you could sign there."

"This is your application for Housing Benefit. You need to sign it there and there." She pointed, appropriately.

I listened as the formalities took place. I was certain that the woman kept looking at me, wondering what sort of a mother I must be to be allowing my son to leave home at sixteen.

Martin and Alex waited in the car. They were to be given the nod when the official stuff had taken place in order that we could begin carting everything in.

I trudged behind to be shown the flat Tom had been allocated. Electric meter, post, laundry, etc. Tom did not seem to be listening. His expression was one of euphoria when he was handed his key.

“There’s a £5 charge if you lose it,” said Carl.

Between us, it did not take long to unload the car.

“You’ve got some sorting out to do tonight Tom.” I flicked my eyes around the flat.

“I’ll tell you something Tom, this isn’t bad,” Martin called from the kitchen as he opened and closed doors. “You’ve got a real chance here. Make sure you don’t blow it.”

A trip around the supermarket was necessary, so we could at least leave him with a full fridge and cupboards

“I can see I’ve got a lot to teach you about shopping.” I said as he tried to sling in whatever took his fancy without even glancing at the price.

As we drove back, I further eased my conscience by buying him cigarettes and crediting his phone. Then we took him and Alex for tea. I was too churned up to eat anything. Eventually, the inevitable had to take place. We had to drop him off.

“I’ll ring you in the morning,” I promised, my voice trembling. “We’ll leave you now and let you get settled.”

“OK Mum.” For a moment I thought he was going to hug me. Briefly, the wall between us crumbled. I hugged him instead.

“You’ll be OK, won’t you?” I battled to hold back the tears. “I do love you; you know. Don’t ever forget that.”

He didn’t answer but for once, he hugged me back. Amidst the angst of his teenage years we’d lost each other as mother and son. From being a baby, he'd never done hugs, but even so we'd become so distant.

"Come on Sarah. Let's leave him to it. He looks done in." Martin's voice sounded from the doorway.

"I'm off home to get a glass of wine." I stood back. "Ring me if you need anything. I'll be back tomorrow."

"Is he staying there forever Mum?" Alex said as we got into the car.

"We'll have to see." The urge to return to the flat and retrieve him was overwhelming.

"Are you OK Mum?"

"I'll be fine." I didn't turn to look at him but was warmed by his concern. We were all exhausted and I needed to pull myself back together. Poor Alex had hardly had any attention from me for two days. But he would now have me all to himself. Not that I had stopped being Tom's mum. In fact, I was feeling a maternal tug towards him more powerfully than I had in years.

Alex got into his pyjamas when we arrived home.

"Tuck me in Mum." His arms wrapped around my neck more tightly than usual. I managed to make it out of his room before the tears surged again.

"I'm taking the dog onto the field," I announced to Martin.

"I'll come with you?" The field overlooked our house. I poured myself a large glass of wine to carry over with me.

"No. I could do with a bit of time on my own. I won't be long."

I sprawled on the grass, as the dog bounced around me, staring over at the stillness of home, aglow in the late sunset. The street was empty, and a bird was singing.

Before long, the tears on my cheeks dried in the breeze. As the sun sank behind the house, I shivered in the sudden chill. I hugged my knees towards me, enjoying the momentary warmth.

A picture of my son crept back into my mind as I imagined him in his flat amongst his things. My heart ached with the loss of him and I prayed he would be OK. At least he was happy. For now, anyway. *That was* all I had ever wanted for him, happiness.

As the sky grew darker, a massive star glowed in front of me. When I was young, my grandma had told me to always wish on the first star I saw when it got dark. But she told me never to tell anyone my wish or it would not come true. For several minutes, I gazed at the star before closing my eyes. I wished like I had never wished before.

MY BOY

I glance at the boy over the street
who seemingly has the world at his feet;
he slings his schoolbag onto his back
containing his books; the ones that you lack.

I watch a boy; with his dog he strides out
"Why isn't he like you?" *I want to shout;*
content with his life as his dog leaps around,
not craving 'props' like you have found.

Another boy passes; jobs on a list,
tears well inside for the boy that I've missed
who cares for his mother - eases her load,
whilst you choose to head along the wrong road.

My attentions diverted by excited noise,
a ball's kicked about by a group of boys;
their carefree laughter rings out as they run,
that's where you *should be, joining in fun.*

A shriek of brakes as a boy cycles by,
his bike gives him wings; makes him able to fly;
why, in your *life, do you not have that pride?*
Your rapid descent makes me sting inside.

I look at these boys, so healthy and strong,
amongst them you'd be, it's where you belong;
weakened and gaunt with pallor so pale,
I'm so scared one day I'll be mourning for real.

EPILOGUE

THIS IS the second edition of 'Don't Call me Mum!' I originally wrote it in 2010 and it was written throughout the first year after Tom had left home at the age of sixteen.I decided to revisit the book with fresh eyes and with a more distant emotional perspective.

Since the book was first published in 2012, I have divorced Tom's stepdad, Martin. I have therefore been able to add in a little more information about the effect of that relationship dynamic, something that I was unable to do at the time as he had 'monitored' the content before publication. I was also able to do a little cosmetic editing on the writing itself.

In some ways, revisiting my journey as Tom's mother unsettled our current relationship as it brought back episodes that I'd managed to bury in my memory box – one of the truest sayings is *time heals* – yet I reopened old wounds by reliving our angst again!

I now wonder how we all survived such a turbulent time – whilst it was happening, it was my way of life – yet going back over it ten years later has highlighted, even to me, how relentless our struggle was.

I wrote the book for two reasons; to challenge the 'blame the parents' mindset and to help other parents who are struggling with ADHD or other similar challenges.

I think we've come a long way since I was taking Tom to every specialist known to man, starting back in 1995. Attitudes have changed and hyperactivity has been accepted as a condition rather than seen as a fallacy. Medication has moved on and support is now more available for any sort of disability; whether developmental, psychological, emotional, physical, cognitive or otherwise. Organisations also seem to work more collaboratively and there is no longer a 'one size fits all' approach taken. I often think it's a shame that we had to become involved with the Youth Offending Team before we got any worthwhile support as a family. Over the years, I was repeated offered a 'parenting course,' which I was totally opposed to at the time but in hindsight, I should have given it a go - it was one of the mistakes I made as a mother to repeatedly turn it down when it may have helped things.

There are many struggling parents out there and I've been delighted to receive feedback from some of them, saying that my book has helped them feel less alone and that they've been able to draw comparisons between their own situation and ours. I've been asked many times, how Tom fared since the end of this book so ten years '*on*' seems like a good time to be writing this epilogue.

At first, after leaving home, he lurched from one catastrophe to another and throughout the first year or so, I worried he'd be dead or in prison by the end of his teens. I supported him closely but for a time, when he was around nineteen, for all our sakes, I had to step back a little. I was providing all his shopping, clothing and keeping him afloat. But he'd sell his clothes and belongings, so it got to the point where I took the difficult decision to somewhat 'let him go' to either 'sink or swim.'

This was the second hardest decision I've taken about him, the first being when he had to move out at the age of sixteen. No mother could have ever felt more guilty, but we had *all* been in danger of losing our home and I had a younger son to think of as well.

Luckily, Tom swam. Yes, he's still hyperactive and chaotic, with the attention span of a flea, but he hasn't been in trouble with the police since he was seventeen. I still irritate him when we're in each other's company for any length of time and most of the time when he visits, he manages to break something!

He's now twenty-six and chooses his friends much more carefully. He has his own flat, a lovely girlfriend and a steady job, selling insurance. His employers give him the flexibility to work within his attention capabilities. He's always been able to 'talk the talk' so is good at what he does. He still has an ambition to be creative so maybe he will take his art back up one day.

Tom has had his trials and scrapes since leaving home, but then doesn't every young person whilst they find their feet? He is absolute proof that time marches on and circumstances change, which is what I want anyone reading this to take from it.

Tom lives around twelve miles away from me now. We both live busy lives so don't see one another as often as we'd like but he's done better than I could have ever imagined. He's turned his life around since he was seventeen and I couldn't be prouder of the brilliant young man he has become.

As for me, I recently got married for the second time to a wonderful man who I wish had been around whilst Tom was growing up. Freedom from past angst has also enabled me to focus on my writing career and I now have ten novels published - domestic thrillers!

I've had lovely messages from other parents who've let me know of similar circumstances, and said that 'Don't Call me

Mum' has helped them feel less alone and offered them hope for the future. I'll close by saying this - you are a parent, yes, but you are also you. I'm living proof of being able to get through incredibly tough times and not just come out on the other side, but then be able to pursue a happy and fulfilling future in all areas of life. Thank you so much for reading about our journey.

Before you go...

Join my 'keep in touch' list to receive a free novella, and to be kept posted of other freebies, special offers and new releases. Being in touch with you, my reader, is one of the best things about being an author.

If you'd like to read my fiction, click here to find The Man Behind Closed Doors on Amazon.

I also get many enquiries about other parents with a tale to tell. If this is you, and you'd like to get your own story onto the page, my book, *Write Your Life Story in a Year* will support you. Check it out on Amazon.

Thank you!

READING GROUP QUESTIONS

1. Talk about how each family member was affected by their homelife.
2. Why do you think an ASBO (Anti Social Behaviour Order) was seen amongst youths as a 'badge of honour' in its time?
3. How could Sarah have dealt with Tom better? In infancy, mid childhood and adolescence?
4. To what extent should parents take responsibility for their child's behaviour?
5. When and how should teenagers take responsibility for their own behaviour?
6. How much do you agree with the 'blame the parents' attitude that existed in this memoir? To what extent did that exacerbate the situation?
7. Sarah's own difficult background was attributed to Tom's behaviour. Discuss the effect of how our own childhood experiences can impact on how we bring up our children.
8. Are there any other factors that contributed to Tom's behavioural issues?

9. Have you had any dealings with the issue of ADHD or conduct Disorder? There is some opinion that they are just labels for 'masking' bad behaviour. How far do you agree with this?
10. What services existed in the story that offered support?
11. What services existed in story that seemed to make the situation more difficult?
12. Do you agree with how the courts dealt with Tom? If not, how could they have done it differently?
13. What is your experience of adolescence? How much do you think it changes from generation to generation?
14. Could things have turned out differently if Tom had been accepted into the state school in his new area, rather than being sent to a pupil referral unit?
15. Discuss drugs use amongst teenagers.
16. Was Tom, through his childhood, *failed by the system*, or do you think the services offered as much support as they could?
17. How would *you* cope if you had an adolescent problem on *your* street like the one described in this story?

THE MAN BEHIND CLOSED DOORS - PROLOGUE

Dogs are good at keeping secrets. That's because they can't talk. I used to get told off for talking all the time. Now I'm told off for not talking. People keep asking questions. About what I saw. What I heard. How I am feeling. I don't want to talk anymore. I wish they would all leave me alone.

The girls at school have stopped trying to play with me and be my friend. That's because I don't have my mummy and daddy. I'm different from them. But I have my dog. She's my best friend. I can talk to her just by thinking things, so I am able to tell her *everything*.

BY THE SAME AUTHOR

Psychological Thrillers

Left Hanging

The Man Behind Closed Doors

The Last Cuckoo

Hit and Run

The Hen Party

Last Christmas

In His Shadow

Frenemy

Last Orders

The Dark Water Series

The Yorkshire Dipper

Drowned Voices

Emergence

How-To Books for Writers

Write a Novel in a Year

Write a Collection of Poetry in a Year

Write a Collection of Short Stories in a Year

Write your Life Story in a Year

Memoir

Don't Call me Mum!

Poetry

Poetry for the Newly Married 40 Something

ABOUT THE AUTHOR

This is the only memoir I have wrote so far though I do have another one scheduled to write. Usually I write domestic thrillers where I shine a light into the darkness that can exist within marital and family relationships. I have been no stranger to turbulent times myself, and this has provided some of the raw material for my novels.

I am a born 'n' bred Yorkshirewoman, and a mum of two grown up sons. In my forties, I have been able to pursue a long-held ambition of gaining an MA in Creative Writing and make writing my full time occupation. Recently I have married for the second time and have found my 'happy ever after.'

This is not something you will find in my novels though! I think that we thriller writers are amongst the nicest people you could meet because we pour all our darkness into our books – it's the romance writers you've got to watch...

I plan to release four novels per year and if you'd like to be kept in the loop about new books and special offers, join my 'keep in touch list' or visit www.autonomypress.co.uk. You will receive a free novella as a thank you for joining!

facebook.com/writermariafrank
twitter.com/writermaria_f
instagram.com/writermaria_f
tiktok.com/@mariafranklandauthor

ACKNOWLEDGMENTS

First and foremost, I want to thank my husband, Michael, for his encouragement with my writing career and advice not to overly edit this second edition of 'Don't Call me Mum!'

I would like to acknowledge my amazing book cover designer Darran Holmes, who has blown the original book cover right out of the water, and Sue Coates, the photographer who took my 'author photo.'

Thanks to my sister, Allison Brown for the eagle-eyed proofread she gave this book and to the rest of my friends and family for assuring me that this memoir was worthy of a polish after being first written in 2010. Also thank you to Rachael and Claire for taking the time to endorse the book for me.

Being a mother has shaped me as a person and offered the material and emotion for writing this book. At the time the experience was hard, but now I'm truly grateful for it. Particularly if it helps *you*, the reader. I wrote this book for you. Thank you for taking the time to read our story. I really hope you enjoyed it.

Printed in Great Britain
by Amazon

32198189R00279